CRUSADE TEXTS IN TRANSLATION

About the volume:

Walter the Chancellor's account of the wars of the Antiochenes against the Muslims in the early twelfth century is a vivid first-hand account of a dramatic period in the history of the northern Crusader states, and an important balance to the more usual focus on Jerusalem. Here it has for the first time been translated into English (from the Latin edition of H. Hagenmeyer). It is prefaced by a substantial introduction, discussing the author and his work in the context of the history and historiography of the Latin settlement, and is followed by a selection of comparative sources.

Walter the Chancellor's history will be of interest both to students of the Crusades and to a wider readership for its perspective on life in a medieval frontier society.

About the authors:

Thomas Asbridge is Lecturer in Medieval History at the University of Reading. His monograph study of the early history of Antioch will appear shortly.

Susan Edgington teaches in further and higher education and has written on many aspects of the crusades. Her major work is an edition and translation of Albert of Aachen's history of the First Crusade.

Walter the Chancellor's
The Antiochene Wars

Crusade Texts in Translation

Walter the Chancellor's
The Antiochene Wars

A Translation and Commentary by

THOMAS S. ASBRIDGE
and
SUSAN B. EDGINGTON

Ashgate

Aldershot • Brookfield USA • Singapore • Sydney

Published by

Ashgate Publishing Limited
Gower House, Croft Road,
Aldershot, Hampshire GU11 3HR
Great Britain

Ashgate Publishing Company
Old Post Road,
Brookfield, Vermont 05036-9704
USA

ISBN 1-84014-263-4

British Library CIP Data
Walter the Chancellor
      Walter the Chancellor's The Antiochene Wars: A Translation and Commentary.
      (Crusade Texts in Translation: 4)
      1. Walter, the Chancellor - Bella Antiochena. 2. Crusades. 3. Antioch (Modern city
      of Antakya) - History. I. Title. II. Asbridge, Thomas S. III. Edgington, Susan B. IV.
      The Antiochene Wars
      956.9'1'02

US Library of Congress CIP Data
A Library of Congress Catalog Card Number has been pre-assigned as:
      99-072047

This volume is printed on acid free paper.

Printed and bound in Great Britain by MPG Books Ltd, Bodmin, Cornwall

CRUSADE TEXTS IN TRANSLATION 4

Contents

Other Texts

Acknowledgements

In a collaborative venture of this kind our first debt of gratitude must be to each other. Help on specific points from colleagues, students and friends has been noted at the appropriate points in the text. In addition we should like to thank especially Professor Bernard Hamilton, who read the text and made many valuable suggestions, and Dr Jonathan Phillips who supported and encouraged us from the inception of the project. We are very grateful to William Zajac who produced the index and bibliography as well as reading the text at different stages and doing his best to eliminate our grosser errors. A grant from the Miss Isabel Thornley Bequest to the University of London helped in the publication of this volume.

Chronology

29 November 1114	Earthquake damages Antioch
Early Summer 1115	Meeting between Roger, Tughtegin and Ridwan
June 1115	Antiochene forces move to Apamea to counter Bursuq
August 1115	Arrival of King Baldwin I and Pons at Apamea
	Bursuq feigns retreat
12 September 1115	Roger assembles Antiochene forces at Rugia
14 September 1115	First battle of Tall Danith, Bursuq defeated
June 1119	Il-ghazi gathers forces at Qinnasrin
c.20 June 1119	Roger advances to Artah
27 June 1119	Il-ghazi attacks al-Atharib
28 June 1119	Battle of the Field of Blood, Roger killed
July 1119	King Baldwin II arrives at Antioch
August 1119	Il-ghazi takes al-Atharib and Zardana
14 August 1119	Second battle of Tall Danith
1121	King David II of Georgia meets Il-ghazi in battle
1122	Death of Il-ghazi

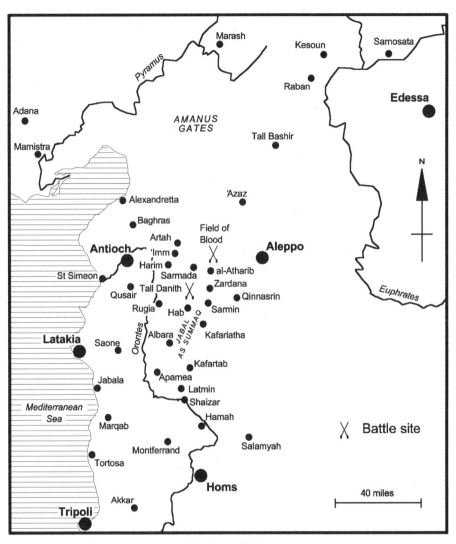

Adana

Mamistra

Pyramus

Marash

Kesoun

Samosata

Raban

Edessa

AMANUS
GATES

Tall Bashir

'Azaz

N

Alexandretta

Baghras

Artah

Antioch

'Imm

Harim

St Simeon

Field of
Blood

Aleppo

al-Atharib

Sarmada

Zardana

Tall Danith

Qinnasrin

Qusair

Rugia

Hab

Sarmin

Albara

Kafarlatha

Euphrates

JABAL-AS SUMMAQ

Latakia

Saone

Kafartab

Jabala

Apamea

Latmin

Shaizar

Orontes

*Mediterranean
Sea*

Hamah

Marqab

X   **Battle site**

Montferrand

Salamyah

Tortosa

Homs

40 miles

Akkar

Tripoli

Northern Syria

Introduction

Walter's subject matter

In the aftermath of the First Crusade and the conquest of the cities of Edessa, Antioch and Jerusalem between 1097 and 1099 the Latins of western Europe established settlements in the Levant which were to endure for almost two centuries. In northern Syria the principality of Antioch was created by Bohemond of Taranto (1098-c.1105) and subsequently ruled by his nephew Tancred de Hauteville (c.1105-1112) and Roger of Salerno (1113-1119).[1] In these first decades the principality became increasingly powerful, second only to the kingdom of Jerusalem in standing amongst the Latin settlements.

Walter the Chancellor, an Antiochene official, wrote a first-hand narrative account of events within the principality between 1114 and 1115 and from 1119 to 1122. His work, *Bella Antiochena* (*The Antiochene Wars*), is the most detailed source for the region in this early period of Latin settlement. Walter was also one of the few writers who did not approach the history of the Levant from the perspective of the kingdom of Jerusalem. Instead he provides us with a unique insight into Latin life in northern Syria during a formative period of Antiochene history.

The first book of Walter's account focuses upon the events of 1115, perhaps the apogee of early Antiochene power, when the principality was invaded by Bursuq of Hamadan. Roger of Salerno's initial response to this threat was to make a temporary alliance with the Muslims Tughtegin (d. 1128), atabeg of Damascus, and Il-ghazi ibn-Artuk of Mardin (d. 1122), who was at the time trying to extend his power over Aleppo. Roger also called upon his fellow Latin rulers in Tripoli and Jerusalem for assistance. A composite force was duly mustered at Apamea in July in order to counter Bursuq's army at Shaizar. The allies were unable to bring him to battle and when his army appeared to break up each member of the alliance returned home. Bursuq had, however, only feigned retreat and returned to attack the Jabal as-Summaq region to the south of Antioch. Roger elected to meet him in battle, with only Antiochene and Edessene troops, at Tall Danith on 14 September where he won a resounding victory which secured the principality's

---

[1] Roger was the son of Richard of the Principate, a southern Italian Norman. See, p. 77, n. 1.

safety and status in the short term.[2]

The theme of Walter's second book is very different. Instead of glorying in victory, he attempts to explain the disastrous Latin defeat and death of Roger in the battle of the Field of Blood on 28 June 1119. This was the first time that a Latin ruler in the Levant had been slain in battle and it was certainly the most serious military setback since the battle of Harran in 1104. Walter recounts the causes and consequences of the Field of Blood in great detail. In early June an Aleppan army under the command of Il-ghazi, Roger's former ally, gathered on the principality's eastern frontier. Roger responded by marching his own forces to Artah, and then on to a site near Sarmada around 20 June. On 27 June Il-ghazi's army attacked the nearby town of al-Atharib and then on the morning of the 28th launched a surprise attack upon the Latin camp. In the ensuing battle the Antiochene army was defeated and Roger slain in hand-to-hand combat.

The Muslim army, now reinforced by Tughtegin of Damascus, proceeded to capture a number of towns on the principality's eastern frontier and raided the region around Antioch itself. Initially the defence of the city was organized by the Latin Patriarch Bernard of Valence (1100-1135), but it was only with the arrival of Latin reinforcements under the command of King Baldwin II of Jerusalem in August that an effective military response could be made. Baldwin met the Muslims in an indecisive battle, again in the region of

---

[2] Walter the Chancellor, *The Antiochene Wars*, I.Prologue-7, pp. 77-108;   Fulcher of Chartres, *Historia Hierosolymitana*, ed. H. Hagenmeyer (Heidelberg, 1913), II.53, pp. 582-3; Albert of Aachen, 'Historia Hierosolymitana', *Recueil des historiens des croisades. Historiens occidentaux*, vol. 4 (Paris, 1879), XII.19-20, pp. 701-2;   William of Tyre, *Willelmi Tyrensis archiepiscopi chronicon*, ed. R.B.C. Huygens, 2 vols (Turnhout, 1986), 11.23, pp. 529-31; 11.25, pp. 532-4;   Matthew of Edessa, *The chronicle of Matthew of Edessa*, trans. A.E. Dostourian (Lanham, New York, London, 1993), III.70, pp. 218-19;   Ibn al-Qalanisi, *The Damascus chronicle of the crusades*, trans. H.A.R. Gibb (London, 1932), pp. 150-51; Usamah Ibn-Munqidh, *An Arab-Syrian gentleman and warrior in the period of the crusades*, trans. P.K. Hitti (New York, 1929), pp. 101-6, p. 149;   Kemal ed-Din, 'La chronique d'Alep', *Recueil des historiens des croisades. Historiens orientaux*, vol. 3 (Paris, 1884), pp. 608-10; Ibn al-Athir, 'Kamel Altevarykh', *Recueil des historiens des croisades. Historiens orientaux*, vol. 1 (Paris, 1872), pp. 296-8;   C. Cahen, *La Syrie du nord a l'époque des croisades et la principauté franque d'Antioche* (Paris, 1940), pp. 272-5;   S. Runciman, 'The kingdom of Jerusalem and the Frankish East 1100-1187', *A history of the crusades*, vol. 2 (Cambridge, 1952), pp. 130-33;   R.C. Smail, *Crusading warfare 1097-1193* (Cambridge 1956), pp. 143-8, pp. 178-9;   H.E. Mayer, *The crusades*, 2nd ed., trans. J.B. Gillingham (Oxford, 1988), p. 71;   J.S.C. Riley-Smith, *The crusades. A short history* (London, 1987), p. 83.

Tall Danith, on 14 August, as a result of which Il-ghazi retreated to Aleppo. The immediate threat to the principality had been staved off, but the grave consequences of the Field of Blood had a profound long-term impact upon the history of Antioch and the Latin East. Roger died without a direct heir and thus Baldwin II was forced to assume the regency of Antioch until the arrival of Bohemond II from southern Italy in 1126. The principality's status within the Levant was shattered, while Baldwin's pre-occupation with northern Syria destabilized his rule in Jerusalem. The Field of Blood is also thought to have prompted the first Latin appeal for military aid from Europe.[3]

These momentous events form the backbone of much of Walter's writing and perhaps the central theme of his work is the attempt to compare, contrast and ultimately rationalize the impressive success of 1115 and the grim failure in 1119. Much of Walter's historical value derives from the step-by-step account of this short period and the rich detail he records in an attempt to explain Antioch's changing fortunes.

Walter was, of course, not the only writer to comment on these events. In order to place his work within its historical context this volume also contains translations of the other Latin sources for events in northern Syria in 1115 and 1119 as well as two early Antiochene charters. This corpus of primary material highlights the wealth of information supplied by Walter, while also demonstrating that other contemporaries could provide different perspectives and revealing some cross fertilization between sources.

In order to provide the reader with some background information this

---

[3] Walter the Chancellor, II.Prologue-12, pp. 109-71;   Fulcher of Chartres, III.3-7, pp. 620-35;   Orderic Vitalis, *The ecclesiastical history*, vol. 6, ed. & trans. M. Chibnall (Oxford, 1978), XI.25, pp. 104-8;   William of Tyre, 12.9-12, pp. 556-62;   Matthew of Edessa, III.79, pp. 223-4;   Ibn al-Qalanisi, pp. 159-61;   Usamah Ibn-Munqidh, pp. 148-50;   Kemal ed-Din, pp. 616-22;   Ibn al-Athir, pp. 323-5;   C. Cahen, *La Syrie du nord*, pp. 283-90; S. Runciman, *A history of the crusades*, vol. 2, pp. 148-55;   R.C. Smail, *Crusading warfare*, pp. 179-81;   H.E. Mayer, *The crusades*, pp. 73-4;   J. Phillips, *Defenders of the Holy Land* (Oxford, 1996), p. 2, pp. 14-15;   H.E. Mayer, 'The Concordat of Nablus', *Journal of Ecclesiastical History*, vol. 33 (1982), pp. 531-43;   H.E. Mayer, 'Jérusalem et Antioche au temps de Baudouin II', *Comptes-rendu de l'Académie des inscriptions et belles-lettres*, Novembre-Décembre 1980 (Paris, 1981), pp. 717-33;   H.E. Mayer, 'Mélanges sur l'histoire du royaume latin de Jérusalem', *Mémoires de l'Académie des inscriptions et belles-lettres*, nouvelle série 5 (1984), pp. 126-30;   H.E. Mayer, 'Die antiochenische Regentschaft Balduins II. von Jerusalem im Spiegel der Urkunden', *Deutsches Archiv*, vol. 47 (1991), pp. 559-66; H.E. Mayer, *Kanzlei der lateinischen Könige von Jerusalem*, vol. 1, pp. 66-7, p. 455;   T.S. Asbridge, 'The significance and causes of the battle of the Field of Blood', *Journal of Medieval History*, vol. 23.4, pp. 301-16.

introduction will outline our knowledge of Walter the Chancellor as an individual, discuss his sources of information and the relationship of his text to other sources, and trace the manuscript tradition of his account. It will also speculate about his reasons for writing and analyse how his different aims and agendas shaped his account. Walter's value as a source will also be discussed, with specific reference to our knowledge of the early history of the principality of Antioch, military practice and cross cultural interaction in the Latin East, and the importance of popular devotion and relics in the medieval Levant.

Walter as a historian

Our knowledge of Walter

Walter, the chancellor of Antioch, is know to us only through *The Antiochene Wars*. He named himself as 'the author Walter' at the start of Book One and then 'I myself, Walter the chancellor' in the Prologue to his second book.[1] He made only one explicit reference to his own actions throughout the account, noting that the chancellor was 'secretly called' by Roger for consultation on the eve of the battle of the Field of Blood.[2] He probably held this office from at least c.1114 to c.1122, the period which he covered in his account, but outside his narrative no evidence exists for the office, or links a name to it, before 1127, when Ralph the chancellor appeared as the third witness to a charter issued by Bohemond II.[3] Although the chancellor's basic role was to head the chancery and oversee the production of documents, Walter did not appear in any charters.[4]

As chancellor we can expect Walter to have had a close relationship with Roger of Salerno, to have been privy at some points to the process of decision making and to have been an eye-witness to many of the events in the principality. He probably accompanied Roger to Apamea, Rugia and Tall Danith in 1115, and at the start of Book Two he noted that he had personally 'experienced' the principality's successes and failures.[5] It is almost certain that Walter was present at the Field of Blood and was taken prisoner by Il-ghazi's forces in the aftermath of the battle.[6] On a number of occasions he mentioned the fact that he had himself been held captive in Aleppo in 1119, noting at one point that his memory might be 'dulled by the experience of the

---

[1] Walter the Chancellor, I.Prologue, p. 77; II.Prologue, p. 109.

[2] Walter the Chancellor, II.3, p. 120.

[3] 'Liber Jurium republicae Genuensis, I', *Monumenta Historiae Patriae*, vol. 7 (Augustae Taurinorum, 1853), pp. 30-31, no. 20.

[4] This does not mean that we should doubt that Walter was chancellor of Antioch. In this period only two chancery staff appear in charters, the notaries Amico de Foro and Peter the subdeacon. H.E. Mayer, *Varia Antiochena: Studien zum Kreuzfahrerfürstentum Antiochia im 12. und frühen 13. Jahrhundert* (Hannover, 1993), pp. 75ff.

[5] Walter the Chancellor, II.Prologue, p. 109.

[6] Walter the Chancellor, II.2, p. 114. He noted that prior to the battle 'we ... forced our way to pitch camp at the Field of Blood'.

prison cell' and later commenting that he would describe the prisoners' 'wretched fate ... just as I saw and heard with my own eyes'.[7] We should, therefore, probably assume that Walter was absent from the principality for at least the remainder of 1119 and thus treat his account of Baldwin II's actions in this period with some caution.

It is probably safe to assume that Walter came from a clerical background. Chancellors were often drawn from this pool of experience, Walter's writing is filled with references to divine will and he has an obvious fascination with piety, and, as we shall see, his account contains a number of scriptural allusions.

i) Walter as a historian

Walter seems to have made a conscious attempt to write a historical record of events in northern Syria which would be of use to future generations. At the start of Book One he wrote that God had 'deigned to instil in me from heaven the power of writing' and, as we shall see, he did try to convey specific messages about divine sanction and human behaviour throughout his work.[8] He also had a fairly keen sense that he was writing a work of historical significance. In Book One he noted that he 'wished to put in writing the sequence of events and commend them to the memory of posterity' in order to preserve a record of the period which 'no previous history has ever told'.[9] In Book Two he reflected on the fact that 'in earlier times ... some historian' would surely have chronicled the events of 1119, but as it was, he noted, 'we are compelled necessarily to speak, since there is no history-writer who can describe the succession of events in full'. He did not wish it to 'seem entirely to slip the memory' and thus he wrote his 'treatise, commending it to the memory of posterity'.[10]

This historical imperative seems to have given Walter a strong awareness of the need for narrative continuity. On a number of occasions in Book Two he commented upon the fact that he must not forget 'the order of events' or indulge 'in too great a digression'.[11] Like many medieval writers

---

[7] Walter the Chancellor, II.Prologue, p. 110; II.7, p. 136; II.15, p. 166.

[8] Walter the Chancellor, I.Prologue, p. 77. See: Walter's purpose in writing *The Antiochene Wars*, pp. 11-12.

[9] Walter the Chancellor, I.Prologue, p. 77; p. 80.

[10] Walter the Chancellor, II.Prologue, pp. 109-10.

[11] Walter the Chancellor, II.2, p. 115; II.6, p. 130; II.8, p. 136; II.13, p. 156.

Walter, of course, made this sort of comment precisely when he was engaged in an aside. He also showed some desire to establish the credibility of his sources, commenting on his own eye-witness status and on one occasion noting that he received his knowledge from 'reliable intermediaries'.[12]

In line with this 'historical' approach, Walter did date most important events within his account, primarily in relation to religious festivals. We learn, for example, that the first battle of Tall Danith took place on the feast of the Exaltation of the Holy Cross, 14 September, and the second battle on that site on the eve of the Assumption of the Virgin Mary, 14 August.[13] Walter's detailed account of day-to-day events also enables us to place other incidents in relation to these specific dates. Thus it is possible to calculate that the town of Zardana fell to Il-ghazi on 13 August.[14] H. Hagenmeyer did assert that Walter dated events by the Pisan calendar, in which the year begins on 25 March, but this appears to have been an erroneous suggestion.[15] Perhaps Walter's most surprising failure is in providing no specific date for the battle of the Field of Blood, the key event of Book Two.[16] This omission is difficult to explain.

ii) Walter's allusions and influences

The assumption that Walter was a cleric is borne out by a study of his citations and allusions. Most of his references are to the Bible, and most of these are from the Psalms and the Epistles, the books of the Old and New Testaments which play a prominent part in the liturgy of the Church. There are, additionally, several quotations from collects and prayers. Walter also used phrases from classical authors, notably Vergil and Ovid. Many of these are the sort of hackneyed expressions which would have been current in

---

[12] Walter the Chancellor, II.8, p. 140.

[13] Walter the Chancellor, I.5, p. 98; II.12, p. 155. Walter also dated the earthquake which affected Antioch to 29 November, the assembly of Latin forces at Rugia to 12 September and the general meeting in Antioch after the first battle of Tall Danith to 1 November. Walter the Chancellor, I.1, p. 80; I.4, p. 96; I.4, p. 97.

[14] Walter the Chancellor, II.11, p. 151. Walter also noted that earthquakes continued to affect northern Syria for five months, that is from November 1114 to March 1115. He specified that Antiochene forces waited two months at Apamea, between mid-June and mid-August 1115. He may also have implied that Robert fitz-Fulk the Leper died on 19 August 1119. Walter the Chancellor, I.1, p. 84; I.3, p. 90; II.14, p. 159.

[15] See: Walter the Chancellor, I.1, p. 80, n. 24.

[16] The specific date of 28 June 1119 is supplied by Ibn al-Qalanisi, p. 160; Kemal ed-Din, p. 617; Matthew of Edessa, III.79, p. 224.

educated society, and it is not possible to claim on this basis that Walter had read the entire works from which these cliches were drawn.[17]

iii) The date of composition

It seems likely that Walter wrote *The Antiochene Wars* in three stages. Book One appears to have been composed before the summer of 1119 because there are no forward references to the disaster at the Field of Blood and, more importantly, because Il-ghazi is styled neutrally as 'emir of the Turcomans', whereas in Book Two he is consistently demonized, from his first appearance being characterized as the 'prince of delusion and dissent'.[18] This would date the composition of Book One between late 1115 and mid-1119.

Book Two may well have been composed in two sections. The text from the Prologue to the end of chapter twelve appears to form a distinct entity, contrasting the defeat at the Field of Blood with the success at the second battle of Tall Danith. Walter also chose to conclude this section with a religious exhortation.[19] The remaining chapters of Book Two, describing the fate of Latin captives, Il-ghazi's defeat by David of Georgia and his eventual death, lack the narrative focus of Walter's earlier work and sit rather uncomfortably with the rest of the text. One might, therefore, tentatively suggest that Walter composed the earlier section of his second book relatively soon after 1119 and then added chapters thirteen to sixteen at a later date. We can, however, suggest no precise dates given that we know neither the date of Walter's release from Aleppo nor the time of his death.

Historiographical background

i) Manuscript tradition

H. Hagenmeyer described seven extant manuscripts of Walter's account. He concluded, no doubt correctly the oldest and best of them (A) was the exemplar of the other six.[20] This codex, now BN. 14378, was prepared

---

[17] We acknowledge with thanks the assistance of Dr Neil Wright, Cambridge University, in the matter of Walter's classical borrowings. H. Hagenmeyer listed many more classical references in his exhaustive annotation of the *Bella Antiochena*, but we have omitted those which appeared to strain resemblances too far.

[18] Walter the Chancellor, I.2, p. 87; II.1, p. 110.

[19] Walter the Chancellor, II.12, p. 156.

[20] *Galterii Cancellarii, Bella Antiochena*, ed. H. Hagenmeyer (Innsbruck, 1896), pp. 52-5.

by William of Grassegals as a gift for Louis VII of France and comprises the works of Fulcher of Chartres, Walter and Raymond of Aguilers. Hagenmeyer conjectured for this collection a date soon after Louis' accession in 1137, or immediately before his departure for the Near East in 1146. In any event, its exemplar - possibly Walter's autograph copy - is lost. In five of the six other codices precisely the same order of contents is preserved; only in the sixth, a fourteenth-century manuscript, is Walter separated from the other two authors. Therefore we might conclude that in manuscript form Walter was probably read in combination with Fulcher and Raymond.

The work was edited by J. Bongars in 1611, using a Bern codex still extant, and this same edition was used in the *Patrologia Latina* of J. Migne (vol. 155) in 1853. In 1876 H. Prutz published a new edition using three manuscripts, and in 1895 P. Riant used all the manuscripts to establish a much better text for the *Recueil des Historiens des Croisades* (*Occidentaux*, vol. 5).[21] The edition used as a basis for this translation is that of H. Hagenmeyer which was published, with exhaustive notes in German, in 1896.[22]

ii) The relationship of *The Antiochene Wars* to other primary sources

Hagenmeyer suggested that Walter drew on another Latin history, that written by Fulcher of Chartres, for the events of 1119.[23] While it is possible that Walter did take a limited amount of information from Fulcher regarding events in the kingdom of Jerusalem, it seems unlikely that he would have needed to do so for the principality of Antioch. He was much closer to those events, and in fact Fulcher only dealt very briefly with the battle of the Field of Blood, expressing a reluctance 'to relate all the wretched events which occurred in this year in the Antiochene region'.[24] William of Tyre certainly drew upon both Walter and Fulcher when writing about events in northern Syria between 1114 and 1119, copying many details directly from *The Antiochene Wars*. As we shall see, William also had a tendency to attempt to reconcile these two sources when they differed on points of detail or

---

[21] *Gesta Dei per Francos*, vol. 1, ed. J. Bongars (Hannover, 1611), pp. 441-67; *Patrologia Latina*, vol. 155, ed. J.P. Migne (Paris, 1853), pp. 995-1038; *Quellenbeiträge zur Geschichte d. Kreuzzüge*, vol. 1, ed. H. Prutz (Danzit, 1876), pp. 1-55; *Recueil des Historiens des Croisades, Historiens Occidentaux*, vol. 5, ed. R. Riant (Paris, 1895), pp. 75-132.

[22] *Galterii Cancellarii, Bella Antiochena*, ed. H. Hagenmeyer, pp. 61-115.

[23] *Galterii Cancellarii, Bella Antiochena*, ed. H. Hagenmeyer, pp. 39ff.

[24] Fulcher of Charters, III.3, p. 621.

interpretation.[25]

It is not clear whether Orderic Vitalis drew any material from Walter. His account bears some marked similarities to *The Antiochene Wars*, particularly in its portrayal of Patriarch Bernard as a 'prudent' advisor and its references to specific individuals such as Robert of Vieux-Pont. Elsewhere it differs strongly, depicting Roger as 'an arrogant prince' who was 'not the equal of his predecessors'.[26] The accounts written by Albert of Aachen and Matthew of Edessa should, almost certainly, be viewed as independent from Walter.

iii) Walter the Chancellor's impact on secondary sources

Walter provided by far the most detailed narrative account of the principality's history in 1115 and 1119. This wealth of information, much of it from an eye-witness perspective, allows the historian to piece together a fairly clear picture of events in this period.[27] R.C. Smail used Walter's account to assess the duration of Roger's campaigning season in 1115 and subsequently reached important conclusions about military levies in the Latin East.[28] It is a testimony to the precision of Walter's account that Smail made so many references to the Antioch wars of 1115 and 1119 in his seminal work on *Crusading warfare 1097-1193* of 1956.[29] Indeed, Smail argued that it was impossible to produce even an approximate reconstruction of the three battles of 1115 and 1119 without examining Walter's account.[30]

[25] See: Roger of Salerno, p. 23;   Walter as a military source, pp. 56-7.

[26] Orderic Vitalis, XI.25, pp. 104-8.

[27] I certainly would not have been able to propose an analysis of the causes and impact of the battle of the Field of Blood without access to the evidence presented in *The Antiochene Wars*. T.S. Asbridge, 'The significance and causes of the battle of the Field of Blood', pp. 301-16.

[28] R.C. Smail, *Crusading warfare*, pp. 147-8.

[29] R.C. Smail, *Crusading warfare*, pp. 143-8, pp. 179-81.

[30] R.C. Smail, *Crusading warfare*, pp. 167-8.

Walter's purpose in writing *The Antiochene Wars*

Walter began each of his two books with a prologue commenting on the purpose of his work. He began Book One hoping that 'when men capable of reason and defenders of the true faith heard the truth, they would cleave strongly to the power and service of their Creator'. Thus he seems to have recorded the successes of 1115 in order to preserve an example to future generations of how 'miracles' and God's favour brought victory. 'For truly', he wrote, 'when they have heard the power of miracles and the deeds of worthy men the wicked will more easily be brought low and the good will also be spurred on to do better.'[1] Thus, perhaps, the most obvious theme in Book One is that Christian warfare must be carried out with divine sanction and pure intention.

His purpose in Book Two is far more problematic. Instead of being able to glory in victory he chose to record Antiochene disaster at the hands of Il-ghazi of Mardin. In the second prologue Walter stated that he would describe the 'grief of griefs' and 'complete unhappiness' of the Field of Blood 'commending it to the memory of posterity'. Walter maintained that he was forced by duty to write of these events. He wrote that 'for this reason we are compelled necessarily to speak, since there is no history-writer who can describe the succession of events in full'. As in Book One, where he asserted that God 'deigned to instil in me from heaven the power of writing and the means of expression', he noted that in Book Two he was writing 'with the assistance of Himself' lest the events of 1119 be forgotten and 'because it may be considered worthy of recital for the good of those who hear it'.[2]

Walter's primary remit seems to have been to rationalize the Latin defeat at the Field of Blood and, not surprisingly given the medieval context, he turns to God to find his explanation. He wrote that pride caused the Antiochenes to be 'both ungrateful to God and unmindful of His kindness' and that 'because we put the success of the earlier war down to the victory of our own forces, in the second detestable war' the Latins were defeated. 'What happened to us' he wrote 'was not the result of that multitude's strength, but the just judgment of God for our sins and wickedness'.[3] Walter tried to draw

---

[1] Walter the Chancellor, I.Prologue, pp. 77-8.

[2] Walter the Chancellor, I.Prologue, p. 77; II.Prologue, pp. 109-10.

[3] Walter the Chancellor, II.Prologue, p. 110; II.2, p. 115.

a distinction between the two wars by claiming that in 1119 the Latins did not act as true 'soldiers of Christ' and he seems to have hoped that by drawing a stark contrast between the success of 1115 and the disasters of 1119, he would demonstrate the importance of spiritual purity in warfare.[4]

As we shall see, however, Walter does appear to have pursued a number of other sub-themes within his narrative. He seems to have been reluctant openly to criticize Roger of Salerno, instead wishing to demonstrate that he died having been spiritually purified. He also goes beyond the explanation of the Field of Blood later in Book Two, to demonstrate the return of God's favour by focusing upon the salvation of the principality under King Baldwin II of Jerusalem and God's omnipotence through the eventual defeat and destruction of Il-ghazi. These aims may have prompted Walter to distort his presentation of figures such as Baldwin II and Patriarch Bernard and at times there is evident tension between his different motifs which produces inconsistency within the text.

Roger of Salerno

Upon first inspection Roger, the ruler of the principality of Antioch from 1113 to 1119, would appear to be the central protagonist of Walter's account. As commander of the Antiochene forces at both Tall Danith in 1115 and the Field of Blood he plays a pivotal role in the narrative of these battles, and in a sense the story of *The Antiochene Wars* is the story of Roger's successes and failures. Walter's attitude to this figure must, therefore, be regarded as a central aspect of his entire work. We must, of course, automatically expect Walter's depiction of Roger to be biased because, as we have seen, he was a high-ranking official in the Antiochene court and a close advisor to the 'prince'.

There are, however, major historical questions regarding Roger's career which are not immediately apparent from a simple reading of Walter's text. Did he rule Antioch as a prince in his own right or simply as regent for the young Bohemond II? To what extent was he personally responsible for the crushing defeat at the Field of Blood which inspired the writing of Walter's second book?

---

[4] Walter the Chancellor, II.Prologue, pp. 109-10.

i) Other Sources

Many of these questions emerge from the evidence presented in other primary sources. Fulcher of Chartres' account of Roger's life differs markedly from that presented in *The Antiochene Wars*. He launched a severe attack upon Roger's character when relating the events of 1119. As we have seen, he initially stated that he did not wish to encumber his history with a detailed account of the disastrous battle at the Field of Blood.[5] He went on to claim that it was not 'surprising if God allowed them to be destroyed, since they were very wealthy in all sorts of riches and in the way they sinned they neither feared Him nor respected men'. Fulcher described two specific sins of which Roger was guilty: adultery and usurpation, while also alluding to his pride and the avarice of the Antiochene nobility as a whole. He claimed that the accusation of infidelity was made by 'his own wife', namely Cecilia of Le Bourcq, implying that Roger's widow spread this rumour after the Field of Blood, perhaps even personally confiding in Fulcher. The charge that Roger 'disinherited his lord, the son of Bohemond, when he was still in Apulia with his mother' would imply that he was never perceived to be prince of Antioch in his own right, but that as regent he prevented Bohemond II from taking up his inheritance.

It is worth remembering, however, that earlier in his text Fulcher had noted that when Tancred died 'Roger, his kinsman, succeeded him' and shortly afterwards described him as 'Roger, prince of Antioch and son of Richard'.[6] Albert of Aachen, the only other contemporary source to discuss Roger's status at this point, also described him as 'the successor and heir of Antioch, son of the sister of Tancred'.[7] Both sources treated Roger as the rightful prince upon his accession in early 1113 and emphasized his legitimacy through the familial link to Tancred. It was only after the Field of Blood that Fulcher suddenly accused Roger of usurpation.

William of Tyre followed Fulcher's characterization of Roger in many respects. He noted that 'it is said that this same Prince Roger was a most corrupt man, unchaste, parsimonious and a known adulterer' and that 'he had made his lord Bohemond the younger, son of the elder Bohemond, who was still in Apulia with his mother, an alien from Antioch, which was his paternal heritage, for as long as he had held the principality'. Writing approximately

---

[5] Fulcher of Chartres, III.3, p. 621. See also: Historiographical background, p. 9.

[6] Fulcher of Chartres, II.47, p. 562; II.49, p. 570.

[7] Albert of Aachen, XII.12.

fifty years later William did attempt to reconcile this image of Roger with his version of his accession. He wrote that 'Lord Tancred of good memory had committed the principality to him on his deathbed, on condition that he would not refuse Lord Bohemond or his heirs if they demanded it back'.[8]

The Armenian writer Matthew of Edessa accused Roger of pride and complacency rather than usurpation. He noted that he had been 'made arrogant by his powerfulness' and with 'the pride of the race from which he was descended' did not make 'a single preparation for defence' advancing to war without 'sufficient troops, without having summoned his Frankish allies'.[9] This emphasis upon the sin of pride does in fact have some resonance with Walter's depiction of Roger's failings.

On this evidence it appears that Roger may have had an unsavoury reputation at the time of his death, that there was doubt about his right to rule Antioch independently and that at the very least he was personally culpable for the defeat at the Field of Blood. Does Walter the Chancellor's depiction of Roger shed any further light upon these accusations? He is, of course, not openly condemnatory in the same way as Fulcher and William, but does he allude to the questions of sin or usurpation, or defend Roger's reputation so adamantly that we might suspect an attempt to divert criticism?

ii) Book One

Walter's depiction of Roger must, by its nature, be split into two distinct sections. In Book One, describing the successes of 1115, Roger can obviously and easily be portrayed as the central, heroic figure. In this first section of the source Walter highlights a number of his positive characteristics. He is consistently described as a wise and respected ruler. When the principality, and more specifically Antioch, suffered severe earthquake damage in 1115 Roger personally oversaw the initial repairs and then appointed Ralph of Acre, duke of Antioch, to head a council on what further measures should be taken to re-fortify the city. Throughout, Roger's actions are shown as shrewd: his initial consultation with Ralph; the

---

[8] William of Tyre, XII.10, p. 558. William also noted this arrangement when describing Tancred's death. He wrote that 'by Tancred's last will, Roger, son of Richard, one of his kinsmen, succeeded to the principality on the following condition: that, when in due time the younger Bohemond, son of the elder Bohemond, should demand Antioch with its dependencies as his rightful inheritance, it should be rendered to him without trouble or gainsaying'. William of Tyre, XI.18, pp. 522-3.

[9] Matthew of Edessa, III.79, pp. 223-4.

acceptance of his recommendations within the council and his subsequent 'very careful' placement of troops with the citadel and city.[10]

At the start of the summer campaigning season, after having 'discussed with his men matters of common utility' at the Iron Bridge, Roger sent scouts into Muslim lands.[11] On their return he first questioned these spies in public and then in his private rooms on 'new and more secret information'. As 'he was aware that wise men have no regrets after taking advice' he convened another council of his advisors, at which Walter may have been present.[12] Walter built up a picture of Roger as a cautious and competent ruler, one who listened to counsel when appropriate, but who was also capable of imposing his own will.

The interaction between Roger and King Baldwin I of Jerusalem provides Walter with another opportunity to demonstrate the former's abilities. Unlike Baldwin of Le Bourcq, at the time second count of Edessa, and Pons count of Tripoli, Roger was not Baldwin I's vassal, and the two are to some extent depicted as equals. Walter did note that after receiving Roger's call to arms Baldwin 'warned the prince with an oath of Christianity and by the bond of brotherly affection' not to attack Bursuq's army before he arrived with reinforcements.[13] This advice prompted Roger to forbid 'all his men generally either to skirmish or even to wage war on pain of having their eyes torn out' because he was joined to the king 'by a sacred Christian oath and by brotherly love'.[14] Roger held to this decision when the Muslims harried his camp at Apamea, warning his troops that 'if anyone dares to ride out now, he will perish by my sword'. Walter did note that this policy of inactivity met with some criticism, writing that 'some of our men also considered it an act of cowardice', but countered that 'men of greater wisdom' understood Roger's purpose, making it clear where his own sympathies lay.[15] Instead of appearing as the king's subject, Roger was praised for accepting and steadfastly adhering to Baldwin's judicious counsel. Once the Latin armies were united military decisions were made by 'a short military council' rather than by the king alone, and Walter stresses that Roger would find victory 'by

---

[10] Walter the Chancellor, I.2, pp. 84-6.
[11] Walter the Chancellor, I.2, p. 85.
[12] Walter the Chancellor, I.2, p. 87.
[13] Walter the Chancellor, I.3, p. 90.
[14] Walter the Chancellor, I.3, p. 92.
[15] Walter the Chancellor, I.3, p. 93.

the prudent disposition and enormous experience of himself and the king'.[16]

Eventually, of course, Roger did defeat Bursuq at Tall Danith without Baldwin I's aid.[17] When the Muslim army returned to threaten the Jabal as-Summaq in September Roger responded by advancing with his household to Rugia, where he was joined by the rest of his forces and a contingent of troops under Baldwin II, count of Edessa.[18] Given the accusations of impatience made against Roger in Book Two, it is interesting that in this instance Walter did not criticize him for not awaiting further Latin reinforcements, instead noting that he acted with 'manly boldness'.[19] Prior to the battle at Tall Danith he is also shown giving a rousing, martial speech in which he informed the army that: 'The time has come when your strength and virtue may be esteemed, when the name of your victory over the barbarians may shine brightly throughout the regions of the world.'[20] Then after the battle Walter recorded that he distributed the accumulated plunder in the correct manner, 'as his sovereignty and the custom of the same court demanded' and was then universally exalted on his return journey to Antioch 'with hymns and songs by all the people throughout countryside and castles'.[21]

The one aspect of Roger's rule which Walter might have criticized was the decision to forge an alliance with Il-ghazi of Mardin and Tughtegin of Damascus. Walter demonstrated his personal objection to this compact when he observed that God caused the break-up of the coalition forces at Apamea because He 'wished to break up the alliance of Belial with our people'.[22] He did not, however, make any personal attack upon Roger in relation to this matter. When the alliance was initially forged he blandly reported that 'they confirmed agreements and became, to all appearances, friends'.[23]

---

[16] Walter the Chancellor, I.4, p. 94; I.3, p. 93.

[17] Walter the Chancellor, I.4-7, pp. 96-106; Albert of Aachen, XII.19-20; Fulcher of Chartres, II.54, pp. 586-9; William of Tyre, XI.25, pp. 533-4; Matthew of Edessa, III.70, p. 219; Usamah Ibn-Munqidh, pp. 105-6; Kemal ed-Din, pp. 609-10; Ibn al-Athir, pp. 297-8.

[18] Walter the Chancellor, I.4, p. 96; I.5, p. 98.

[19] Walter the Chancellor, I.4, p. 96.

[20] Walter the Chancellor, I.6, p. 100.

[21] Walter the Chancellor, I.7, p. 106.

[22] Walter the Chancellor, I.4, p. 95. See also: The depiction of Islam and eastern Christendom, p. 66.

[23] Walter the Chancellor, I.2, p. 88.

In Book One Walter also portrayed Roger as a pious individual. Before leaving Antioch at the start of the summer campaigning season he undertook a series of spiritual preparations: 'he heard divine office, prayed in the churches of the blessed intercessors St Mary the Virgin, Peter and Paul, George and very many others'. He then received some form of licence from Patriarch Bernard, which Walter described as the 'permission and patriarchal blessing', probably associated with the concept of justified violence.[24] Roger was fortified by a second patriarchal 'benediction' prior to the battle of Tall Danith, and then underwent a further series of rituals alongside the rest of his army, including Mass, confession and a sermon.[25] Roger is not, however, singled out amongst the army as being particularly penitent or devout at this point, and Walter does appear to have been generally keen to record instances of spiritual activity. It is also worth noting that although Walter recorded Roger's personal involvement in battle in Book One, he does not emphasize his individual military prowess or courage, nor attribute the victory in 1115 solely to his actions. Instead Roger is placed on a relatively equal footing with men such as Baldwin of Le Bourcq, count of Edessa, Guy Le Chevreuil, Robert fitz-Fulk the Leper, Robert of Sourdeval, the young Alan and Guy Fresnel, who are all shown fighting with bravery and competence.[26] This rather restrained use of heroic imagery is particularly interesting given Walter's idealized treatment of Baldwin of Le Bourcq in Book Two.

iii) Book Two

In Book Two the depiction of Roger is, of necessity, different, just as Walter's reasons for recording the events of 1119 were different. As we have already noted, most of the other Christian sources blame Roger directly for the Field of Blood. Walter certainly does not condemn him out of hand, nor criticize him heavily for the disaster, indeed he begins the book by styling him as the 'very worthy Prince Roger of Antioch'.[27] Instead he struggles to maintain him as a central figure in the narrative, and thus continues to make use of heroic imagery, while still attempting to explain the defeat on 28 June by indicating how Roger was responsible. There are two main areas in which Walter enters into veiled, and sometimes even direct, criticism of Roger.

---

[24] Walter the Chancellor, I.2, p. 86.
[25] Walter the Chancellor, I.4-5, pp. 96-100.
[26] Walter the Chancellor, I.6-7, pp. 102-5.
[27] Walter the Chancellor, II.Prologue, p. 109.

a) Roger as a military leader

The first concerns the practical errors in judgement and leadership which, in Walter's account, led to the disaster. Chief amongst these was the decision to advance to the camp at the Field of Blood. Roger left the site at Artah, where 'the lie of the land was abundant and healthy with regard to food and drink' and where the low lying Jabal Talat to the east, which consisted of 'mountains ... intermixed with the dense vegetation', provided a formidable natural defence against attack from Aleppo.[28] Walter stresses that after the Latins camped at the site of the Field of Blood, near Balat, they were 'under pressure day after day through lack of food and natural drink' because there was a 'shortage of both in those parts'.[29]

Walter is less direct in his analysis of the other main effect of the move from Artah. Most of the other sources state categorically that Roger had called for aid from Jerusalem and Tripoli and then criticize him for crossing the Jabal Talat before their arrival.[30] Walter is rather evasive on this point. He did note that Roger 'could have consulted there (at Artah) Baldwin ... by waiting cautiously for him and his men' and went on to note that Roger left Artah saying 'no one should wait there any longer'.[31] It is, however, only when Rainald of Mazoir is noted to be awaiting 'Baldwin, king of Jerusalem, who was hurrying to the aid of Christianity' in the immediate aftermath of the Field of Blood, that it becomes clear that the king had been summoned before the battle.[32] Walter thus neglects the theme of impatience, favoured by Matthew of Edessa and Orderic Vitalis, although, as we shall see, he may have accused Roger of the sin of pride in order to explain the decision to advance without reinforcement.

By largely omitting references to the summons of fellow Latins, Walter focuses his primary, practical criticism upon the strategic error of moving from Artah to Balat. He noted that 'rejoicing in his unadvised mind ... he (Roger) decided to cross over with the tents from the suitable place to a useless position', and this in many ways becomes his central explanation for

---

[28] Walter the Chancellor, II.1, p. 111.

[29] Walter the Chancellor, II.2, p. 114.

[30] Fulcher of Chartres, III.4, pp. 624-5;   William of Tyre, 12.9, p. 556;   Orderic Vitalis, XI.25, p. 106;   Matthew of Edessa, III.79, pp. 223-4. Only Matthew of Edessa noted that Roger marched to Balat 'without having summoned his Frankish allies'.

[31] Walter the Chancellor, II.1, p. 111.

[32] Walter the Chancellor, II.5, p. 129.

the subsequent disaster.[33] Even here, though, he does not enter into the same direct or severe condemnation of Roger favoured in the other Christian sources.

Roger is partially distanced from criticism by Walter's suggestion that bad advisors swayed his opinion. He made bad decisions - 'venturing where he should not venture and daring to do what should not be done' - but he was prompted to make these choices 'when he was advised by certain barons, whose possessions the enemy were accustomed to lay waste every single year'.[34] Thus Walter deflects some of the blame onto the 'barons' with lordships on the eastern frontier with Aleppo, perhaps indicating individuals such as Alan of al-Atharib and Robert fitz-Fulk the Leper, lord of Zardana, who had a vested interest in seeing the border zone strongly protected.

As we shall see, Roger's other main error, according to Walter, was in failing to heed Patriarch Bernard's advice to remain at Artah. In *The Antiochene Wars* Walter is able to use Bernard as his mouthpiece, presenting him as a divine advocate, and thus he avoids personal attack upon Roger by directing his opinions through the figure of the patriarch.

Even in Book Two, and in the context of the Field of Blood, Walter does praise Roger's practical leadership where possible. He provides a detailed account of the council held by Roger on the night of the 27 June, highlighting the fact that he entered into consultation regarding the best course of action, and went on to note the prudent preparations made for war, including the reinforcement of al-Atharib, the dispatch of scouts and the return of the baggage train to Artah.[35] Then, just before the start of the battle on 28 June, Walter noted how Roger carefully prepared and deployed his forces and went on to emphasize his military experience by recording that 'just as often before he had drawn up his battle-lines one by one, so then he also commanded them to march in ranks'.[36] Roger is also shown rallying the morale of his troops in a series of reported speeches, exhorting them to 'fight today in a successful battle as soldiers for God' and then 'In the name of Our Lord Jesus Christ, as befits knights, [to] set off eagerly for the sake of defending God's law'.[37]

---

[33] Walter the Chancellor, II.1, p. 113.
[34] Walter the Chancellor, II.1, p. 112.
[35] Walter the Chancellor, II.3, pp. 118-21.
[36] Walter the Chancellor, II.4-5, pp. 123-5.
[37] Walter the Chancellor, II.4-5, pp. 124-5.

Walter also places some emphasis upon Roger's personal bravery and prowess in battle, and shows him adhering to a chivalric ideal. Even when he made the fateful decision to seek battle on the 28th his actions are described as befitting 'a knight of vigorous nature' and he calls on his troops to show a 'knight's courage and love of God'.[38] In the ensuing battle he is also depicted 'fighting energetically' just prior to his own death.[39] The rather incongruous scene which takes place just before the start of battle, in which Roger is described hunting 'as befits a prince', may also be linked to Walter's desire to portray him within a chivalric context.[40]

b) Roger as a sinner

As we have seen, Fulcher of Chartres accused Roger of a number of sins, including adultery, avarice and usurpation. There is some evidence to suggest that Walter was aware of Roger's reputation and the criticisms which might be levelled against him, indeed he noted early on that 'a mass of offences drove that prince' to disaster.[41] The first half of Book Two is filled with references to sin, confession and repentance and it is necessary to isolate which of these are specific to Roger in order to determine the image Walter wished to project.

In his attempts to explain the disaster of 1119 Walter indicates that the Field of Blood was God's punishment for the sins of the Latins, a form of 'divine vengeance' or 'the just judgement of God for our sins and wickedness'.[42] In part Walter seems to be suggesting that the general sins of the Antiochenes brought on defeat, but at some points these sins appear to be linked specifically with Roger.[43]

In the lead-up to the battle Walter made a number of comments about the sinfulness of man and the penitent attitude of the Latins. Before the army moved from Artah to Balat Patriarch Bernard 'delivered a sermon to that same prince and to all the people ... he prayed for all of them with fatherly compassion, that he might reform their behaviour by his attention' and by

---

[38] Walter the Chancellor, II.3, p. 118.
[39] Walter the Chancellor, II.5, p. 127.
[40] Walter the Chancellor, II.3, pp. 121-2.
[41] Walter the Chancellor, II.Prologue, p. 109.
[42] Walter the Chancellor, II.Prologue, p. 109; II.2, p. 115.
[43] A strong tradition developed during the twelfth century, particularly in the crusading context, that the general sins of man brought about divine vengeance in the form of military defeat. See E. Siberry, *Criticism of Crusading 1095-1274* (Oxford, 1985), pp. 72-95.

their observance of 'the law of the churches'. He 'exhorted his listeners not to boast of their virtues' and informed them that 'by resisting sins and guilty passions, they might begin to become warriors of God'.[44] On the night of 27 June, Walter noted that a 'moon-struck' woman prophesied the defeat of the Antiochenes, causing many in the army 'to bewail in earnest the sins they had owned up to' and the following morning, just prior to the Field of Blood, 'all with one voice freely acknowledged in public confession and public lamentation that they had sinned against God's law'.[45]

Out of this general tide of sin and confession two themes emerge which might be more personally associated with Roger. The sin of pride is closely linked by Walter to the events at the Field of Blood, and at the start of the twelfth century this was viewed as one of the most serious sins committed by man.[46] In the Prologue to Book Two Walter warns his readers 'not ever to take pride in their own good deeds' and notes that God deserted the Antiochenes in 1119 'because we put the success of the earlier war down to the victory of our own forces'.[47] His message is that the disaster was caused by overconfidence brought on by the victory against Bursuq in 1115, and thus in a spiritual sense by relying upon one's personal ability rather than the intervention of God, and in a practical sense by Roger's decision to seek battle, as he had four years earlier, without the assistance of Jerusalem and Tripoli. Walter goes on, drawing upon the New Testament to note that 'by some ill omen we were snatched into danger, not waiting for the proud to be brought low according to their deserts and the humble to be exalted.'[48] This sin of pride is by implication closely associated with Roger's military leadership.

There are also strong echoes of the personal sins described by Fulcher of Chartres. Some of Walter's language and his persistent presentation of Roger as the penitent suggest a level of guilt that goes beyond the normal sinfulness of man. Walter remarks that 'although the performance of his duties had been neglected ... he did not delay to make amends'. Roger is then shown admitting that 'he had lived steeped in worldliness' and the patriarch 'enjoined

---

[44] Walter the Chancellor, II.1, pp. 111-12.

[45] Walter the Chancellor, II.3, pp. 120-21.

[46] B. Hamilton, *Religion in the Medieval West* (London, 1986), pp. 132-4.

[47] Walter the Chancellor, II.Prologue, p. 110. This ties in quite closely with Matthew of Edessa's references to Roger's 'pride' and 'arrogance'. Matthew of Edessa, III.79, p. 223.

[48] Walter the Chancellor, II.2, p. 114.

the prince and all his people generally to lament their evil deeds'.[49] In a private confession at dawn on the 28th Roger is reported describing his sins in an extremely sensory manner when he 'poured forth tears before the altar for all the sins he had committed against God by way of sight, hearing, taste, smell or touch' and in a speech just prior to the battle he spoke of the debt owing to God because the army had 'violated His honour in us' and 'sinned through sweetness'.[50] Perhaps most conclusively Roger is shown in his final confession rejecting the 'pleasures of the body in the past, present and future'.[51] Roger seems therefore to be portrayed as a man whose sins go beyond those of all mankind, or personal pride, to suggestions of sins of the flesh or adultery, and we must at the very least conclude that Fulcher of Chartres' accusations cannot be discredited out of hand.

c) Roger as a penitent

So, Walter certainly does not depict Roger as being free from sin. On the contrary, in his pursuit of an explanation for the Field of Blood he shows Roger to be proud and perhaps adulterous, but his purpose does not really require him to criticize Roger's character. Instead his primary message alongside that of sin is that Roger died as a penitent having carried out confession. In fact in Book Two he is shown making a series of confessions in the run up to the Field of Blood. Walter noted that before leaving Artah Roger 'did not blush to confess his sins ... quite privately in his tent' to the patriarch, archdeacon, deacon and court chaplains, as a result of which Bernard 'acting on behalf of St Peter and only for true penitence' encouraged Roger and his whole army to renounce their sins.[52] Then at dawn on 28 June at Balat Roger may have been involved in the general confession to sins 'against God's law' before Peter archbishop of Apamea. Walter did then note that Roger carried out a second private confession in his tent, where he 'poured forth tears before the altar for all the sins he had committed against God' and 'confessed to the archbishop out loud all his sins individually, of whatever kind or number, and he received a like penance'.[53] Just prior to the commencement of battle Roger is finally shown 'publicly renouncing' sins of

---

[49] Walter the Chancellor, II.1, pp. 113-14.
[50] Walter the Chancellor, II.3-4, pp. 121-2.
[51] Walter the Chancellor, II.4, p. 123.
[52] Walter the Chancellor, II.1, pp. 113-14.
[53] Walter the Chancellor, II.3, p. 121.

the flesh 'to God and the bishop' after which 'the archbishop received him on behalf of blessed Peter' and 'absolved him of all his sins in the name of the Lord and in the name of true repentance'.[54] Thus in Walter's account Roger undergoes two private confessions, one public individual confession and a possible fourth general confession. There can be little doubt that he wanted to press home the idea that Roger was cleansed of his sins before he died. He was therefore able to record that when he was killed 'settling his due debt of death in the name of the Lord ... he gave up his body to the earth and his soul to heaven' and thus achieved salvation.[55]

There is then an important distinction between Walter's and Fulcher of Chartres' attitude to Roger's sins. Both reflect upon his failings, either through implication or explicit reference, but Walter stresses above all that he died after having been purified by repeated confession, whereas Fulcher treats him as an unrepentant sinner who was 'destroyed' by God.[56] The image of Roger as a penitent was adopted by William of Tyre, and incidentally acts as a perfect example of the way in which Walter's account influenced later writers and of William's technique of combining and reconciling different historical strands. William drew first upon Fulcher of Chartres when recounting Roger's death, noting his reputation for corruption, usurpation and adultery. He went on, however, to blend Fulcher's powerful accusations with Walter's insistence upon confession, recording that 'it is said that on that expedition, on which he was stabbed and died, he had made confession of his sins to God with contrite and humble heart ... and so he rode into the trial of battle as a true penitent'.[57]

d) Roger as prince of Antioch?

It may be possible to detect echoes of the accusations of adultery, pride and avarice made by Fulcher of Chartres in Walter's text, but there is no real evidence to suggest that he was aware of Roger's reputation as a usurper and attempting to counter or conceal it. Throughout both books he is styled as the 'prince of Antioch' and there are numerous examples of his ability to wield authority effectively within the principality. Equally Walter did not enter into any discussion or justification of Roger's status, perhaps suggesting that in this

---

[54] Walter the Chancellor, II.4, p. 123.
[55] Walter the Chancellor, II.5, p. 127.
[56] Fulcher of Chartres, III.3, pp. 621-4.
[57] William of Tyre, XII.10, pp. 558-9.

case he did not feel the need to defend his reputation, and in all the descriptions of the sins associated with Roger there is nothing that hints at usurpation. Does Walter's account then suggest that Roger was seen as the rightful prince of Antioch in his own lifetime?

Major questions are, in fact, raised by Walter's account of the council held in Antioch after the Field of Blood which sought to solve the succession crisis prompted by Roger's death. During this meeting in the *curia* of St Peter 'it was decreed that the king ... should hand over the princedom of Antioch to the son of Bohemond, whose rightful inheritance it was (*cuius iuris erat*)'. He went on to note that 'this decree exists, sanctioned and confirmed by the words and hand of the king', which suggests that a charter was issued at this point confirming this arrangement.[58] This implies that Walter upheld both Roger's and Bohemond II's claim to the principality.

A range of evidence does demonstrate that Roger styled himself as prince of Antioch in his own right. In 1114 he issued a charter in which he described himself as 'Roger prince of Antioch by the grace of God'.[59] On 4 June 1118 he issued another again naming himself 'Roger, by the grace of God, prince of Antioch' and attesting as 'Roger prince of Antioch'.[60] This charter also made two references to the 'realm of Antioch (*regno Antiocheno*)', but it seems likely that in this instance the idea of a region under one individual's authority was being expressed, rather than any concept of an actual kingdom of Antioch. The charter relating to the grants made to the Genoese by Bohemond and Tancred, which Roger confirmed at some point between 1113 and 1119, was also witnessed 'Prince Roger'.[61] It is possible that the use of these titles was simply the result of Roger's chancery imitating that of Tancred.

Roger also issued Antiochene copper coins in his own name. One of his issues, depicting St George on horseback slaying the dragon, carried an inscription 'Roger prince'.[62] This coin cannot be precisely dated and thus it

---

[58] Walter the Chancellor, II.10, pp. 144-5.

[59] *Chartes de Terre Sainte provenant de l'abbaye de N. D. de Josaphat*, ed. H. F. Delaborde (Paris, 1880), pp. 26-7, no. 4.

[60] *Cartulaire général de l'ordre des Hospitaliers de S. Jean de Jérusalem (1100-1310)*, ed. J. Delaville Le Roulx (Paris, 1894), vol. 1, p. 38, no. 45.

[61] *Italia Sacra*, vol. 4, ed. F. Ughelli, pp. 847-8.

[62] D.M. Metcalf, *Coinage of the Crusades and the Latin East in the Ashmolean Museum, Oxford* 2nd. ed. (London, 1995), pp. 24-5;   M. Rheinheimer, 'Tankred und das Siegel Boemunds', *Schweizerische Numismatische Rundschau*, vol. 70 (1991), pp. 86ff.

is not clear how early he began using this title on his issues. It does, however, provide further evidence that he was using the title of 'prince', and is in fact the first surviving Antiochene issue to bear the inscription '*princeps*'. It is also significant that during the dispute over the ecclesiastical province of Tyre, Pope Paschal II acknowledged Roger's status, describing him as 'the prince of Antioch (*Antiocheni principis*)'.[63] It is, however, difficult to establish the exact significance attached to the title of 'prince of Antioch' at this time because Walter tells us that even Baldwin II, who appears to have acted only as regent of the principality, 'assumed the rank of prince, by right indeed' when he arrived at Antioch.[64]

It is possible that Roger was treated as the legitimate prince of Antioch during his lifetime, but that his premature death in 1119, leaving no direct heir of his own, precipitated a major crisis of leadership in Antioch. Given Walter's assertion that Roger made a will in June 1119 it is even possible that he actually designated Bohemond II as his heir.[65] Perhaps it was only after the Field of Blood, when a new ruler needed to be found, that Bohemond's claim to the principality received support in the East. From August 1119 onwards it seems clear that King Baldwin wanted to off-load the burden of ruling Antioch, and the Latin population of the principality would also have been keen to find a new full-time ruler. It would not be surprising if, in this political climate, the council held at Antioch in August decided to support Bohemond's claim. The statement that the principality was his by right of inheritance may have been designed to prevent any argument about Bohemond's selection.[66] The council was clearly determined to avert any dispute and Walter emphasized that its decrees were enacted out of 'great necessity'.[67] It should be noted that the council's decision to limit strictly Bohemond's ability to alter patterns of landholding in the principality may be an indication that there was a section of the Latin population which did not fully support his selection and were worried about the changes which his

---

[63] *Papsturkunden für kirchen im Heiligen Lande*, ed. R. Hiestand (Göttingen, 1985), p. 120, no. 15.

[64] Walter the Chancellor, II.9, p. 143.

[65] Walter the Chancellor, II.1, p. 113, n. 23.

[66] Walter the Chancellor, II.10, p. 144. Walter may have been obliged to record this because it appeared in the charter issued during the council.

[67] Walter the Chancellor, II.10, p. 144.

arrival might bring.[68]

Fulcher of Chartres' accusation that Roger withheld Bohemond's inheritance from him could have been made in the 1120's in order to conform with claims circulated then to support Bohemond's rights to inheritance. Once in the East Bohemond would not have wanted his claim challenged, and Fulcher may, therefore, have deemed it wise to portray Roger as a usurper and Bohemond as the legitimate prince of Antioch. Indeed, Fulcher actually describes Roger as 'Prince ... of Antioch' after the section of text containing his accusation of usurpation.[69] This inconsistency may well indicate that he interpolated the preceding passage.

In reality there is insufficient evidence to come to any concrete conclusion regarding Roger's status. It is unfortunate and in some ways surprising that other sources, such as Fulcher of Chartres, contain no record of the Antiochene council which resolved the succession. It is conceivable that, as William of Tyre suggested, Roger was only ever considered regent of Antioch, but it is also possible that he styled himself and was accepted as prince during his lifetime and that Bohemond II's claim was only supported when a new claimant to the principality was needed.

Baldwin of Le Bourcq

Baldwin of Le Bourcq, count of Edessa from 1100 to 1118 and then king of Jerusalem until his death in 1131, plays a high-profile role in the second book of Walter's account. As we might expect, in the Jerusalemite sources of Fulcher of Chartres and William of Tyre the king assumes a prominent and generally positive role in the salvation of the Antioch after the Field of Blood.[70] Although Walter was not writing to glorify the kingdom, his agenda does lead him to a similar, perhaps even more favourable, presentation of Baldwin's actions.

As we have seen, Walter's primary stated aim in Book Two was to explain why God allowed the disaster at the Field of Blood to take place. He also seemed determined to demonstrate that divine favour returned once the

---

[68] Walter the Chancellor, II.10, p. 145. This provision will be discussed in more detail below.

[69] Fulcher of Chartres, III.7, p. 635.

[70] Fulcher of Chartres, III.4-7, pp. 624-35;   William of Tyre, XII.11-12, pp. 559-62.

Latins freed themselves of pride and put their trust in God, thus balancing the catastrophic destruction of the Antiochene army with an affirmation that Christianity was in fact almighty. His principal instrument in this regard seems to have been Baldwin II. Having been a virtual nonentity in Book One, as count of Edessa, Baldwin became the perfect hero of Book Two, the agent through whom God manifested his renewed support for the Latins. From his arrival in northern Syria in the mid-summer of 1119 Walter's attitude to Baldwin is made clear when he describes him as 'the renowned king; to all the Christian people he was great in prospect, greater in arrival, greatest in the protection he brought'.[71] The laudatory depiction of Baldwin is so extreme that he begins to appear as a paragon of Christian kingship, styled as 'the king, who was second only to the Lord as lord and defender of Christendom'.[72] As we shall see Walter portrayed his character by combining the 'heroic' elements of effective leadership, chivalric knighthood and pious devotion.

i) Baldwin as the saviour of Antioch

In Walter's account Baldwin is responsible for saving the principality from disaster. Almost immediately after recording Roger's death, he informs us that his history will go on to explain how God 'by the agency of Baldwin, second king of the Latins of Jerusalem, delivered from the lion's mouth the people of the Antiochene lordship when they were almost destroyed by the enemy's devastation'.[73] Baldwin is described as 'hurrying to the aid of Christianity' when he marched into northern Syria, perhaps implying that he was moved to act by his piety.[74] Fulcher of Chartres similarly asserted that when the king received Roger's appeal for aid 'he immediately rushed to the assistance of the Antiochenes', but at the same time Fulcher does admit that he waited until the successful completion of his current campaign against the Damascenes.[75]

Walter also suggested that Baldwin had an official responsibility to act as the custodian of the Latin settlements in the Levant, describing him as the man 'whose prerogative it was to protect the fatherland' and noting that when

---

[71] Walter the Chancellor, II.9, p. 143.
[72] Walter the Chancellor, II.11, p. 151.
[73] Walter the Chancellor, II.6, p. 130.
[74] Walter the Chancellor, II.5, p. 129.
[75] Fulcher of Chartres, III.4, p. 625.

he fought it was 'for his fatherland ... as befits a king'.[76] Similarly, Baldwin was reported to have assumed temporary control of the principality out 'of great necessity' and 'for the love of justice and the common good'.[77] Thus, through his intervention in Antiochene affairs Baldwin was characterized as both the instrument of God and a dutiful ruler, whilst Walter stressed he had no ulterior motives such as megalomania or avarice.

In accordance with this image, Walter presented Baldwin as a shrewd and effective military leader. During the march to Antioch we are told that he decided to forgo the opportunity to pursue a nearby Muslim force in favour of reaching the city more rapidly.[78] Following his arrival Baldwin did attempt to pursue a Muslim force which was fleeing the region, but after a short distance he realised that 'they were a long way off and not halting in any place', gave up the chase and returned to Antioch. Walter took care to emphasize that this was neither a cowardly nor foolish action, but one that met with 'the approval of the clergy and the entire nobility'.[79]

Baldwin's authority within the principality after the council in Antioch is demonstrated by the general summons by which he 'swiftly assembled his people in the name of war, from regions far and near and wherever possible'.[80] William of Tyre tells us, for example, that Alan lord of al-Atharib was 'summoned along with his retinue by the lord king' and responded to the call to arms.[81]

Walter portrayed Baldwin as a military veteran, describing him as 'he who had often experienced the enemy's existence and wars'.[82] Thus we read that, when Muslim skirmishers were harrying the army at Tall Danith and causing the Latins to break formation, Baldwin 'relying on the vigour of his manly good sense ... perceived that they were not conducting themselves in the manner of warriors' and brought order to the Latin ranks. Similarly, the army was prepared for a surprise attack on the night of the 13th-14th because the king 'arranged for their tents to be gathered up by night, [and] the soldiers to be put on alert'.[83] Walter goes on to describe the marching formation

---

[76] Walter the Chancellor, II.9, pp. 141-3.
[77] Walter the Chancellor, II.10, p. 144.
[78] Walter the Chancellor, II.9, pp. 141-2.
[79] Walter the Chancellor, II.9, p. 143.
[80] Walter the Chancellor, II.10, p. 145.
[81] William of Tyre, XII.11, p. 559.
[82] Walter the Chancellor, II.11, p. 151.
[83] Walter the Chancellor, II.11, p. 149, p. 152.

adopted by the army when preparing to leave Tall Danith, noting that 'after the king's command everybody was put in his rightful place'.[84] Perhaps the greatest contrast with Roger is achieved by the portrayal of the king as a cautious military campaigner. After describing the loss of Zardana and the threats posed to the Latin army Walter concluded that Baldwin finally decided to ride towards Hab and seek battle, commenting that 'truly only then he welcomed war, and it was inevitable'.[85]

Through his desire to praise the king and present Tall Danith as a resounding victory, which was indicative of the renewal of divine favour, Walter does at times appear to have distorted his account of Baldwin's actions and to shield him from possible criticism. He did not, for example, provide an adequate explanation for the king's decision not to relieve the siege of Zardana. He specifically stated that when Baldwin camped at Tall Danith on *circa* 12 August he learned from 'the report of people who had heard and seen them that the infidels had besieged Zardana'. Earlier in the text Walter ruminated upon the shame caused by the surrender of al-Atharib, noting that 'the king was overcome ... was stunned and saddened. For he realized [that] ... the disgrace of its surrender was irreparable.' In spite of this, Baldwin, perhaps shrewdly, decided to wait in a defensible position instead of racing to defend the town, and as a result its citizens accepted Il-ghazi's duplicitous offer of safe conduct 'assenting to the abominable petition by this agreement'. Many were apparently killed when the town capitulated, and although Walter did note that Baldwin 'suffered greatly once more on account of the damage and disgrace to Christians' when he heard this news on the night of the 13 August, he never really addressed the fact that the king probably knowingly sacrificed Zardana in favour of military necessity.[86] At this point the desire to show the sad fate of the Latins of al-Atharib and Zardana seems to conflict slightly with the idealized picture of king.

The progress and outcome of the battle of Tall Danith are also problematic. Walter did admit that its result was inconclusive in that 'both sides considered they were both vanquished and victors' and that some

---

[84] Walter the Chancellor, II.12, p. 152.

[85] Walter the Chancellor, II.11, p. 152.

[86] Walter the Chancellor, II.11, pp. 148-51. We cannot know exactly when Zardana fell. Indeed Walter may be suggesting that the town had surrendered before Baldwin reached Tall Danith when he noted that Il-ghazi offered terms 'before the king arrived'. The important point is that Baldwin apparently still thought that the town was under siege when he arrived in the region.

sections of the Latin army fled the field bringing tidings of defeat to Hab, Tripoli and Antioch.[87] Matthew of Edessa seems to have thought that the battle was drawn, recording that 'the Christians destroyed a number of Turks, then the two armies took flight, both of them, without either being victorious or defeated, for each side had suffered many losses, the infidels as many as 5,000 men'. He did, however note that 'the king of Jerusalem had inflicted heavy blows on the infidels'.[88]

In spite of this Walter is still keen to present the battle as 'the triumph of Christianity' and Baldwin as an unquestionably competent general.[89] It is possible, however, to detect some hints of the king's difficulties in the battle. Even though he had taken time to describe the careful disposition of Latin troops, Walter still notes that Muslim ferocity 'made the very splendid battle-line of the count [Pons of Tripoli] become mixed up with the royal battle-line' during the battle. He does not pass any judgement over this lapse of military discipline even though elsewhere he pinpointed the Turcopoles' loss of formation at the Field of Blood as one of the battle's turning points.[90] Walter also admits that there was enough uncertainty about the outcome of the battle that Baldwin felt it necessary to send a messenger bearing his ring to Antioch 'so that he might proclaim by this sign the victory of the Holy Cross and announce that the king had won the field of battle'.[91]

Walter seems to have been at pains to explain how by 'ill-luck' a groom who was 'carrying one of the king's banners' was captured during a minor skirmish away from the main battle and 'without the king's knowledge'.[92] He also informs us that after the battle 'the king was forced

---

[87] Walter the Chancellor, II.12, p. 154. The other Latin sources are perhaps more blatant in claiming victory at Tall Danith. Fulcher admits that 'for a long time victory was doubtful for either side', but then asserts that 'God scattered the Turks', leaving Baldwin to stand 'manfully on the battlefield' for two days. Fulcher of Chartres, III.5, pp. 629-30. William of Tyre attempted to estimate the battle's casualties, noting that 'about seven hundred of our infantry are said to have fallen there, and a hundred of our cavalry, but of the enemy the number was as high as four thousand, not counting the mortally wounded and prisoners'. William of Tyre, XII.12, p. 561.

[88] Matthew of Edessa, III.79, p. 224; Kemal ed-Din, pp. 620-21. These indicate that the Muslims inflicted serious casualties upon the Latins, 'destroying almost all their infantry, a part of their cavalry and pushing them all back to the castle of Hab'.

[89] Walter the Chancellor, II.12, p. 156.

[90] Walter the Chancellor, II.12, p. 153; II.5, p. 127.

[91] Walter the Chancellor, II.12, p. 156.

[92] Walter the Chancellor, II.12, p. 155.

by shortage of food and drink to set out in the evening for Hab, returning to the battle-field in the morning'. In this period in the Latin East there seems to have been a tradition that victory in battle was often allotted to the side left in possession of the field.[93] Thus the loss of the royal standard and Baldwin's departure probably help to explain the question marks over Tall Danith's outcome, and it is possible that Walter manufactured the excuse regarding a lack of supplies in order to cover up the king's over-hasty withdrawal. Walter certainly seems to have been sensitive to criticism as he went on to note that on 15 August Baldwin 'even remained on the battle-field long enough to be certain from sure announcements and sure signs that the infidels had been defeated'.[94]

Walter also used Tall Danith as an opportunity to portray Baldwin as a chivalrous and skilful warrior. In contrast to the Field of Blood and even the earlier battle at Tall Danith in 1115 in which he did not describe Roger's personal prowess playing a crucial role in events, here he shows Baldwin effectively turning the tide of battle. At a key moment Walter noted that 'the king ... relying on his manly courage' sought out the strongest part of the Muslim line 'and there, calling upon the protection and assistance of the Holy Cross, he charged at great speed, overthrew the infidels and forced them to scatter' as a result of which 'he put to flight by his attack first the vanguard then the rearguard'.[95] If such a charge did take place Baldwin would surely have been accompanied by his own battle-line, but in Walter's account it almost appears that he won Tall Danith single-handedly.

ii) Baldwin as a pious ruler

Walter depicted Baldwin as a paragon of the pious Christian king, using imagery which has echoes of the First Crusade and which serves to further compare and contrast him with Roger. After his initial arrival at Antioch, Baldwin apparently paused 'to pray devoutly to God, as befits a king, in the church of St Peter' so that after absolution and 'strengthened by the Church's counsel' he could pursue the nearby Muslim forces more effectively.[96] Walter went on to use strong religious imagery when describing

---

[93] Our thanks to W.G. Zajac for his advice on this matter.

[94] Walter the Chancellor, II.12, p. 155.

[95] Walter the Chancellor, II.12, p. 154.

[96] Walter the Chancellor, II.9, p. 143. Baldwin was also said to have been permitted 'to undertake the expedition freely' at this point.

Baldwin's departure from Antioch en route for al-Atharib and the eventual battle of Tall Danith. After gathering his forces he is reported to have set off 'in a spirit of humility and with a contrite heart' and to have 'put on a woollen garment and marched barefoot'. This bears comparison with the descriptions of Raymond of St Gilles' barefooted departure from Ma'arrat-an-Nu'man during the First Crusade.[97] The image of the pious penitent is further reinforced by the indication that Baldwin also venerated local saints prior to his departure, 'hastening to entreat the Almighty in the churches of His blessed intercessors'. Throughout this passage Walter stressed that the king was motivated by piety rather than pride or personal interest. He tells us that Baldwin hoped to 'begin and finish to the honour and praise of His [God's] name' not his own, that it would be through 'the power of the Holy Cross' that he would defeat 'the tyrants and assailants of Christianity', and that he set out making 'no false claim of victory or human praise for himself, but entrusting all to God'.[98] This highlights the supposed contrast with Roger's pride and self-reliance and thus helps to explain the different fortunes of these two protagonists.

The theme of piety is continued during and after the battle of Tall Danith. Whilst in the thick of the fighting Baldwin is shown 'calling upon the protection and assistance of the Holy Cross' at the moment, discussed earlier, when Walter depicted him singlehandedly securing victory.[99] He went on to record that after the battle Baldwin returned to Antioch, where 'as was fitting, he was given a victor's welcome, further than usual outside the city'.[100] This statement further highlights this victory by comparing it with Roger's success in 1115. He then returned to the church of St Peter in Antioch in order to give thanks for a success which had been 'to the praise and glory of the Highest King and the Highest Lord'.[101]

iii) Baldwin's status within the principality

There are major question marks regarding Baldwin's position and power in Antioch during the summer of 1119. Although all the sources agree

---

[97] J.S.C. Riley-Smith, *The First Crusade and the idea of crusading* (London, 1986), p. 84.

[98] Walter the Chancellor, II.10, pp. 146-7.

[99] Walter the Chancellor, II.12, p. 154.

[100] Walter the Chancellor, II.12, p. 156.

[101] Walter the Chancellor, II.12, p. 156.

that he assumed some form of leadership within the principality it is not clear whether this was as regent or fully fledged prince. Fulcher of Chartres noted that Baldwin stayed in Antioch after Tall Danith 'since the situation there demanded it', so that he could stabilize the structure of landholding within the principality by redistributing vacant fiefs and organizing the marriage of widows. Fulcher went on to state that whilst 'up to now he had been king only of the Jerusalemites, so with the death of Prince Roger of Antioch he was made king of the Antiochenes by the addition of a second realm'.[102] No other evidence suggests that the principality was actually absorbed into the kingdom of Jerusalem at this point, and Fulcher may have been exaggerating the king's authority in order to fit in with his warnings about tyrannical abuse of power. This is not to deny that Baldwin may have temporarily exercised kingly might within the principality. William of Tyre tells us that the population of Antioch 'by common desire and freely given assent handed over to the king the care and every kind of authority over the Antiochene principality, so that in this way he would have a free hand in the principality, just as he had in the kingdom, to establish, remove and deal with all things in the role of judge'.[103] The problem is that at this early date in the history of the Latin East we have no clear definition of the powers of a king or prince and thus cannot classify Baldwin's role in northern Syria simply on the basis of action.

Instead of clarifying matters, Walter's closer testimony actually serves to complicate the argument. When the king arrived at Antioch in August 1119, Walter stated categorically that Baldwin took the title of prince, noting that 'he was called by God and elevated by His gift and assumed the rank of prince, by right indeed'.[104] Elsewhere Walter's statements correlate more closely with the other sources. He remarked that God 'had subjected nearly all the kingdom of the eastern Christians' to Baldwin, and then noted a little later in the text that 'with His assent the king had taken on the governance of the kingdom'.[105] He does seem to have been empowered to confer princely authority upon Bohemond II as Walter tells us that 'for the love of justice and the common good, (he) would hand over the principality of Antioch, with his own daughter, to Bohemond's son' when he arrived in the Levant, but, as we

---

[102] Fulcher of Chartres, III.7, pp. 634-5.
[103] William of Tyre, XII.12, p. 562.
[104] Walter the Chancellor, II.9, p. 143.
[105] Walter the Chancellor, II.10, p. 144, p. 147.

have seen, Walter also noted that the principality 'belonged of right' to the young Bohemond. Perhaps Baldwin assumed the title of prince as a temporary measure, before any concrete decision about the succession had been reached, but even so there are no surviving charters, coins or seals where he styled himself in this way. Given Walter's heroic depiction of the king it is also possible that he exaggerated his status.

There can be little doubt that Walter portrayed Baldwin in an extremely favourable light, perhaps in order to contrast what he saw as the king's piety and humility with Roger's arrogance and ultimate destruction. As a consequence, we must be wary of bias or distortion not only in Baldwin's depiction, but also in the account of the battle of Tall Danith and, to some extent, the provisions made for the Antiochene succession.

Bernard of Valence, patriarch of Antioch

Although Patriarch Bernard (1100-1135) may not play as prominent a role as Roger or Baldwin II in *The Antiochene Wars* he does represent the most spiritually perfect and unsullied figure of the account.[106] As we shall see, Walter characterized him as the spiritual leader of Latin Antioch, the bastion of moral rectitude within the principality and the sagacious advisor of temporal rulers. He appears as such an irreproachable individual that he almost assumes saintly qualities and his opinions take on divine licence. The major historiographical problem with this laudatory depiction is that we have little in the way of a corrective to balance or judge Walter's account. *The Antiochene Wars* is in fact the most important source for much of Bernard's career, and he certainly never plays so prominent a role in any other surviving narrative.

This is not to suggest that we cannot piece together some evidence of his life and status with the principality. Bernard, the former chaplain of Adhémar of Le Puy, the papal legate on the First Crusade, first came to prominence in northern Syria when at the end of 1099 he was consecrated as the first Latin bishop of Artah.[107] Within six months he was elevated to

---

[106] See: Walter the Chancellor, I.1, p. 82, n. 31.

[107] Ralph of Caen, 'Gesta Tancredi in Expeditione Hierosolymitana', *Recueil des historiens des croisades. Historiens occidentaux*, vol. 3 (Paris, 1866), p. 704.

become the first Latin patriarch of Antioch, replacing the previous Greek incumbent, John IV the Oxite.[108] Traditionally the patriarchate of Antioch was below only Rome and Constantinople in importance, ruling over the church of all Asia except for Palestine. In theory, Antioch had precedence over the patriarchate of Jerusalem and Bernard was the pre-eminent spiritual figure in the Levant. In fact the patriarchs of Antioch and Jerusalem entered into heated dispute over control of the ecclesiastical province of Tyre during Bernard's career.[109] Although he did not win a total victory in this conflict Bernard did demonstrate that he could defend his authority not only in the Levant but also against the pope in Rome.

Bernard held the office of patriarch for thirty-five years, during which period seven individuals ruled the principality and his stable position at the head of the church appears to have allowed him to develop considerable personal authority in northern Syria. Charter evidence demonstrates that Bernard was involved in the secular government of the principality. He attended the princely court, appearing high in the witness lists of a number of important charters issued by the princes of Antioch.[110] He was also capable of playing an important diplomatic role in the region. As patriarch, he had authority over both the principality of Antioch and the county of Edessa and thus seems to have acted as a negotiator between the two political powers during the inter-Latin struggles of 1108 and 1127.[111]

Bernard does therefore appear to have been a figure of considerable spiritual and political importance and thus we cannot automatically discredit Walter's evidence. We must, however, exercise caution when assessing the patriarch's role and be aware that Walter may have exaggerated his standing because of personal admiration for his character and, perhaps, to fulfil certain needs within his narrative.

i) Bernard as a spiritual father

From his first appearance in 1114 Bernard is portrayed as the central figure of spiritual authority in northern Syria. After a major earthquake

---

[108] William of Tyre, VI.23, p. 340.

[109] J.G. Rowe, 'The Papacy and the ecclesiastical province of Tyre', *Bulletin of John Rylands Library*, vol. 43 (1960-1961), pp. 160-89.

[110] *Italia Sacra*, IV, pp. 847-8; William of Tyre, X.24, p. 484; *Carte dell'Archivio Capitolare di Pisa (1101-1120)*, vol. 4, ed. M.T. Carli (Rome, 1969), pp. 80-83, no. 37-8.

[111] Ibn al-Athir, p. 262; William of Tyre, XIII.22, p. 615.

affected 'Antioch and its region' on 29 November, Walter asserted that the Latin and eastern Christian population of the city turned for guidance to the patriarch, 'renouncing their past and present pleasures to Lord Bernard'. Walter reflected that the patriarch and his clergy then began 'very humbly entreating God' and as a result 'the Lord took pity on the rest of his Antiochene people'. At this point Bernard also seems to have performed Mass and delivered a sermon containing some instruction on correct Christian behaviour.[112]

Shortly afterwards, when news of Marash's destruction reached the city, public confidence was shattered and it fell to Bernard to counsel the population. In a prime example of Walter's exaggerated praise of the patriarch's character he described him as the 'most experienced of all men of the place and time'. He went on to note that he drew upon 'philosophical teaching' to inform his sermon and was able to calm those 'who were now almost despairing of life' through the 'sweetness of holy preaching'. Bernard was also responsible for setting out the method of ritual purification of the population when 'he proclaimed a three-day fast for all the people' designed to demonstrate their contrition.[113] This bears some comparison with the activities of Adhémar of Le Puy during the siege of Antioch in 1098.[114]

Bernard again played a central role in the rituals of spiritual preparation for the campaign leading to the 1115 battle of Tall Danith. Walter tells us that, when giving a sermon to the army at Rugia, 'the virtuous patriarch ... spoke clearly and plainly words more pleasing to God than to men' and 'as befits a father' he pointed out their sins and took their confessions.[115] It is also possible that he offered some form of indulgence to the Latin army at this stage.

Then, before returning to Antioch 'the reverend patriarch celebrated the ritual of Mass', absolved the army of their sins and 'strengthened them all with his patriarchal benediction'.[116] Throughout this section Bernard is naturally at the centre of spiritual affairs, and Walter did emphasize the fact that absolution, benediction and ultimately salvation are conveyed by God

---

[112] Walter the Chancellor, I.1, pp. 81-2.

[113] Walter the Chancellor, I.1, p. 83.

[114] Raymond of Aguilers, *Le 'Liber de Raymond d'Aguilers'*, ed. J.H. & L.L. Hill (Paris, 1969), p. 54.

[115] Walter the Chancellor, I.4, p. 46.

[116] Walter the Chancellor, I.5, p. 97.

through the patriarch. Independent evidence demonstrates precedents for this spiritual role. In 1104, before the battle of Harran, Bernard and Archbishop Benedict of Edessa heard the confessions of the Latin soldiers, and in 1105, before the battle of Artah, he preached a sermon and prescribed a three day fast which was then observed.[117]

ii) Bernard and the practice of warfare

Walter also seems to have been keen to point out that while Bernard might sanction or even direct violence, he did not contravene canon law by actually participating in warfare. Thus, prior to the battle of Tall Danith in 1115, he returned to Antioch rather than continue with the army and Walter informs us that 'he humbly commended them for the cure of souls to the bishop of Jabala'. Bernard was physically distanced from military affairs, in contrast to William of Jabala, who, we are told, 'was going off to war at the same time' as the rest of the army. Instead of direct action, the patriarch is shown 'earnestly entreating the Lord and interceding with Him' in order to gain victory for the Latins.[118]

Walter's determination to distance Bernard from direct military action is clearest during his description of the defence of Antioch in 1119 after the Field of Blood. He suggested that in early August 'the impending loss of the city of Antioch' was feared, because after the disastrous battle 'it was deprived of military service and almost the entire military force of Frankish citizens was lost'. Rather than an external attack, however, the Latins apparently feared the rebellion of the city's indigenous eastern Christian population.[119] In this context, Walter tells us, 'of necessity, all came down to the clergy' and primarily to the patriarch. His organisation of the city's defences at this point has probably become the most noted episode of his career in modern historiography, and Walter certainly highlighted his personal authority and wisdom in his account of events.[120]

He describes Bernard 'acting wisely about these and other things' and states that 'strengthened by God's power' he decided 'that he himself would

---

[117] Albert of Aachen, IX.39; IX.47.

[118] Walter the Chancellor, I.5, p. 97.

[119] For further discussion of Walter's attitude to eastern Christians, see pp. 67-8.

[120] B. Hamilton, *The Latin Church in the Crusader States. The Secular Church* (London, 1980), pp. 21-2; C. Cahen, *La Syrie du nord*, p. 288; S. Runciman, *A history of the crusades*, vol. 2, p. 151.

take charge of the entire city for himself and the clergy'. With this authority he decreed a form of curfew, whereby non-Latins were not permitted to carry arms nor travel within the city at night without some form of light to mark them out. He also organized the city's defences and took the extreme step of using 'armed clergy' to augment Antioch's weakened forces. It appears that to some extent Walter approved of this measure, because he noted that 'the clergy ... acted the part of military service wisely and vigorously ... and with God's strength'. Perhaps he believed that necessity justified this action and that Antioch's survival demonstrated divine approval. He certainly suggested that these measures met with approval within the city noting that 'all the citizens carefully obeyed as one the orders of this wisest of fathers and teachers'.[121]

In spite of this positive attitude Walter still took pains to distance Bernard from direct involvement in military activity. He noted that while the others defended the city 'that same patriarch, preferring to fight with prayers rather than weapons, constantly beseeched God from the heart for the safety and defence of the Christian people'.[122] At the same time he made regular visits to 'his armed clergy and knights' to improve their morale and perhaps to direct their minds to the concept of right intention in warfare. Thus, Walter managed to depict Bernard as the central force behind the defence of Antioch while maintaining his pure Christian image.

iii) The depiction of Bernard in relationship to Roger and Baldwin

Walter's portrayal of Bernard is perhaps most interesting in terms of his relationship to the source's other two key protagonists, Roger and King Baldwin II. Walter may, to some extent, have used the patriarch to reconcile the different agendas within his account by characterizing him as the mouthpiece of God or indicator of divine judgement. Thus in Book One Bernard's positive relationship with Roger serves to emphasize divine support for the success of 1115, while in Book Two Walter is able to explain the defeat at the Field of Blood and avoid excessive direct criticism of Roger by channelling the objections to his actions through Bernard. Similarly, in rendering Baldwin and Bernard's relationship in such a positive light, Walter heightens the comparison between Baldwin's ample respect for 'divine' opinion, and his consequent success, with Roger's pride and failure.

---

[121] Walter the Chancellor, II.8, pp. 138-9.
[122] Walter the Chancellor, II.8, p. 139.

a) Roger

In Book One Walter stresses that Roger had great respect for the patriarch. Before leaving Antioch to meet Il-ghazi and Tughtegin in 1115 Roger made a series of preparations which included visiting Bernard to receive what is described as 'permission and patriarchal blessing'. Upon first inspection this suggests that he felt obliged to seek some form patriarchal sanction for the forthcoming military campaign. He also seems to have conferred some powers of regency upon Bernard, as we are told that 'he commended to God and the lord patriarch himself the city and all his possessions' before departing.[123] There is no definite evidence to suggest that Bernard was officially appointed as regent of Antioch on other occasions. During the early crisis brought on by Bohemond I's capture in 1100 he is not mentioned, while in the years after the Field of Blood Baldwin does not seem to have empowered the patriarch to act in his stead. He did continue to act as a high profile advisor in this period, however, counselling Joscelin of Courtenay, count of Edessa, to relieve Zardana in 1122 and to travel to Jerusalem to gather forces which might help to free the then captive King Baldwin II.[124]

The theme of respect for Bernard is reiterated later in Book One when, after Roger advanced to Rugia, Walter noted that 'with utmost devotion he entreated the lord patriarch to join him there'. This wording suggests that he wanted his audience to view Roger and Bernard as, at the very least, equals. He also related that Roger wished the Latin army to be 'empowered by divine office and by his [Bernard's] benediction' so that 'they could more freely and more safely fight in God's service', again suggesting the concept of violence sanctioned by the patriarch.[125] Bernard's approval of the 1115 campaign, and thus Roger's victory, is again emphasized by the fact that 'the reverend patriarch' headed the procession which greeted the returning army outside Antioch.[126]

As we have seen, however, in Book Two Walter's purpose seems to have been more complex. It appears that, above all, he wanted to explain why the Latins were defeated at the Field of Blood, and the cause that he focused upon was spiritual impurity. In the prologue to Book Two he suggested that

---

[123] Walter the Chancellor, I.2, p. 86.
[124] Walter the Chancellor, II.16, pp. 170-71; Kemal ed-Din, p. 635, p. 644.
[125] Walter the Chancellor, I.4, p. 96.
[126] Walter the Chancellor, I.7, p. 106.

the Antiochenes, suffering from the sin of pride, had been 'ungrateful to God and unmindful of His kindness'.[127] Later he noted that true soldiers of Christ ought 'not to boast of their virtues, but to reform their behaviour', in effect to dedicate themselves to spiritual purity rather than military prowess.[128] Walter's attempts to contrast the two campaigns in spiritual terms were not really effective because he was also determined to demonstrate that in 1119 Roger and his forces died with pure hearts, having heard a number of sermons, taken Mass, made public confession of their sins and venerated a relic of the True Cross. He was also not prepared to criticize directly or severely his former hero Roger in relation to the disaster at the Field of Blood.

Walter appears to use Patriarch Bernard to reconcile these conflicting agendas. Having established him as the embodiment of Christian purity, 'a man of venerable life and most distinguished in demeanour', Bernard's words and opinions take on a divine sanction and he can almost be characterized as the mouthpiece of God.[129] Thus Walter was able to explain the Field of Blood by carefully describing how Roger failed to heed the advice of the patriarch and he channelled criticism of Roger's decisions through Bernard.

At the start of Book Two Walter reiterated Roger's respect for the patriarch by informing us that after advancing to Artah he 'humbly' asked him to join him there. He also recorded, however, that Roger immediately made the crucial error of ignoring Bernard's 'holy doctrine and advice' to await reinforcement by King Baldwin II and Pons of Tripoli before crossing the Jabal Talat, and thus to delay the move from the well protected camp at Artah to the exposed site at Balat.[130]

Then, using 'the liveliness of his powerful mind', Bernard gave a sermon in which he stressed the army's sins and the importance of right intention in the coming warfare. The underlying implication seems to be that the patriarch disapproved of the hasty advance from Artah, because once Roger 'disregarded the warnings of the fatherly priest' and proclaimed that 'no one should wait there any longer', Bernard launched into a second speech in which he advocated caution rather than bravado and plainly pointed out the

---

[127] Walter the Chancellor, II.Prologue, p. 110.
[128] Walter the Chancellor, II.1, p. 112.
[129] Walter the Chancellor, II.1, p. 111.
[130] Walter the Chancellor, II.1, pp. 110-11. Thus, in Walter's account, one of the most important strategic observations is actually made by a clerical figure.

dangers ahead. As a result 'the prince, frightened in every possible way by the voice of the holy man' hastened to make a private confession and a will. He did not, however, change his mind about advancing to Balat, and Walter seems to have been rather unclear about whether Bernard was primarily concerned with the spiritual purity of the army or Roger's intentions, because the patriarch made no further attempts to change his mind but simply advised the Antiochenes to fight as true 'soldiers of Christ'. This confusion was perhaps caused by Walter's overlapping agendas. He did suggest that Bernard had an almost divine foreknowledge of the Field of Blood, noting that he predicted events 'just as happened to the prince and the majority of his men not long afterwards', and then left Artah 'pouring forth tears and constant sobs from the depths of his heart' seemingly in response to his prescience.[131]

Walter almost seems to suggest that he gave up trying to prevent the imminent disaster when he noted that 'the aforesaid father, therefore, having compassion for his [Roger's] weakness and that of all the people, acting on behalf of St Peter, and only for true penitence urged the army to renounce sin.' Then, for the second time, Walter reflected upon Roger's fate by recording 'and would that this had saved him!'[132] From a historical point of view it is possible that Walter combined the knowledge that Bernard advised caution prior to the Field of Blood, but did not fully refuse to provide spiritual backing to the expedition, with his desire to present Roger and his army as purified penitents, while at the same time censuring the military errors which led to the disaster of 1119.

b) Baldwin

Bernard's relationship with King Baldwin II serves to contrast the latter's attitude and fortunes with those of Roger. Where Roger failed to heed the advice of the patriarch and met with disaster the king gained full ecclesiastical support and God's sanction and thus enjoyed what Walter presents as a resounding victory. Walter stressed that Baldwin set great store by the patriarch's opinion, noting that when the king arrived in northern Syria in August 1119 he hurried to Antioch, at least in part so that he might 'take counsel with the patriarch', and we are told that he was subsequently 'invigorated by the patriarch's advice'.[133]

---

[131] Walter the Chancellor, II.1, pp. 111-14.
[132] Walter the Chancellor, II.1, p. 113.
[133] Walter the Chancellor, II.9, pp. 142-3.

Then, before the campaign which culminated in the battle of Tall Danith, 'the patriarch and the clerical order, whose right it is to advise' again stressed the importance of right intention in the coming war noting that 'if they [the Latins] fought lawfully with true righteousness on their side' they would gain victory. Baldwin apparently took this guidance to heart, as Walter tells us that 'the king and the rest busied themselves amending their behaviour'. Just before leaving Antioch the Latin army attended Mass in the church of St Peter, where 'the patriarch celebrated the divine office', he then 'advised them and prepared them for battle and signed them with his heavenly patriarchal benediction'. Finally, on their departure 'the patriarch once again took up the Holy Cross in his consecrated hands and once again signed them all with its power'.[134]

Therefore, in stark contrast to the preparations prior to the Field of Blood, Walter stresses that there were no clerical objections to the king's proposed campaign and that the patriarch offered the army both his sanction and a full absolution of sins. As we have seen, however, Bernard's actual treatment of the two expeditions may not have been that different.

As Bernard is the most eulogized figure within Walter's account we must obviously exercise caution when attempting to assess the historical accuracy of his characterization. This is not to suggest that we must discount the patriarch's importance. His depiction has some resonance with the career of Adhémar of Le Puy, with whom had a strong personal connection, and it is possible that like the papal legate Bernard did exercise a significant influence upon the secular world around him.[135]

---

[134] Walter the Chancellor, II.10, p. 144, p. 147.

[135] We should be aware that with all three figures discussed here it is impossible to precisely delineate between historical 'reality', the personal views of Walter the Chancellor and the historical constructs which he may have created in order to reconcile the different narrative strands and agendas within his account. The analysis offered here is, of course, only an attempt to assess the aims and views of the author and, given the relative paucity of evidence for his life and the events he recorded, it can only be presented as hypothesis.

The historical value of Walter's account

Walter and the early history of the principality of Antioch

One of the remarkable qualities of Walter the Chancellor's account is that, as a member of Antiochene court, he wrote from the perspective of the principality rather than the kingdom of Jerusalem. In this early period only Ralph of Caen, the biographer of Tancred of Hauteville, can be said to have had a similar focus, and he dedicated most of his account to the history of the First Crusade rather than the Latin settlement of northern Syria.[1] For the period between 1114 and 1122, and most importantly for the dramatic events of 1119, *The Antiochene Wars* is the only known Latin source written within the principality. This is in particular contrast to Fulcher of Chartres' *History of Jerusalem*. Walter's unique interest in and knowledge of the principality's history helps to clarify the narrative of events and contributes to the study of institutions and prosopography.

i) Antiochene institutions

Walter the Chancellor is practically the only source which provides any information about the early history of the principality's institutions. The paucity of other evidence does add value to Walter's account, but it also makes it virtually impossible to judge the accuracy of his statements. Even though he does not seem to have been especially concerned with self-aggrandizement, we must obviously exercise particular care when assessing the evidence for his own actions as an Antiochene official.

Walter mentions Roger's household on a number of occasions and gives some insight into its role. This group might be loosely termed as the prince's closest advisors and probably consisted of the great officers, namely constable, marshal, chancellor, chamberlain and perhaps seneschal.[2] The household may also have had separate domestic and military sections, which consisted of the prince's servants and knights. J.O. Prestwich has pointed out that in Norman England, an area to which we might look for institutional

---

[1] Ralph of Caen, pp. 587-716.

[2] Given that the principality was ruled by a succession of southern Italian Normans in this early period it is not surprising that Antiochene institutions appear to have been largely drawn from a Norman template.

comparison, the king's military retinue (*familia regis*) had already started to become a distinct body from the royal household (*domus regis*) in this period.[3] It is possible that a similar distinction was developing in the principality as Walter does mention both *domestici* and *familiares*, but this variation in terminology may not be deliberate.

Walter noted that in 1115 Roger made a hurried advance from Antioch to Rugia in order to meet the renewed threat posed by Bursuq, 'taking only the household members of his retinue'.[4] He was later joined by a full levy of Antiochene and Edessene forces, but Walter's evidence suggests that even in an emergency the prince would not be separated from his household. Although Walter does not specifically record that the Antiochene household participated in the first battle of Tall Danith, he does note their presence beside Roger after the victory.[5] In 1119 the prince's household apparently stayed with him prior to and during the disaster at the Field of Blood. After holding a council with his advisors on 27 June, Roger summoned his 'household (*domestici*)', and ordered them to see that the council's decisions were carried out. Later that same night Roger used his 'household (*familiares*)' to transmit the decisions relating to civil matters which he and the chancellor of Antioch had just made.[6] Walter went on to note that Roger was accompanied into the battle of the Field of Blood by at least some of his household, recording that at the moment of his death he was fighting alongside 'a few of his men (*comitatus*)', which can probably be understood to mean his military household or retinue.[7]

Walter does not mention a constable of Antioch, the chief military officer with the principality, which is strange given his subject matter. We do know that the office was filled in this period because a charter issued by Roger of Salerno at some point between 1113 and 1118 was attested by one 'Adam the Constable'.[8] He made one brief reference to a marshal, noting that just before the battle of the Field of Blood Roger 'summoned his marshal (*agaso*)' and messengers and then 'commanded the entire army to prepare for

---

[3] J.O. Prestwich, 'The military household of the Norman kings', *English Historical Review*, vol. 96 (1981), p. 7.

[4] Walter the Chancellor, I.4, p. 96.

[5] Walter the Chancellor, I.7, p. 105.

[6] Walter the Chancellor, II.3, p. 120.

[7] Walter the Chancellor, II.5, p. 127.

[8] *Italia Sacra*, vol.4, ed. F. Ughelli, pp. 847-8.

battle'. This mobilization was carried out in three stages, under the direction of three horn-blasts and it is possible that these were the marshal's responsibility.[9] In the West and in the kingdom of Jerusalem the marshal was the constable's lieutenant, and frequently acted with him or by his command; in Normandy the marshal was primarily associated with the care and maintenance of horses.[10]

Walter also recorded that a certain Alberic was the third messenger to return to the main Latin army, having been amongst the forty knights who were sent on a scouting party under the command of Mauger of Hauteville.[11] Alberic was described as 'vice-seneschal (vice-dapifer)'. In general terms the seneschal was a lord's chief lieutenant, controlling financial administration and the judicial system, and also supervising all matters relating to castles, including the transfer of garrisons. It was not specifically stated that Alberic was the vice-seneschal of Antioch, acting in place of the seneschal, but this is the most likely possibility. Thus, although there is no specific reference to a seneschal within the principality until 1149, when it was held by Eschivard of Sarmenya, it was probably filled by 1119.[12]

The first information about the chancellor of Antioch is provided by Walter the Chancellor himself. His account suggests that, as chancellor, he had a close personal relationship with Roger of Salerno, holding what would appear to be an important consultative position. The Norman chancellor was also closely linked to the ruler, being noted in the *Constitutio Domus Regis* to have always been 'in the household', never 'out of the household'.[13] Walter recorded that on the eve of the battle of the Field of Blood, Roger 'secretly called his chancellor' in order to discuss 'what should properly be done for the business in hand about those things which seemed burdensome to the warriors'.[14] This passage provides us with a number of important insights into the role of the chancellor. First, the fact that he apparently met the prince in private emphasizes the close nature of his relationship with Roger, although Walter may have exaggerated this factor. Secondly, it appears that the sphere

---

[9] Walter the Chancellor, II.4, p. 123.

[10] J.L. La Monte, *Feudal Monarchy in the Latin kingdom of Jerusalem, 1100 to 1291* (Cambridge, Mass., 1932), p. 119.

[11] Walter the Chancellor, II.4, p. 124.

[12] C. Cahen, *La Syrie du Nord*, p. 463.

[13] F. Lot & R. Fawtier, *Histoire des Institutions Françaises au Moyen Age*, vol. 1 (Paris, 1957), p. 27.

[14] Walter the Chancellor, II.3, p. 120.

of the chancellor's authority encompassed chiefly non-military matters, and that the extent of his power was primarily consultative rather than active. The responsibility for implementing the decisions made in this meeting apparently devolved upon Roger's chamberlain and his household knights. The former may have been summoned because the 'precious vessels' which needed to be transported to Artah constituted part of the princely treasury, of which he had custody.

Walter's account provides a brief but illuminating glimpse into the early administration of the city of Antioch. He recorded that in order to deal with the crisis precipitated by the earthquakes which racked northern Syria in the early summer of 1115, Roger of Salerno met with Ralph of Acre, duke of Antioch. The duke then called a council of 'the greater' and 'the lesser' to which the viscount, magistrate, herald and judge were summoned.[15] It is probably safe to assume that these individuals were city officials involved in the administration of Antioch, although little more can be said of their roles.

Walter's evidence suggests that in 1115 the duke exerted the greatest authority, after the prince, over the civil governance of the city. During their initial meeting Roger and the duke discussed what action should be taken to repair the extensive damage to Antioch and what ought to be done by 'the lord and his warriors for the exigencies of war'. A policy was formulated at this meeting, which the duke subsequently passed on to the *maiores et minores* at the council which he called. Walter recorded that after having heard the 'lord's decree' all those present agreed to a course of action, almost certainly that suggested by Roger, whereby the responsibility, probably both financial and physical, for repairing damage to walls and towers would be assigned to those holding land and honours and in accordance with their relative resources.[16]

The fact that Roger first consulted Ralph of Acre on this matter and that Ralph was then responsible for calling and presiding over the civil council clearly indicates the duke's importance. The degree of autonomy which the duke possessed is, however, open to question. Although he did summon the council, Walter recorded that it was done 'by the lord prince's authorized command'.[17] Roger discussed the matter with Ralph of Acre, and apparently the prince did not simply tell Ralph what to do but formed a policy with him,

---

[15] Walter the Chancellor, I.2, p. 85.
[16] Walter the Chancellor, I.2, pp. 85-6.
[17] Walter the Chancellor, I.2, p. 85.

yet this solution was presented by the duke to the subsequent council as 'his lord's decree'. From this single example it is impossible to form any concrete theory about the duke of Antioch's ability to exert independent control over the civil government of the city, but in this case it appears that Ralph consulted closely with the prince before implementing any policy and acted primarily as his representative and with his authority.

Independent charter evidence seems to confirm Ralph's position. A copy of Tancred's charter of 1101 granting the Genoese privileges and quarters in Antioch and Latakia was reconfirmed in the palace of St. Peter between 1113 and 1118 by Roger of Salerno and a group of men including Ralph *dux*.[18] Ralph was the second witness after Roger, an indication of his importance. The significance of his office is underlined by Ibn al-Qalanisi's decision to report the death of the duke of Antioch in 1117 or 1118.[19]

Walter's account also demonstrates that in this early period landholders made use of their own households and had begun to develop local administrative frameworks to assist with the governance of their lordships. In 1119 Alan of al-Atharib was reported to have defended al-Atharib against the army of Il-ghazi in that year with a 'household'.[20] He then travelled to Antioch in the company of 'his retinue'.[21] Walter implied that Alan also had rear vassals by recording that he travelled to Antioch in 1119 'with his knights (*cum suis militibus*)'.[22] Geoffrey the Monk was described leading 'a distinguished battle-line' into the battle of the Field of Blood.[23] These references suggest that households, or perhaps more loosely, close groups of followers, 'retinues (*comitatus*)', had become attached to both Alan and Geoffrey by 1119.

ii) The prosopographical study of the principality

Walter's account is a relatively rich source of prosopographical information. In a medieval context specific information about individuals other than kings, princes and other rulers is quite rare. *The Antiochene Wars*

---

[18] *Italia Sacra*, vol. 4, ed. F. Ughelli. p. 478.

[19] Ibn al-Qalanisi, p. 157.

[20] Walter the Chancellor, II.2, p. 117.

[21] William of Tyre, XII.11, pp. 559.

[22] Walter the Chancellor, II.10, p. 145.

[23] Walter the Chancellor, II.5, p. 126. Geoffrey may also have had his own seneschal, as Walter mentions 'Arnulf, seneschal of Marash' amongst the captives in Aleppo. Walter the Chancellor, II.15, p. 165.

furnishes some valuable details of the principality's population. Excluding
Roger, Patriarch Bernard and himself, Walter names twenty-two individuals
who were specifically connected to the principality.[24] Of these, one can be
confirmed from the sources to have held ecclesiastical office within the
patriarchate of Antioch, another, as we have seen, can be confirmed as the
duke of Antioch, while a further nine can be shown to have held land within
the principality.

Walter noted that 'Peter the archbishop of Apamea' acted as the
foremost ecclesiastical figure in the run-up to the battle of the Field of
Blood.[25] Peter of Narbonne was in fact consecrated as bishop of Albara in
1099, during the First Crusade.[26] His career was subsequently furthered by
his elevation to the archiepiscopal see of Apamea. This town was captured by
Tancred in 1106,[27] and by 1110 Peter had been consecrated as its archbishop.
In a charter of 1110 he appeared both as 'archbishop of Apamea', and
'archbishop of Albara'.[28] As he clearly retained control of both dioceses, and
the two titles appear to have been interchangeable throughout his life, Walter
has correctly identified him.[29]

Walter associates only one of the nine independently identifiable
Antiochene landholders with his known lordship. Alan, who is probably the
same 'young man Alan' referred to in 1115, is described as 'lord of that same
castle (al-Atharib)'.[30] He appears elsewhere in both Latin and Islamic
sources, perhaps gaining a reputation in the Muslim world because his
lordship lay on the frontier with Aleppo.[31] Throughout the rest of his account

---

[24] Sanson of Bruera, who was amongst the captives executed by Il-ghazi may have been
an Antiochene captured at the Field of Blood or a Jerusalemite taken prisoner at the second
battle of Tall Danith. Walter the Chancellor, II.16, pp. 166-7.

[25] Walter the Chancellor, II.3, p. 119.

[26] *Gesta Francorum et aliorum Hierosolimitanorum*, ed. & trans. R. Hill (London 1962),
p. 75.

[27] Albert of Aachen, X.22-24;   Kemal ed-Din, p. 595.

[28] *Le Cartulaire de chapitre du Saint-Sépulchre de Jérusalem*, ed. G. Bresc-Bautier (Paris,
1984), pp. 197-9, n. 86.

[29] Walter also identified Bishop William of Jabala, 'a man worthy of praise in every
respect', whom he suggests acted as Patriarch Bernard's legate during the second campaign
of 1115. Walter the Chancellor, I.5, pp. 77-8. No other source mentions William, however,
and the next known incumbent of the see was Bishop Romanus in 1133. *Regesta Regni
Hierosolymitani (MCVII-MCCXCI)*, ed. R. Röhricht, 2 vols (Oeniponti, 1893-1904), n. 143

[30] Walter the Chancellor, I.7, p. 104;   II.2, p. 117.

[31] William of Tyre, XII.11, pp. 559. This appears to have been drawn from Walter.
Kemal ed-Din, p. 628, p. 635, p. 639;   Ibn al-Athir, pp. 166-7.

Walter seems to be uninterested in associating individuals with lordships, and in all probability Alan was only connected with al-Atharib because of the events which took place there during the narrative. He does imply that the colourfully named Robert fitz-Fulk the Leper was associated with Zardana, because news of that town's fate is transmitted by one of his priests.[32] Robert, whose lordship included Zardana, Saone and Balatanos appears in a number of other narrative and documentary sources.[33] Other known figures include Guy Le Chevreuil, whom Albert of Aachen described as 'prince of Tarsus and Mamistra';[34] Guy Fresnel the lord of Harim;[35] Rainald Mazoir, lord of Marqab;[36] and Geoffrey the Monk, count of Marash.[37] Robert of Sourdeval,[38] Robert of Vieux-Pont[39] and Robert of St Lô[40] are all known to have held land within the principality, but were not associated with a specific town or castle by any source.

In spite of his seeming reluctance to record lordships, Walter does make a significant contribution to our prosopographical knowledge of the principality. It is significant, if not necessarily surprising, that he makes no apparent errors when associating known individuals with Antioch. We can therefore have some confidence when describing otherwise unknown figures such as Theoderic of Barneville, Mauger of Hauteville and Eudes of Forest-Moutiers as inhabitants of the principality.[41]

Walter as a military source

Given the title of Walter's account it is not surprising that military events make up a large proportion of the source. For someone who probably

---

[32] Walter the Chancellor, II.11, pp. 150-51.

[33] *Carte dell'Archivio Capitolare di Pisa (1101-1120)*, vol. 4, pp. 80-83, n. 37-8; *Chartes de Terre Sainte provenant de l'abbaye de N. D. de Josaphat*, pp. 26-7, n. 4; Usamah ibn-Munqidh, p. 149;   Kemal ed-Din, pp. 620-2.

[34] See p. 102, n. 157.

[35] See pp. 104-5, n. 173.

[36] See p. 125, n. 79.

[37] See p. 126, n. 86.

[38] See p. 104, n. 168.

[39] See pp. 116-17, n. 41.

[40] See p. 127, n. 90.

[41] Walter the Chancellor, I.5, p. 99;   II.3, p. 119;   II.4, p. 124.

had a clerical background, Walter proves himself to be an interested and generally capable historian of warfare, recording details of strategy, battle tactics, military tradition and technology and attempting to render coherent descriptions of the major battles in 1115 and 1119.

i) Military practice and tradition

Walter shows awareness of the military strategies adopted by the Latins. Early in Book One he noted that Roger 'made for the borderlands' early in the summer of 1115 'as is the custom of that region' in order to protect the principality more effectively from invasion during the campaigning season.[42] He may, however, have been wrong to suggest that Roger's decision to counter Bursuq's invasion by advancing to Apamea was prompted by a desire to travel 'to those places from which he could sooner attack the enemy head on'[43]. As Walter himself went on to record, Roger pursued a defensive rather than aggressive strategy at Apamea, avoiding battle while holding his forces in a protected position and awaiting reinforcement. Apparently some of the Latins viewed this as an 'act of cowardice', but Walter showed his own approval by noting that others 'of greater perspicacity' realised that he was sensibly awaiting King Baldwin I, 'whose arrival was very near'. Walter was here commenting more upon the importance of leadership than manpower, because he stated that victory would be won by the 'prudent disposition and enormous experience of himself (Roger) and the king ... for, as experience shows, a handful of warriors with boldness and ingenuity will more often prevail in war than an ill-disciplined and unreliable multitude of armed men'.[44] In 1119 King Baldwin II appears to have used a similar holding strategy at Tall Danith, perhaps in the hope of drawing Il-ghazi into battle on unfavourable terrain, but on this occasion Walter makes no comment regarding his intentions.

Walter's most direct remarks about Latin strategy come in the period leading up to the Field of Blood, when he reflects upon the decision to advance from Artah to Balat. As we have seen, this criticism is channelled through Patriarch Bernard and focused upon the relative strategic merits of the two sites. At Artah, Walter noted, 'the lie of the land was abundant and healthy with regard to food and drink, and offered open and safe approaches

---

[42] Walter the Chancellor, I.2, p. 84.
[43] Walter the Chancellor, I.2, p. 89.
[44] Walter the Chancellor, I.3, pp. 92-3.

to our side; to the enemy quite the opposite' because of the physical barrier presented by the Jabal Talat.[45] In contrast the camp at the Field of Blood was poorly provisioned and, as it turned out, approachable from three directions.[46] In essence Walter criticized Roger for not pursuing the customary strategy of holding one's forces at a well defended site from which the surrounding region could be policed, while avoiding direct confrontation with the enemy until their forces broke up. This formula had been used successfully by Tancred in 1111 to counter Maudud of Mosul's invasion, and was further developed by King Baldwin II in the 1120s while defending the principality's eastern frontier.[47]

Walter also entered into some discussion of Latin military tactics and conventions associated with battle. On a number of occasions he mentioned the use of scouts and spies and emphasized the importance of intelligence and reconnaissance. Thus in 1115 Roger heard of Tughtegin and Il-ghazi's arrival at Aleppo from scouts and later set out for Apamea 'having sent out scouts towards the enemy'.[48] On 27 June 1119 Roger sent out forty knights under Mauger of Hauteville to patrol the region around Balat and a further ten knights to man a nearby watchtower.[49] On another occasion Walter suggested that Roger used a screen of patrols to protect his forces whilst on march, noting that 'after guards had been posted all around, the prince confidently ordered his columns to march'.[50]

One mention is made of logistics, when we are told that Roger advanced towards Aleppo in 1115 'having sent ahead weapons and other necessities of war and provisioning'.[51] Walter also demonstrated some awareness of the danger and vulnerability associated with holding an army in a field-camp. Roger apparently fortified the site at the Field of Blood, although Walter suggests that this measure was counter productive as it caught the attention of Muslim spies.[52] Then when the camp was threatened on 28

---

[45] Walter the Chancellor, II.1, p. 111;   T.S. Asbridge, 'The significance and causes of the battle of the Field of Blood', pp. 301-16.

[46] Walter the Chancellor, II.2, p. 114;   II.4, p. 122.

[47] Fulcher of Chartres, II.45, pp. 553-4;   III.11, p. 649;   Matthew of Edessa, III.51, p. 207;   Albert of Aachen, XI.40-2;   Kemal ed-Din, pp. 631-3.

[48] Walter the Chancellor, I.2, p. 85, p. 87;   I.3, p. 89.

[49] Walter the Chancellor, II.3, p. 119.

[50] Walter the Chancellor, I.5, pp. 97-8.

[51] Walter the Chancellor, I.2, p. 86.

[52] Walter the Chancellor, II.2, p. 114.

June an infantry screen was thrown up around the mounted forces, indicating that in this static position the Latin knights needed to be protected from Muslim harrying.[53] In August 1119 Baldwin II apparently took pains to prepare his forces for a night assault whilst camped on the slopes of Tall Danith.[54]

Walter implies that victory in battle was traditionally determined either by the capture of an enemy's standard or by the ability to hold the field after fighting had stopped. As we have seen, he may have exaggerated this latter factor in order to validate Baldwin II's victory in 1119. Even in 1115, however, it is noted that Roger held the field for three days after defeating Bursuq at Tall Danith. At the same time the ruler of Antioch amassed all booty, chose his own portion and then distributed the remainder amongst the army 'as the custom of that same court demanded'.[55] This reference suggests that rules did exist governing the division of spoils, and that it was the responsibility of the prince rather than the constable or the marshal. This is partially confirmed by Albert of Aachen's assertion that Tancred gathered and distributed the plunder taken after the battle near Artah in 1105.[56] There is no other evidence, however, to indicate how divisions were calculated nor whether vassals, or others taking part in a military action, received an agreed proportion.

ii) The concept of knighthood

Walter seems to have been interested in the idea of knightly and chivalric activity and the process of hand-to-hand combat. We have already seen how he associated personal heroism and gallantry with Roger and Baldwin II, but he also explored these elements in a more general context. In the run-up to the battle of Field of Blood he commented upon knightly activity during skirmishing outside al-Atharib on 27 June. The Latins are depicted 'relying on their courageous boldness' as they 'drew their shields close to their sides, brandished their lances, sank in their spurs - all these at once as befits knights - and charged into the middle of the enemy'. They then fought, 'dealing violent blows in knightly fashion' and 'eagerly inflicted blows worthy

---

[53] Walter the Chancellor, II.4, p. 124.
[54] Walter the Chancellor, II.11, p. 152.
[55] Walter the Chancellor, I.7, p. 106.
[56] Albert of Aachen, IX.47.

of their knighthood'.[57] Walter also made a telling comment about the importance of the knightly class. He observed that during the skirmish 'the last came first in striving both to be seen and to exceed the first in knightly deeds', that is, the non-knightly classes, perhaps including the infantry, tried to gain prestige in battle. 'But', he notes, 'as I may truly declare, it was not the hangers-on, but the true-born knights' who fought most effectively and sought 'to do good and to become knights of Christ'.[58] Walter reiterated the importance of knightly renown when noting that those involved in the skirmish later declared 'that the deeds of the past day had brought honour to their knighthood; as a consequence, as is the fixed habit of knights, everyone lamented who had not been there'.[59] Indeed, he may well have felt that one of the purposes of his account was to record honourable deeds, as he showed Roger urging his army to 'remember with how much praise, how much honour - indeed, with how much written remembrance the deeds of good men are committed to memory by the whole world'.[60]

On a number of occasions Walter also attempted to describe combat at close quarters. Just before the first battle of Tall Danith in 1115 Roger encouraged his troops 'to practise their knightly profession' and 'to couch their weapons' before battle, which must be a reference to the use of lances.[61] Roger is later shown commenting on the two main weapons used by knights, saying 'when our lances are broken, let us approach closer as quickly as possible with unsheathed swords'.[62] This theme of using first lance and then sword appears again in both Books One and Two.[63]

iii) The description of battle

Walter attempted one of the most difficult tasks facing any military historian - to record full scale battles. As we have seen, he was probably an eye-witness to the first battle of Tall Danith and to the Field of Blood, and would certainly have had access to participants of both conflicts as well as those involved in the second battle of Tall Danith in 1119.[64] Even so he does

---

[57] Walter the Chancellor, II.2, pp. 116-17.
[58] Walter the Chancellor, II.2, p. 117.
[59] Walter the Chancellor, II.3, p. 118.
[60] Walter the Chancellor, I.6, p. 100.
[61] Walter the Chancellor, I.5, p. 99.
[62] Walter the Chancellor, I.6, p. 100.
[63] Walter the Chancellor, I.6, p. 103; II.2, p. 117.
[64] See: 'Our knowledge of Walter', pp. 5-6.

have considerable, if not unexpected, difficulty in describing the actual progress of battle. This is a common trait amongst almost all medieval sources. His real value lies in the detailed record of battle formations and commanders. He made particular note of the vanguard, or frontline, in battle, which was, in a medieval context, a position of both considerable honour and responsibility. Thus he recorded that in the first battle of Tall Danith in 1115, the Latin van was held by Count Baldwin II of Edessa and Guy Le Chevreuil. We also learn that Roger of Salerno commanded his own battle-line, which contained Turcopoles, and Robert fitz-Fulk led a 'cohort', while Robert Sourdeval, Bochard, Guy Fresnel, Alan of al-Atharib and the battle-line of St Peter were all prominent participants. It is not clear what distinguished a 'cohort' from a 'battle-line'. Walter does try to describe how the battle unfolded, noting, for example, that the Latin vanguard first attacked Bursuq's army on the left flank, but, as he himself admits, the conflict soon became quite chaotic. He wrote that the din of battle was so intense, that 'the wailing and the clash of weapons on both sides so deafened the warriors that a friend could not recognize his friend, nor a brother his brother'.[65]

Walter again provides some record of participants at the Field of Blood. He noted that on this occasion the vanguard was held on the right by the battle-line of St Peter, while to the left Robert of St Lô led a cohort which included Turcopoles. According to Walter this latter force contributed to the loss of the battle by routing. Rainald Mazoir was despatched into the region around Sarmada at the head of three companies, while further battle-lines were commanded by Geoffrey the Monk, Guy Fresnel and Roger of Salerno himself.[66] Walter does convey a sense of how difficult it was to control a medieval army in the field. He entered into a fairly lengthy description of how the Latins were mustered into battle formation through a series of bugle blasts, twice noting that standard bearers indicated the position of each section of the army, and he recorded that just before the battle Roger personally drew 'up his battle-lines one by one' and 'commanded them to march in ranks'. Communication between these forces was achieved through messengers who 'were sent from column to column, flying like javelins or even like arrows, as the custom of warriors requires'.[67] Messengers are again mentioned during the march of King Baldwin II and Pons of Tripoli from Laitor towards

---

[65] Walter the Chancellor, I.6-7, pp. 102-6.
[66] Walter the Chancellor, II.5, pp. 126-9.
[67] Walter the Chancellor, II.4, p. 123; II.5, pp. 125-6.

Antioch, in this instance providing communication between the rear and van-guard of their forces.[68]

Walter provides a less detailed record of the personnel involved in the second battle of Tall Danith in 1119, at which he was probably not present, naming only Baldwin and Pons. He did attempt to describe the Latin battle-formation in considerable detail, but his comments are not always entirely clear. When preparing to march into battle from Tall Danith 'nine battle-lines were drawn up at the royal command' with Pons on the right flank and the 'barons', presumably the Antiochene nobility, on the left. Walter also noted that 'three lines were placed in the vanguard and the infantry was positioned to the rear, so that they could protect them and be protected by them; the royal force, prepared for the protection of the former and the latter, fell in the necessary order for all'. On the basis of this evidence it is difficult to know whether the infantry or royal force held the rear-guard.[69]

Walter's attempts to describe pitched battles may not always have been successful, but he generally provides far more military detail than his closest contemporary source Fulcher of Chartres, and was often copied almost verbatim by later writers such as William of Tyre.[70]

iv) Manpower

It is also worth comparing Walter's estimates of military manpower with those furnished by other sources. In this context he shares one important failing with other Latin sources, namely the inability to provide realistic estimates of Muslim numbers. In Book One he made little attempt to record the number of troops involved in the first battle of Tall Danith, at one point noting that the Muslim commander Tamirek was 'accompanied by a magnificent battle-array of three hundred', but generally concluding that the 'number of slaughtered enemies' was 'innumerable' whilst 'among us few casualties were counted'.[71] He did, however, record that a total of 2,000

---

[68] Walter the Chancellor, II.9, p. 141.

[69] Walter the Chancellor, II.12, p. 152;   William of Tyre, XII.12, pp. 561, attempted to clarify this description, noting that Baldwin 'put the infantry companies in the middle, and the lord king himself, ready to reinforce the rest, followed with four battle-lines'.

[70] Fulcher of Chartres, II.54, pp. 586-91; III.3, pp. 620-24; III.5, pp. 629-31;   William of Tyre, XI.25, pp. 533-4, XII, 9-12, pp. 556-62.

[71] Walter the Chancellor, I.6, p. 103; I.7, p. 106.   According to Fulcher of Chartres 'it is estimated that three thousand of them (the Muslim forces) were killed, many captured' during the first battle of Tall Danith.

Antiochene troops gathered at Apamea earlier that year.[72] Albert of Aachen
was equally vague about Bursuq's forces, noting that he had '40,000 Turks',
but recorded that King Baldwin I brought 500 knights and 1,000 infantry and
Count Pons 200 cavalry and 2,000 infantry to Apamea, while Roger and
Baldwin II of Edessa brought 10,000 cavalry and infantry.[73] Fulcher of
Chartres estimated that 3,000 Muslims were killed at Tall Danith but made no
mention of Latin manpower, while William of Tyre simply noted that Bursuq
'assembled an infinite horde'.[74] Of the non-Latin sources, Matthew of Edessa
described 700 cavalry amongst the Antiochene and Edessene forces at Tall
Danith, whilst Ibn al-Athir provided quite a conservative estimate of 500
knights and 2,000 infantry.[75]

    Walter provided more detailed estimates of manpower in Book Two.
He wrote that at the battle of the Field of Blood 'there were reputed to be 700
knights and 3,000 foot-soldiers' on the Latin side, as well a large number of
mercenaries, but made what appears to be a wild estimate of 100,000 soldiers
in Il-ghazi's army, at one point noting that Geoffrey the Monk's battle-line
alone was confronted by 10,000 enemy troops.[76] Fulcher of Chartres noted
that '7,000 of the Antiochenes were killed' during the battle, but may have
been trying to emphasize God's displeasure with Roger when he wrote that of
Muslim casualties there were 'not even twenty'.[77] William of Tyre followed
Walter's estimates of Latin manpower exactly, while Orderic Vitalis mirrored
Fulcher's reference to 7,000 troops.[78] Matthew of Edessa rather arbitrarily
estimated that there were 80,000 troops in Il-ghazi's army, but was very
specific in listing '600 Frankish cavalry, 500 Armenian cavalry and 400
infantry' in Roger's army, alongside 'a rabble recruited from among all sorts
of people' of 10,000.[79] Ibn al-Qalanisi numbered the Latin forces at '20,000
horse and foot', but could only note that there were 'vast numbers' of troops
in Il-ghazi's forces.[80] Ibn al-Athir recorded the presence of 3,000 Latin

---

[72] Walter the Chancellor, I.3, p. 89.

[73] Albert of Aachen, XII.19.

[74] Fulcher of Chartres, II.54, p. 588;   William of Tyre, XI.23, p. 530.

[75] Matthew of Edessa, III.70, p. 219;   Ibn al-Athir, pp. 297-8.

[76] Walter the Chancellor, II.5, p. 126.

[77] Fulcher of Chartres, III.3, pp. 621-2. This estimate is, however, repeated by Kemal ed-
Din, p. 618, who also noted that 15,000 Latins were killed during the battle.

[78] William of Tyre, XII.9, pp. 556-7;   Orderic Vitalis, XI.25, p. 106.

[79] Matthew of Edessa, III.79, p. 225.

[80] Ibn al-Qalanisi, pp. 160.

knights and 9,000 footmen.[81]

Walter's account of Baldwin II's march to Antioch provides a excellent example of his differential approach to Latin and Muslim manpower. When dealing with Islamic forces he consistently deals in multiples of a thousand, so we are told that Il-ghazi sent 10,000 troops to harry the king's advance, a figure repeated by William of Tyre, and that 4,000 Muslims had camped near Laitor while a further 3,000 attacked St Simeon. In contrast Walter notes that precisely thirty seven Latins were killed while defending Antioch's Bridge Gate from a Muslim assault in the same period.[82]

Even though Walter tried to represent the second battle of Tall Danith as a resounding victory he had to concede that fatalities took place on both sides, recording that 'it is thought, five or seven hundred of our infantry and a hundred of our knights died' while amongst the Muslim forces 'as they themselves claimed ... two or three thousand fell to the swords of the Christians'.[83] Matthew of Edessa upped the estimate of Muslim dead to 'as many as 5,000 men,[84] while Fulcher noted that between them Baldwin II and Pons brought 250 knights to relieve Antioch, and wrote that during the battle 'we had 700 soldiers, the Turks had 20,000'.[85] Kemal ed-Din recorded that the Latins had numerous footmen and 400 knights in the army, but went on to represent the battle as a Muslim victory.[86]

As an eye-witness source we might expect Walter to have had a fairly clear picture of the manpower available within the principality. Although his figures were often repeated by other sources he does not stand out from writers such as Fulcher of Chartres in terms of his numerical accuracy. His estimates of Muslim manpower are also unconvincing, in contrast to the Islamic writers who were often able to provide reasonable approximations of Latin numbers.

v) The depiction of Islamic military practice

Unlike many other contemporary writers Walter showed a fairly keen interest in the military tactics, technology and techniques of the principality's

---

[81] Ibn al-Athir, p. 324.

[82] Walter the Chancellor, II.8, p. 140; II.9, pp. 141-2; William of Tyre, XII.11, p. 559.

[83] Walter the Chancellor, II.12, p. 155.

[84] Matthew of Edessa, III.79, p. 224.

[85] Fulcher of Chartres, III.4, p. 627.

[86] Kemal ed-Din, pp. 620-21.

enemies.[87] He suggested that, like the Latins, the Muslims used scouts to gather intelligence, noting that spies disguised as bird-sellers were able to observe the Antiochene camp at the Field of Blood.[88] He was aware that Muslim armies often used missile weapons to harry their opponents, mentioning the use of bows in 1115 and arrows and javelins in 1119.[89] He also described how the Muslims attempted to use a feigned retreat to draw the Latins out of formation during the skirmishing outside al-Atharib in 1119. In a rather remarkable aside he noted that although some thought this tactic to be 'dishonest' others considered it to the 'result of creative genius', revealing that he felt some appreciation of this technique.[90] Elsewhere he described the Muslims as 'men of crafty cunning'.[91] During his account of the second battle of Tall Danith he recorded that the Muslim's drew up their battle-lines 'in their customary way', but unfortunately did not go on to describe what this entailed.[92]

Walter also made some interesting observations about Muslim siege techniques. He noted the difficulties involved in supplying the siege of Zardana, describing how Muslim troops were sent out in foraging bands, descending on the region like 'swarms ... [of] ravening wolves'.[93] On two occasions he mentioned the use of petraries, siege-engines utilizing either torsion or counter-weights to propel stone projectiles, and noted that Bursuq was preparing further siege-engines to assault Zardana prior to the first battle of Tall Danith.[94] He provided a detailed if not entirely clear description of the techniques involved in undermining a wall while recording the siege of al-Atharib in August 1119. He noted that Il-ghazi first 'sent men from different sides to dig out a cave made underground' and then 'prepared fuses by grafting together dry pieces of wood so that when they reached the towers and

---

[87] For some discussion of Muslim military practice, see: R.C. Smail, *Crusading Warfare*, pp. 75-83.

[88] Walter the Chancellor, II.2, pp. 114-15. Walter also suggested the more general Muslim use of spies when he mentioned the presence of 'messengers' in Christian garrisons. Walter the Chancellor, I.2, p. 85.

[89] Walter the Chancellor, I.3, pp. 92-3; I.6, p. 103; II.10, p. 146; II.12, p. 153.

[90] Walter the Chancellor, II.2, p. 116. He did, however, condemn Bursuq as 'a general of deceitful cunning' when he feigned retreat from the region of Shaizar in 1115. Walter the Chancellor, I.4, p. 93.

[91] Walter the Chancellor, II.2, p. 115.

[92] Walter the Chancellor, II.9, p. 140.

[93] Walter the Chancellor, II.11, p. 150.

[94] Walter the Chancellor, I.4, pp. 95-6; II.10, p. 146.

put in that same kindling they would collapse, being supported by posts'.[95] This process involved the excavation of a tunnel, supported by wooden stays, beneath a wall. Once the tunnel had been filled with firewood it could then be burnt out, causing it and the wall above to collapse.[96]

The depiction of Islam and eastern Christendom

Walter demonstrated a relatively strong interest in eastern Christendom and Islam. While his account reflects many of the prejudices we might expect from a writer living in a 'crusader' settlement, it also exhibits some unexpected knowledge and, on rare occasions, even-handedness.

i) Walter's general knowledge of Islam

Walter seems to have been conscious of the ethnic divisions within Islam, even if his observations were not always accurate. He differentiated between the Persians, whom he called Parthians, who invaded the principality in 1115 and Tughtegin of Damascus and Il-ghazi of Mardin, whom he described as 'Turks'.[97] In this period, however, the Great Seldjuk Sultanate held power in Baghdad and thus the army sent under Bursuq of Hamadan could also be described as 'Turkish'.[98]

Walter also showed some knowledge of individual Muslim leaders. He correctly identified Tughtegin with Damascus, but described him as 'the king of Damascans' when he was, in title at least, atabeg of the city.[99] Il-ghazi was initially styled simply as the 'emir of the Turcomans', but was later accurately associated with 'Mardin, a particular castle in his own territory'.[100] In Book One Walter initially made the vague statement that 'the

---

[95] Walter the Chancellor, II.10, p. 146.

[96] H. Kennedy, *Crusader Castles* (Cambridge, 1994), pp. 103-6, comments upon the extensive Muslim use of mining during sieges and recounts Usamah ibn-Munqidh's anecdote regarding this practice during the 1115 investment of Kafartab. He does, however, conclude that in this early period it may have been necessary for the Muslims of Syria to import specialist miners from Iran.

[97] Walter the Chancellor, I.Prologue, p. 77; I.2, p. 88.

[98] P.M. Holt, *The Age of the Crusades: The Near East from the eleventh century to 1517* (London, 1986), pp. 10-11.

[99] Walter the Chancellor, I.2, p. 87.

[100] Walter the Chancellor, I.2, p. 87; II.16, p. 168.

sultan of Khorasan' had 'taken command of the army of all Persia',[101] but
went on to note that 'Bursuq, general of the Persians' led the invading Muslim
force. Walter does not seem to have known, however, that Bursuq ruled the
town of Hamadan.[102] A similar lack of precision is evident in the fact that
the 'lord' of Hamah was not named, even when the sack of his town was
described at some length,[103] and that the emir of Shaizar and brother were
unidentified even when their delicate negotiations with Bursuq were
recorded.[104] During the first battle of Tall Danith Bursuq's brother was
mentioned but not named; there too a certain Tamirek, who may have been
Tamirek of Sinjar, made an appearance.[105]

In Book Two Walter noted, rather vaguely, that Il-ghazi was joined by
'Turkish chieftains from all around' before the battle of the Field of Blood,
he also failed to name Il-ghazi's son, but did at least record that 'the king of
the Arabs himself, whose name was Dubais' joined Il-ghazi at Zardana and
that Tughtegin fought alongside him at the second battle of Tall Danith.[106]

Walter showed some understanding of political relationships within the
Islamic world. He was aware that Tughtegin had been implicated in the
murder of Maudud of Mosul in 1113, and thus felt threatened by
Baghdad.[107] He concluded, however, that 'the fact of the matter' was that
in 1115 Tughtegin and Il-ghazi felt no real allegiance to 'Ridwan's son', the
unnamed Sultan-shah of Aleppo, but intended 'to hand [the city] over to the
sultan'.[108] He was probably in error here as the Arab sources suggest that
these two hoped to maintain Aleppo's semi-independent status in order to
prevent Baghdad gaining a foothold in northern Syria.[109] Walter was perhaps
unsure of their intentions because he went on to note that Tughtegin eventually
opted to ally with the Latins 'rather than to make an agreement with the
Persians, whom he knew to be much more cruel towards him in peace than

---

[101] Walter the Chancellor, I.2, pp. 86-7.

[102] Walter the Chancellor, I.3, p. 90.

[103] Walter the Chancellor, I.3, p. 91.

[104] Walter the Chancellor, I.3, p. 91.

[105] Walter the Chancellor, I.6, pp. 101-2.

[106] Walter the Chancellor, II.2, p. 115; II.7, p. 135; II.11, p. 150; II.12, p. 154.

[107] Walter the Chancellor, I.2, p. 88. It is worth noting that Fulcher of Chartres also
described Maudud's murder, the suspicions regarding Tughtegin and their impact upon events
in 1115. Fulcher of Chartres, II.51, pp. 577-8; II.53, pp. 582-3.

[108] Walter the Chancellor, I.2, pp. 87-8.

[109] Kemal ed-Din, p. 608;   Ibn al-Athir, p. 296.

in war'.[110] He continued to indicate Aleppo's precarious political situation by suggesting that Il-ghazi might feel the need to impress the 'sultan' of Baghdad with his Latin prisoners in 1119, and that factionalism was present in the city after the second battle of Tall Danith.[111]

Like many Latin writers Walter had a rather confused and hostile vision of Islamic religious practice. On a number of occasions he described Muslims resorting to divination, noting that the 'Persians' 'had consulted the auguries of sun and moon' before deciding to invade northern Syria in 1115 and that while in the region of Shaizar Bursuq's forces 'were awaiting the augury of the crescent moon'.[112] Later he mentioned the use of 'astrological rituals' by Muslims.[113] He also implied that Islam was a polytheistic religion when recording that the Muslims 'summoned the aid of divination and of false gods to appear for them' at Tall Danith 1115.[114] Walter also misrepresented religious hierarchy within Islam by superimposing Christian practice, describing the imam of Damascus as its 'patriarch'.[115]

ii) The depiction of Islamic character

As we would expect, Walter showed a fairly strong bias against Muslims and used a range of standard *topoi* to illustrate their character. His account contains many examples of general vilification. 'The enemy' he noted 'one day made a dreadful attack, as was their tyrannical practice, on the castle of Kafartab' in 1115.[116] Later he commented that 'Bursuq and all his men' were 'steeped in the rottenness of error'.[117] 'The barbarity of the enemy' was also observed during a skirmish outside al-Atharib in 1119.[118]

On a number of occasions Walter also accused Muslims of being cowardly and militarily ineffective.[119] He described the Turks as being

---

[110] Walter the Chancellor, I.2, p. 88.

[111] Walter the Chancellor, II.7, pp. 134-5; II.13, p. 157.

[112] Walter the Chancellor, I.2, p. 86; I.3, p. 90.

[113] Walter the Chancellor, II.7, p. 134.

[114] Walter the Chancellor, I.6, p. 101.

[115] Walter the Chancellor, II.15, p. 165. Muslim sources could also make similar 'errors'. Ibn al-Athir, for example, described Patriarch Bernard of Antioch as the 'imam' of that city. Ibn al-Athir, p. 262.

[116] Walter the Chancellor, I.4, p. 95.

[117] Walter the Chancellor, I.6, p. 101.

[118] Walter the Chancellor, II.2, p. 118.

[119] As we have seen, he made some positive comments about Islamic military practice. See: Walter as a military source, pp. 57-9.

'brought low by fear' by the approach of the principality's forces in early 1115.[120] He compared Latin and Muslim military prowess, noting that although Roger brought 2000 troops to Apamea while his Muslim allies had 10,000, 'this side, which was greater in number, was indeed less in worth'.[121] Later he suggested that Bursuq's forces were full of arrogance before the first battle of Tall Danith, and then described how 'Bursuq, wounded by the dart of divine terror' decided in his fear 'to escape with whatever he could'.[122]

Muslims were also characterized as drunken and avaricious. Walter noted that, while approaching Shaizar, Bursuq's army had 'taken drink and other pleasures' and then later that 'they once again took to drinking day after day'.[123] At the Field of Blood Muslim troops are depicted breaking up the Antiochene relic of True Cross through greed for the precious adornments of its reliquary.[124] Then, after the battle we are told that 'very wicked men' were 'possessed by greed for gold and silver and the prince's jewels' and that an 'emir clad in gold' was killed by a certain Euterpius.[125]

As we have seen, Walter was probably amongst the captives held at Aleppo in the aftermath of the Field of Blood. He commented at length upon the treatment of these prisoners, recounting Muslim cruelty on a number of occasions. Many of these observations related specifically to Il-ghazi or Tughtegin, but others were more general in nature. At one point, for example, when Muslim troops had been ordered to torture the Latins, Walter noted that 'the wicked men joyfully obeyed the wicked command of their lord.'[126] Later we are told, 'they rolled in the spilt blood [of Latins] as a pig wallows in mud; not yet sated with the slaughter of men' they begged Il-ghazi 'to be able to destroy the chosen prisoners with a like slaughter at his command'.[127] At one point 'a certain emir' did intervene to stop the wholesale slaughter of the Latins, but this was only so that the more prestigious captives could be singled out for ransom or display.[128] Walter

---

[120] Walter the Chancellor, I.2, p. 88.
[121] Walter the Chancellor, I.3, pp. 89-90.
[122] Walter the Chancellor, I.6, p. 101.
[123] Walter the Chancellor, I.3, p. 90.
[124] Walter the Chancellor, II.5, p. 128.
[125] Walter the Chancellor, II.6, pp. 130-31.
[126] Walter the Chancellor, II.6, p. 132.
[127] Walter the Chancellor, II.7, p. 135.
[128] Walter the Chancellor, II.7, pp. 134-5.

did, however, allot some motive to these atrocities, having a Muslim state that the Latins were punished 'because and to the degree that they and their kin and compatriots have sinned against our most holy law'.[129] In a remarkable aside Walter even acknowledged that Christian 'kings, princes and other powerful people of the world, and even powerless men' were also capable of torturing prisoners and being 'inspired by the Devil'. Thus, he wrote, 'I think it is better for me to keep quiet about the kind and quantity of their tortures than to express them, lest Christians bring the same to bear on Christians and turn them into accustomed usage'.[130] Walter clearly felt that evil was not the preserve of Islam.

a) Tughtegin of Damascus

Walter also provided two particular case studies of Islamic character. Tughtegin was portrayed as the key Islamic figure in the Latin-Muslim alliance of 1115, but also as a coward who only entered into the pact because 'he feared the formidable power of both of them, Christians and Persians'.[131] After the second battle of Tall Danith in 1119 Walter again informs us that Tughtegin and Il-ghazi were 'frightened by the flight and destruction which had happened to them, and … were paying attention only to drinking'.[132] The atabeg of Damascus is particularly criticized for his involvement in the mistreatment of Latin prisoners. He was described as 'the minister of the Antichrist' and 'Tughtegin, the investigator and discoverer of various tortures'.[133] His execution of Robert fitz-Fulk the Leper is confirmed by other sources, but we might doubt whether he really did have a gold-plated drinking cup made from Robert's skull or that he bathed in the blood of slaughtered Latin captives to maintain his youth.[134]

b) Il-ghazi of Mardin

Il-ghazi is probably the fourth most important individual within the narrative structure of Walter's account, after Roger, Baldwin II and

---

[129] Walter the Chancellor, II.7, p. 135.
[130] Walter the Chancellor, II.15, p. 166.
[131] Walter the Chancellor, I.2, p. 88.
[132] Walter the Chancellor, II.15, p. 163.
[133] Walter the Chancellor, II.14, p. 160; II.15, p. 165.
[134] Walter the Chancellor, II.14, pp. 161-2, n. 246.

Bernard.[135] As we have seen, he barely made an appearance in Book One, but in Book Two he was generally presented as the personification of evil, being styled variously as 'the prince of the impious', 'the master criminal' and 'the wicked leader' to name but a few.[136] As the actual agent of the defeat at the Field of Blood and the atrocities committed in its aftermath, Il-ghazi was, not surprisingly, subject to the harshest criticism by Walter. Walter also dedicated the closing sections of his account to demonstrating that Il-ghazi was eventually punished by God for his actions.

It is almost impossible to find even a moment of neutral portrayal of his character in Book Two. During his negotiations with Rainald Mazoir at Sarmada Il-ghazi was described as 'astute' and shown giving Rainald his ring 'as a sign of my good faith and oath according to our blessed law' that he would be freed after one month.[137] Walter did not record Rainald's fate, but we know that he was free by 1122 when he witnessed a charter issued by King Baldwin II.[138] Perhaps Walter failed to record his release because he did not want to show Il-ghazi keeping his word.

He certainly depicted him as duplicitous in other negotiations. At Artah, we are told, he made 'a truce' of surrender with the Latin bishop and his men, guaranteeing them safe passage to Antioch. Walter noted, however, that 'he partly kept this promise and partly broke it' by arranging for them to be looted en route by their 'escorts'. Il-ghazi may not have organized this robbery, as Walter grudgingly admitted that he subsequently sent any recovered priestly vestments on to the Latins.[139] Later in 1119 at Zardana, Walter described how 'he strove more to deceive the townspeople by his deceitful cunning: he even promised them on his honour and on an oath binding in his law' that in return for surrender he would assure safe and free passage back to the principality. Once the town was occupied, however, 'happily he ordered his armies to put to death savagely the Christians as they departed'.[140]

Walter also accused Il-ghazi of being a drunkard. 'He was keen on drink' he wrote, noting how, after the Field of Blood, he 'lay drunk by the

---

[135] See: Walter's purpose in writing *The Antiochene Wars*, pp. 11-12.

[136] Walter the Chancellor, II.6, p. 132.

[137] Walter the Chancellor, II.6, p. 129.

[138] 'Chartes de l'abbaye de Notre-Dame de Josaphat', *Revue de l'Orient Latin*, vol. 7 (1890), pp. 118-19, n. 8.

[139] Walter the Chancellor, II.8, p. 136.

[140] Walter the Chancellor, II.11, p. 149.

madness of wine in his palace' and was often preoccupied with 'horrific drinking'.[141] At one point we are told that he was 'overcome by wine as was his custom, and he lay as if dead in the stink of his own ordure for a period of fifteen days. And he was very often exhausted by this kind of disgraceful passion.'[142] Walter allegations of excessive drinking are, to some extent, confirmed by other sources, but even so it would seem unlikely that one night of alcohol was enough to debilitate Il-ghazi, as Usamah ibn-Munqidh suggested: 'for twenty days'.[143]

In keeping with his general approach to Muslim character, Walter reserved his most scathing condemnation of Il-ghazi for his involvement in the abuses of Latin prisoners. He was shown as the central figure and mastermind of these atrocities, and on numerous occasions he is described as sadistic and inhuman.[144] Walter noted that while watching the Latins being tortured 'the wicked man was delighted by their torments and he laughed at them as if he were refreshed by some food to fuel his cruelty. And yet he was not satisfied and he was thinking up crueller things.'[145] As a consequence of his attack upon the principality and direction of torture which may have personally affected Walter, Il-ghazi is portrayed in an extremely negative light. If others can be identified as the heroes of The Antiochene Wars then he must surely be classed as the villain of Book Two.

In keeping with this theme, Walter seems to have been determined to demonstrate that God punished Il-ghazi for his actions. Indeed, this was probably the primary reason why he continued his account to 1122. Divine retribution first struck after the miraculous transportation of the son of the viscount of Acre's body from Aleppo. 'When this happened', Walter wrote, 'the wicked one lost his powers, foaming with blood which poured out, he was crushed and fell, harshly disfigured by a savage kind of passion'.[146] After God had afflicted him with this fit, Il-ghazi was defeated in battle by King David II Georgia, who is shown as God's tool of justice, returning wounded to 'his homeland half-dead, unarmed and famished'.[147] Walter

[141] Walter the Chancellor, II.8, p. 138; II.15, pp. 163-4.
[142] Walter the Chancellor, II.16, p. 168.
[143] Usamah ibn-Munqidh, p. 149.
[144] Walter the Chancellor, II.6-7, pp. 132-6.
[145] Walter the Chancellor, II.7, p. 134.
[146] Walter the Chancellor, II.16, pp. 167-8.
[147] Walter the Chancellor, II.16, pp. 168-70.

chose to conclude his entire account with Il-ghazi's ignominious death in 1122. He described in shameful and humiliating detail how in 'his infirmity, his filthy soul issued forth from his anus along with a flux of dung from his belly' and was dragged 'into the halls of deepest hell'.[148] This final image was surely designed to leave the reader in no doubt regarding God's omnipotence and Il-ghazi's damnation.

iii) Walter's attitude to interaction with Islam

It is not surprising that, given Walter's generally hostile attitude towards Islam, he seems to have struggled to accommodate Roger of Salerno's 1115 alliance with Tughtegin and Il-ghazi within his account. He did not openly criticize this pact, probably for fear of embarrassing Roger, but did demonstrate his disapproval through a number of relatively subtle comments. Walter suggested that the Muslims were not really committed to this temporary truce, noting that Tughtegin wished 'to be united with the Christians in a pretended peace, so that he might lead them to disaster'. He implied that a difference existed between the external facade and 'reality', writing that the two sides 'confirmed agreements and became, to all appearances, friends', and later met at 'Apamea where they seemed to meet with a welcome, even a bond of complete love, like sons and parents in companionship'.[149] Walter's opinion seems clear, however, when explaining why the alliance between Antioch, Jerusalem, Tripoli, Damascus, and perhaps Aleppo, broke up in August. He noted that 'we realize that this was not done by the power of these men, but no doubt by His influence who wished to break up the alliance of Belial with our people'.[150] In Walter's opinion God had judged this to be a pact with the Devil.[151]

---

[148] Walter the Chancellor, II.16, p. 171.

[149] Walter the Chancellor, I.2, p. 88; I.3, p. 89.

[150] Walter the Chancellor, I.4, p. 95.

[151] The existence of this alliance is confirmed by a range of other sources, but there is some disagreement on points of detail. Matthew of Edessa, III.70, p. 219, recorded that both Tughtegin and Il-ghazi came to camp near Shaizar 'with many troops' and 'joined the Franks'. Fulcher of Chartres, II.53, pp. 582-3, however, believed that Tughtegin allied with Roger and Baldwin I, and that this treaty was made in the first instance at Apamea. Albert of Aachen, XII.20, even asserted that Tughtegin fought in alliance with Roger at the first battle of Tall Danith. Usamah ibn-Munqidh, p. 149, noted that Il-ghazi joined the Latins at Apamea, and observed that he was accompanied by Robert fitz-Fulk the Leper, a known friend of Tughtegin. Ibn al-Qalanisi, p. 147; Kemal ed-Din, pp. 608-9; Ibn al-Athir, pp. 296-7, all recorded an alliance between the Latins and Tughtegin, Il-ghazi and Shams al-Kwaiss, a

Walter was, however, the only contemporary Latin source to confirm that a system of tribute payments was established between Antioch and her Muslim neighbours in this early period. Muslim sources demonstrate that from c. 1111 onwards both Aleppo and Shaizar made regular tribute payments to the principality, an arrangement which not only enriched Antioch but also increased its political influence in northern Syria.[152] On the whole, Latin sources remained silent on this form of contact, perhaps through design or lack of knowledge, but Walter did make the passing comment that Shaizar 'had formerly been tributary and served our men'.[153] Perhaps even more notably he also suggested that Robert fitz-Fulk had paid his own tribute to Tughtegin, when the atabeg stated: 'I remind you that in the past you paid tribute to me from your possessions'.[154]

iv) The depiction of the principality's eastern Christian population

Walter's account reveals some important information about the indigenous Levantine Christians who lived under Antiochene rule. He made it clear that the city of Antioch itself had a polyglot population, made up of 'Latins, Greeks, Syrians, Armenians, strangers and pilgrims'.[155] In spite of the fact that this population shared the Christian faith, Walter did demonstrate a degree of distrust and disaffection towards non-Latins. While reporting the earthquakes and associated disasters of 1114 he noted that the eastern Christian citizens of Antioch 'deserved to be afflicted by such a vengeance' and were being punished for the sins of 'gluttony', 'unchastity', 'lust' and perhaps also avarice.[156] Although Walter did, at one point, note that all the diverse elements of the population of 'one accord ... claimed the earthquake had happened because of their own sins', he still focused most blame upon eastern Christians.[157] We might, therefore, question Walter's rather jaded view of Levantine customs, such as his suggestion that prostitution was rife

---

general from Aleppo. This culminated in a united force congregating at Apamea for two months, although Ibn al-Athir dated its dispersal to the middle of September.

[152] Ibn al-Qalanisi, p. 99, p. 106, p. 132; Kemal ed-Din, p. 598; Ibn al-Athir, p. 279, p. 298; Usamah ibn-Munqidh, p. 150.

[153] Walter the Chancellor, I.2, p. 89.

[154] Walter the Chancellor, II.14, p. 161.

[155] Walter the Chancellor, I.1, p. 81.

[156] Walter the Chancellor, I.Prologue, pp. 78-80.

[157] Walter the Chancellor, I.1, p. 81.

amongst the indigenous population.[158]

Walter did on occasion concede that eastern Christians might play a positive role within the principality. At the end of Book One he included them in the Antiochene celebrations of the victory at Tall Danith, writing that 'people of different nations are bent upon garlanding the town with flowers'.[159] We are also informed that in 1115 Roger decided 'to send scouts of different races into those regions belonging to the Persians', which suggests the use of eastern Christians.[160] The man named Joseph, who was associated with Artah, may also, on the evidence of his name, be tentatively identified as a Levantine Christian. At one point Walter described him as 'a very wise individual' because of his cunning deception of Il-ghazi.[161]

In common with other Latin settlements in the East it appears that much of the indigenous population of Antioch was used as an agrarian workforce, as Walter equated the 'the farmers of Syria' with 'the eastern Christians'.[162] B. Kedar has suggested that Walter also acknowledged that the Latins, like the Greeks and Muslims before them, exploited the principality's indigenous Christian population. This observation depended upon his translation of the Latin word 'intolerabiliori' as 'more intolerable'. We have, however, suggested the alternative translation of 'irresistible'.[163]

This is not to say that Walter's account contains no recognition of Latin exploitation. In an oft quoted passage, Walter noted that Antioch was more vulnerable to internal dissent than external assault after the Field of Blood, which forced Patriarch Bernard to disarm 'the peoples of different nations' within the city and impose a form of curfew. In a less well known, but significant aside, Walter went on, however, to state that he understood why the city's indigenous population might wish to overthrow Latin rule, writing: 'nor was it remarkable if the Antiochenes wanted to return evil for evil ... for indeed the people of Antioch had been deprived of their goods by the force and deviousness of our people and were ... often overcome by despair'.[164]

---

[158] Walter the Chancellor, I.Prologue, p. 79.

[159] Walter the Chancellor, I.7, p. 107.

[160] Walter the Chancellor, I.2, p. 85.

[161] Walter the Chancellor, II.8, pp. 137-8.

[162] Walter the Chancellor, I.Prologue, p. 78.

[163] Walter the Chancellor, I.Prologue, pp. 79-80;   B.Z. Kedar, 'The subjected Muslims of the Frankish Levant', *Muslims under Latin rule, 1100-1300*, ed. J.M. Powell (Princeton, N.J., 1990), p. 168.

[164] Walter the Chancellor, II.8, p. 138.

Walter's attitude to religion and piety

The centrality of Christianity in medieval Europe is demonstrable through a wide range of features, from cathedral building and the growth of monasticism to the popularity of pilgrimage and crusading. Walter's account, with its continual references to divine judgement and popular devotion, provides an excellent example of how Christian faith could influence almost every aspect of Latin writing in this period. Walter may, of course, have come from a clerical background. He certainly claimed to have been inspired by God to write *The Antiochene Wars*, he presented the victory of 1115 as a 'miracle' and the events of 1119 as acts of God.[165] We must therefore expect him to emphasize the importance of religion. As we have seen he comments extensively upon the need for spiritual purity amongst the Latins, describing many sermons and the rituals of Mass and confession. This may, to some extent, have been influenced by his depictions of Roger of Salerno and King Baldwin II and his desire to explain the disaster at the Field of Blood.

Walter also gives us an insight into the importance of some aspects of 'popular' religion, namely the cult of saints and the cult of relics.[166] Evidence of these types of devotion, which were certainly not limited to the 'popular' masses, can perhaps lead us beyond Walter's view of events as divinely overseen to a closer understanding of how personal piety was expressed in a medieval context.

The premier saint within the principality was St Peter. Tradition held that he had founded the first Christian church at Antioch and therefore the city was a major centre for his cult. Evidence of devotion to St Peter within the principality ranges from his appearance on coins to the existence of the military group described by Walter as 'the battle-line of St Peter'.[167] He

---

[165] Walter the Chancellor, I.Prologue, p. 77; II.Prologue, pp. 109-10.

[166] For further discussion of the impact of 'popular' religion upon medieval Europe see: R. & C. Brooke, *Popular religion in the Middle Ages: Western Europe 1000-1300* (London, 1984); P. Brown, *The Cult of Saints* (Chicago, 1981); B. Ward, *Miracles and the Medieval mind: Theory, Record and Event 1000-1215*, rev. ed. (Aldershot, 1987); M. Bull, *Knightly Piety and the lay response to the First Crusade* (Oxford, 1993); P.J. Geary, *Furta sacra: theft of Relics in the Central Middle Ages* (Princeton, NJ, 1990).

[167] D.M. Metcalf, *Coinage of the Crusades*, pp. 22-8; Walter the Chancellor, I.7, p. 105; II.5, p. 126. See also: T.S. Asbridge, 'The significance and causes of the battle of the Field of Blood', p. 308.

mentioned the cult specifically in the aftermath of the earthquakes which afflicted the principality in 1115, noting that the fearful citizens of Antioch rushed 'to the very church of St Peter the apostle, seeking the protection of his eternal patronage'. He went on to suggest that devotion to the saint was dependent upon need and circumstance, writing that 'that very same saint whom they had failed to appreciate when things were going well, they recognized as omnipotent and well-disposed in bad times'.[168]

Walter also provides the only surviving evidence that, like the kingdom of Jerusalem, Antioch possessed a relic of the True Cross, that is a piece of wood believed to have been part of the cross upon which Christ was crucified.[169] It appears to have played a major devotional role within the principality, appearing prominently at both the first battle of Tall Danith and the Field of Blood. Walter noted that on the morning of 14 September 1115, the feast of the Exaltation of the Cross, after the Latin army had celebrated Mass, 'everyone flocked to adore the most holy wood of that same Cross of Our Lord.'[170] Then, just prior to the battle, Bishop William of Jabala 'bearing in a spirit of humility the Cross of holy wood in his reverend hands, circled the whole army' and proclaimed that 'they would claim victory in the coming battle through its virtue'. Everyone in the army then 'fell to their knees three times before the Lord's Cross, and, kissing it reverently, they entrusted themselves to Him'.[171]

Walter similarly depicted the Latin army venerating the Antiochene relic of the True Cross at the Field of Blood. After the troops had been ordered into battle-lines they congregated before the temporary chapel erected in the camp 'where the Cross was'. There Archbishop Peter of Apamea 'bearing the Cross of Our Lord in reverent hands' exhorted them to battle 'with this sign of the health-giving Cross going before'. After making confession Roger himself asked for a priest to carry the Cross into battle

---

[168] Walter the Chancellor, I.1, p. 81. In the medieval period the veneration of saints does seem to have been quite heavily based upon necessity and demand. Saints, as more 'human' manifestations of divine will, could be entreated for assistance, but also castigated if they did not bring the desired result. See: P.J. Geary, 'Humiliation of Saints', *Saints and their cults: studies in religious sociology, folklore and history*, ed. S. Wilson (Cambridge, 1983), pp. 123-40.

[169] A. Frolow, *La relique de la vraie croix; recherches sur le développement d'un culte*, 2 vols (Paris, 1961).

[170] Walter the Chancellor, I.5, p. 98.

[171] Walter the Chancellor, I.5, pp. 99-100.

beside him. Then, just before the fighting began he 'venerated the symbol of the Holy Cross and kissed it most reverently'.[172] Walter needed, of course, to deal with the difficult fact that, although the Antiochenes were accompanied into battle by this potent relic on 28 June 1119, they were still defeated by Il-ghazi. It was perhaps this factor which encouraged him to report that a miracle associated with the True Cross took place during the battle. According to Walter, when Roger was killed by a sword blow the priest carrying the relic was also slain. The Muslim troops were then greedy 'for the gold and precious stones', which presumably refers to the decorated reliquary in which the fragment was carried, and therefore smashed it up. The 'strength of God's power hidden in the Cross' then manifested itself, however, and the Muslims were 'stricken by that timber of death' and consigned to 'the fires of hell'.[173] Not surprisingly the Antiochene relic of the True Cross was lost after the battle and disappears from the written record. The principality did possess other relics, some of which were brought out of Antioch by Patriarch Bernard to greet Roger in 1115, but given the prestige known to have been associated with the Jerusalemite relic of the True Cross the loss of 1119 must be seen as another important consequence of the Field of Blood.[174]

King Baldwin II did in fact bring the Jerusalemite True Cross to northern Syria in 1119. Its appearance in Walter's account is most notable because the language and style associated with its description match those of the Antiochene relic. This suggests that, in Walter's opinion at least, the two were of equivalent status. The Jerusalemite True Cross appears on a number of occasions during the spiritual preparations for the second battle of Tall Danith.[175] Walter then reports that on 14 August Evremar archbishop of Caesarea was miraculously saved by the power of the True Cross, which he had carried into the battle, asserting that 'by its protection, even though he was struck by an arrow, as many bear witness, he remained unharmed, only a drop of his blood being visible as testimony.' He goes on to note that Evremar then protected the king, whose horse had been wounded, and turned the tide of battle, by pointing the relic at the Muslim forces, cursing them 'by

---

[172] Walter the Chancellor, II.4, pp. 123-4; II.5, p. 125.

[173] Walter the Chancellor, II.5, p. 128.

[174] Walter the Chancellor, I.7, p. 106. The most recent discussion of the Jerusalemite relic appears in: A.V. Murray, '"Mighty against the enemies of Christ": The relic of the True Cross in the armies of the kingdom of Jerusalem', *The Crusades and their sources: essays presented to Bernard Hamilton*, ed. J. France & W.G. Zajac (Aldershot, 1998), pp. 217-38.

[175] Walter the Chancellor, II.10, p. 147; II.11, p. 151; II.12, pp. 152-6.

the holy power of this Cross' and willing that they 'be scattered and put to flight by divine vengeance'.[176] Walter seems to imply that the presence of these relics in battle demonstrated divine sanction of that conflict.

Walter's account contains one reference to a miracle which was not directly related to the True Cross, but played a prominent role in the closing stages of his narrative. During his extended description of the fate suffered by Il-ghazi's Latin prisoners, Walter noted that a knight named Sanson of Bruera dreamt that Christ marked him and twenty-four other captives with the sign of the Holy Cross, but left the rest of his companions unmarked. He apparently woke and related this vision to his fellow captives. On the following day all those who had been marked were executed and 'adorned with the name martyr', but 'by the power and a miracle of the Lord' the decapitated body of 'the son of the viscount of Acre' was transported 'to another place'. This strange event apparently prompted Il-ghazi to have some form of fit or seizure, preventing him from killing any more prisoners and eventually leading to his own death.

Walter describes these events as 'something I consider should not be kept quiet' and noted that this 'miraculous thing which happened to the prisoners in prison I am spreading abroad for the compassion of people living now and as a written memorial for people in the future'.[177] Walter was perhaps trying to provide some focus for the last four chapters of his account, which are comparatively confused and rambling, but which probably record his own memories of captivity. Through this miracle he was able to explain how some prisoners, perhaps himself included, were saved from death and how God ultimately exacted his revenge upon Il-ghazi. We might, therefore, view this miracle as the most personal expression of piety within Walter's account as well as an important narrative device.

---

[176] Walter the Chancellor, II.12, pp. 153-4.
[177] Walter the Chancellor, II.15-16, pp. 166-8.

Summary

Walter was chancellor of Antioch between c. 1114 and c. 1122 and probably came from a clerical background. He was almost certainly an eye-witness to most of the events he recorded, although he was probably captive in Aleppo for at least the latter part of 1119. He may have composed *The Antiochene Wars* in three stages, with breaks between Books One and Two, and chapters twelve and thirteen of Book Two.

His account seeks to explain the principality's varying fortunes on the basis of divine will. It is dominated by the actions of four main protagonists: in spite of his failures in 1119 Roger of Salerno is rarely criticized; King Baldwin II's salvation of the principality receives universal praise; Patriarch Bernard of Antioch's role as spiritual leader and advisor allows him to act as a mouthpiece for Walter's own views; and Il-ghazi of Mardin's victory at the Field of Blood is balanced by his eventual punishment by God.

Walter's writings also contain a relative wealth of information about the prosopographical and institutional history of Latin Antioch, and offer a range of important observations on military practice. Like many Latins who wrote about the Levant in this period, Walter produced a negative and distorted image of the Islamic world, although he showed some respect for Muslim tactics in war. His occasional comments about contact with indigenous Christians are punctuated by the fairly remarkable admission that the Latins had exploited their eastern co-religionists.

Above all, Walter's work offers a uniquely detailed account of Latin life in northern Syria at the start of the twelfth century. His writing informs our understanding of the principality of Antioch's early history and helps to explain how the Latins were able to survive the threats posed by Muslim aggression.

Walter the Chancellor's
The Antiochene Wars

The First War

Here Roger,[1] lord and general[2] of the Antiochenes was victor, as the author Walter[3] shows.

Prologue

It is the reward for our labour and equally it is to our advantage to hear how, with what miracles, and by what favour God as judge exceeded our hopes by waging war on the Persians[4] through the agency of Roger, prince[5] of Antioch. For truly, when they have heard the power of miracles[6] and the deeds of worthy men the wicked will more easily be brought low and the good will also be spurred on to do better. And so may I pray for His assistance, at whose prompting all good things are done, who granted to that same prince the inspiration of his advice and the force of his encouragement,[7] with the help of which he succeeded in shattering the pride[8] of the heathens and vanquishing their fierceness, and when I wished to put in writing the sequence of events and commend them to the memory of posterity, He also deigned to instil in me from heaven the power of writing and the means of expression,

---

[1] Roger of Salerno, ruler of the principality of Antioch (1113-1119). He was the son of Richard of Salerno, who had participated in the First Crusade and had subsequently held Edessa from c. 1105-8 and Marash from c. 1109. Michael the Syrian, XV.10, p. 195; Albert of Aachen, XI.40. Roger was also a familial relation of the previous ruler of Antioch, Tancred (c. 1105-1111). Fulcher of Chartres, II.47, p. 562. Albert of Aachen describes Roger as 'the son of the sister of Tancred' and therefore his nephew. Albert of Aachen, XII.12. See charters (a) and (b) pp. 205-8.

[2] From the Latin 'dux'. This is the only occasion upon which Walter styles the ruler of Antioch as *dux*. Elsewhere he consistently styles him as 'prince', and as we shall see, by 1115 the 'duke (*dux*)' of Antioch seems to have been an official within the city. See below: Walter the Chancellor, I.2, p. 85.

[3] Walter, chancellor of Antioch (c.1114-c.1122). See: Our knowledge of Walter, pp. 5-8.

[4] See: The depiction of Islam and eastern Christendom, p. 59.

[5] This title is consistently used to describe Roger's status. See: Roger of Salerno, pp. 23-6.

[6] The 'miracles' related by Walter are primarily associated with relics of the True Cross. See: Walter's attitude to religion and piety, pp. 69-72.

[7] Isaiah, 11.2: 'spiritus consilii et fortitudinis'.

[8] Walter is particularly interested in the sin of pride and its consequences. See: Roger of Salerno, p. 21.

so that when men capable of reason and defenders of the true faith heard the truth, they would cling strongly to the power and service of their Creator, while their opponents, smitten by divine dread, both in the present and in the future, trusting not in God but in themselves, would expose their backs to God's arrows,[9] and would not dare to return to the same task. Nevertheless, having looked into the necessary aspects of the battle, and having selected the material which is equal to my powers,[10] it seems to me essential, before the account of the battle, first to outline the evils which happened earlier, so that by an examination of the previous reasons for the events which follow, our achievement may more easily be appreciated.[11]

First, therefore, hordes of locusts, stirred up far and wide by way of a metaphor for the enemy, stole nearly all the things necessary to feed the farmers of Syria. Then they were dispersed partly by crawling along the ground, partly through the air, and they afflicted almost the whole region of the eastern Christians to the same devastating effect;[12] and although they knew that they deserved to be afflicted by such a vengeance, yet they not only did not look to appease God their creator, they clung to their past vices, indeed they even went beyond the bounds of shame,[13] adding crime upon crime. For certain men who hated fasting and loved lavish banquets, slaves to gluttony for enticing foods, were eager to copy the life and life-style not of those who live well but of those who eat well. Some indeed were influenced to unchastity and frequented houses of ill-fame, they strove even to pollute the respect of the public audience with shameless words, sowing doubt, and they were reckoned rather disgusting or scandalous.

Moreover, some of those who had come by ill-gotten gains, having used up

---

[9] Job 6.4.

[10] Vergil, *Aeneid*, 12.230: 'viribus aequi'. Ovid, *Trist*. 5, 7, 47: 'viribus aequum'.

[11] In this first section Walter explores some of the central themes of his narrative: the idea that God inspired both the Latin successes of 1115 and Walter's own desire to write about them; his interest in recording a chronological record of events; and the fact that this account is designed to act as an exemplar to future generations. He also seems to suggest that he will be presenting only a selection of the evidence available to him. See: Walter's purpose in writing *The Antiochene Wars*, pp. 11-12.

[12] The sins and retribution described in this section seem to be focused upon the indigenous eastern Christian population of northern Syria, rather than the Latins who had settled in the Levant. See: The depiction of Islam and eastern Christendom, pp. 67-8.

[13] Ovid, *Epist*. 16, 70: 'fines pudoris transire'.

all their own wealth, ardently sought for vessels to be made, suitable for their
voluptuous excesses, artfully engraved in the style of Solomon;[14] and for
their wives, so gossip has it, they paid craftsmen to have coverings carefully
made in Arabian gold and a manifold variety of precious jewels for their
shameful parts, not to clothe the appearance of their shame or to restrain the
flame of lust, but so that that which was forbidden might inflame more hotly
those people who did not desire legitimate pleasures. Since they were willing
to excite their lust in this way, and set out to bedizen women and to exploit
them, as we have indicated before, they added crime upon crime.[15]

For the women, to be sure, nothing was sacred, nothing serious in their
pursuit of wickedness: for the silly women, having scorned their husbands'
beds, served unchastity in the lewd brothel; they lay in wait day and night
with special drinks on street corners and where three or four roads meet; they
put themselves about in the streets and the squares, lascivious in the way they
looked and walked, and they stood where they would catch the eye of passers-
by; they were available for a price whatever the weather and would lie down
with anyone who wanted. Moreover, they scarcely allowed those who were
unwilling, those whom they were unable to provoke to their own level of
lewdness, to escape, even when they paid the asking price.[16]

Since these people did not lament the evil deeds they had done and they did
lamentable deeds willingly and openly, the originator of supreme justice
allowed them to be afflicted with signs, prodigies, plagues, trouble and even
enemy peoples for the duration of many years, not to destroy them but to save

---

[14] This seems to be a general reference to the glories of Solomon; see Matt. 6.29.

[15] For a comparison between Walter's examination of sin and Fulcher of Chartres's
revelations about Latin sins in the period leading up to the Field of Blood, see Roger of
Salerno, pp. 13-14, pp. 20-23.

[16] Walter comes close to condemning all womankind through his attacks on prostitution.
The idea that women were a source of sin and evil was, however, prevalent in the medieval
world, and had seen earlier expression when, during the First Crusade, all women were
thrown out of the Latin camp surrounding Antioch. J.S.C. Riley-Smith, *The First Crusade and
the idea of crusading*, p. 88. Walter did, however, later note that women were amongst those
who adopted a pure and penitential life-style after the earthquakes of 1114. Walter the
Chancellor, I.1, pp. 83-4.

them.[17] For while the Greeks ruled they were persuaded to be enslaved to their empire.[18] When those same people had been driven forth from Asia they had yielded to the dominion of the ruling Persians; eventually, God willing, they succumbed to the irresistible power of the Gauls.[19] When their behaviour was set right neither by the Persians nor the Gauls, the aforesaid Syrians and their rulers[20] suffered so great a destruction and ruin from the earthquake[21] which befell them as no previous history has ever told.[22]

I.1   *The great earthquake in Antioch and its effect on the inhabitants.*[23]

Therefore in the 1115th year from the incarnation of our Lord Jesus Christ, on the eve of the feast of St Andrew the apostle[24] and in the silence at the

---

[17] The concept of adversity as a means to salvation gained considerable currency during the twelfth century. It was used, for example, by St Bernard to explain the failure of the Second Crusade. See: E. Siberry, *Criticism of Crusading*, p. 78; G. Constable, 'The Second Crusade as seen by Contemporaries', *Traditio*, vol. 9 (1953), pp. 213-79.

[18] The Byzantine empire had held the city of Antioch until 1084. Walter's use of the word 'enslaved' to characterize Greek rule suggests that he subscribed to the general antipathy towards Byzantium which was prevalent amongst the Latins of Antioch in this period. The Greeks disputed possession of the city and had, in the first decade of the principality's existence, constantly contested control of the fertile region of Cilician Armenia and the port of Latakia. See: R.J. Lilie, *Byzantium and the Crusader States 1096-1204*, trans. J.C. Morris & J.E. Ridings (Oxford, 1993), pp. 61-87.

[19] For discussion of B.Z. Kedar's alternative views on this phrase see: The depiction of Islam and eastern Christendom, p. 68.

[20] Walter seems to suggest that the Latins also deserved to be punished because they had failed to reform the eastern Christian population of the principality. See: The depiction of Islam and eastern Christendom, p. 68.

[21] In common with many medieval writers, Walter here interprets a natural disaster as a punishment or sign of God's displeasure. Northern Syria was, however, prone to consistent tectonic activity in this period.

[22] Walter seems to have believed himself to be writing a unique historical account. See: Our knowledge of Walter, p. 6.

[23] These italicized chapter headings do not appear in the manuscripts of Walter's text. Chapter breaks and titles were introduced by Riant in his edition of 1895 and the headings used here roughly follow his.

[24] 29 November 1114. *Galterii cancellarii, Bella Antiochena*, ed. H. Hagenmeyer, p. 126, n. 1, translating this date as 1115, wrongly suggested that Walter followed the Pisan calendar, which dates the start of the year from 25 March. Other sources confirm that by the standard dating system this earthquake occurred in 1114. Fulcher of Chartres, II.52, pp. 578-80; Matthew of Edessa, III.67, p. 216, place the earthquake earlier in the year; Kemal ed-Din,

dead of night,[25] when human frailty[26] was accustomed more suitably and more sweetly to sleep, there was an immense and terrible earthquake in Antioch and its region. And as a matter of fact, in that same unexpected earthquake men were horribly knocked around, and they felt, saw, heard the collapse of walls, towers and different buildings deeply threatening themselves and others; some thought to escape the collapse by running away, some to slide down from the walls, certain men gave themselves up and threw themselves down from high houses. More, indeed, were caught piecemeal in their sleep by the collapse, in such a way that even if a part of the wall remained intact, they were nowhere to be seen. Others, indeed, were terrified; they abandoned their homes, scorned their wealth, left everything, and behaved as if demented in the streets and squares of the town. They stretched their hands towards the heavens because of their manifold fear and powerlessness, and cried tearfully without ceasing in different languages: 'Spare us, Lord, spare your people!'[27]

When morning came, and the vast scale of the wretched disaster was clear beneath the ruin both of men and of other things, everyone of one accord - Latins, Greeks, Syrians, Armenians,[28] strangers and pilgrims - claimed the earthquake had happened because of their own sins.[29] At once they took advantage of good advice and had recourse to the very church of St Peter the apostle,[30] seeking the protection of his eternal patronage. And so that that very same saint whom they had failed to appreciate when things were going well, in bad times they recognized as omnipotent and merciful, his utter

---

p. 607; Ibn al-Athir, p. 295; Ibn al-Qalanisi, p. 149. See: Our knowledge of Walter, p. 7.

[25] Vergilian, e.g Georgics, 1.247: 'intempesta silet nox'.

[26] Cicero, Tusc. 5.4: 'fragilitas humani generis'.

[27] Joel, 2.17: 'Parce, Domine, parce populo tuo'.

[28] Walter provides a number of insights into the religious and ethnic diversity of the inhabitants of Antioch. Note his above comment on the number of different languages spoken in the city. See: The depiction of Islam and eastern Christendom, p. 67.

[29] In spite of Walter's earlier concentration upon the sins of the Eastern Christians, he here seems to admit that the Latin population was also guilty of sinfulness.

[30] The Basilica of St Peter, the main Christian church of the city of Antioch. During the First Crusade the Latins discovered the Holy Lance, believed to be a relic of the spear which pierced the side of Christ, buried within this building. Raymond of Aguilers, pp. 68-75; Gesta Francorum, pp. 59-60. Walter provides a number of insights into the close association between Antioch and St Peter, who according to tradition had chosen the site to found the first Christian church. See: Walter's attitude to religion and piety, pp. 69-70.

goodness performing with justice, and those same men confessed that they had grievously sinned and, renouncing their past and present pleasures to Lord Bernard, the first Latin patriarch,[31] they promised most devoutly to mend their ways, and by his faith, merits and prayers, with his own clergy and the rest of the faithful very humbly entreating God, so we truly believe, the Lord took pity on the rest of his Antiochene people.

When the divine office had been celebrated, a sermon delivered and some instructions imposed as to how they should behave or what they ought to do, just as they were thinking nothing very serious had happened, they were suddenly frightened by terrible news. For certain people who had escaped by God's favour in the town of Marash[32] testified that that same town had been entirely destroyed with its lord[33] and bishop,[34] also the clergy and all the people.[35] And not long afterwards testimony from the town of Mamistra,[36] previously ruined with its citizens and the greater part of the town on the feast of St Brice,[37] increased their fear. What of al-Atharib?[38] What of the other

---

[31] Bernard of Valence, the first Latin Patriarch of Antioch (1100-1135). Bernard had previously held the new episcopal see of Artah for approximately six months in 1100. Ralph of Caen, p. 704. See: Bernard of Valence, patriarch of Antioch, pp. 34-42, for a discussion of Bernard's career and his portrayal in Walter's account. See also: B. Hamilton, *The Latin Church in the Crusader States*, pp. 21-30.

[32] Marash, from the Latin 'Miragium', a large town to the far north of Antioch which had originally been part of the county of Edessa, being held by Joscelin of Courtenay in 1104. Ralph of Caen, 148, p. 710. By 1111 it seems, however, to have become more closely associated with the principality of Antioch. Albert of Aachen, XI.47. See also: G.T. Beech, 'The crusader lordship of Marash in Armenian Cilicia, 1104-1149', pp. 35-52.

[33] This may be a reference to Richard of Salerno. He had been appointed as ruler of Marash in 1108. Michael the Syrian, XV.10, p. 195. Albert of Aachen noted that in 1111 a man named Richard was 'prefect (*praefectus*) of the town of Marash'. Albert of Aachen, XI.40. It is, however, strange that Walter makes no further comment on the death of the 'lord' of Marash if the town were still held by the same Richard in 1114, given the fact that he was Roger of Salerno's father. G.T. Beech, 'The crusader lordship of Marash in Armenian Cilicia, 1104-1149', pp. 40-42, argues that Richard must have already been dead in 1112.

[34] The name of the Latin bishop of Marash is unknown.

[35] Fulcher of Chartres also recorded that an earthquake affected Marash in this period. Fulcher of Chartres, II.52, pp. 579-80.

[36] A town to the north-west of Antioch, on the Cilician Plain. Sometimes also referred to as Misis or Mistra. Occupied by the First Crusaders in 1097. Ralph of Caen, pp. 636-9; Albert of Aachen, III.15-16.

[37] 13 November 1114.

Antiochene lands? A comparable torment was imagined happening in quite disparate places. Therefore fear was mingled with terror and thus redoubled for the wretched masses, because they absolutely did not know where they should stay or where they should flee. For each day, the earthquake threatened for hopeless hours; and for this reason they said this to one another: 'Oh the wretched necessity of being born, the miserable need to die, our hard necessity to live!' Although these people knew that the power of God could nowhere and never be escaped, yet they decided it was easier to cohabit with the animals outside than to live inside in constant fear of the impending collapse of the buildings. For this reason they adopted tents for homes in the streets, in the squares, in gardens, in thickets, with other dwellings abandoned. More, indeed, left the towns and took their huts from place to place, staying on the plains.

And yet the patriarch, most experienced of all men of the place and time,[39] drawing discursively on the necessary divisions of philosophical teaching, pacified the hearts of the desolate people, who were now almost despairing of life, by means of the encouraging sweetness of holy preaching. And then finally he proclaimed a three-day fast for all the people,[40] with sighing and in a spirit of contrition, adding also that they should avoid evil works and pay attention to all good things. What, therefore, of the result? The people who had been brought back into the Lord's service were described in this manner: they flee feasting; they abhor drunkenness; they shun the baths;[41] they curse immorality; having laid aside everything, even care of the body, they have changed their style of dress into sackcloth and ashes;[42] they roam from street to street, from church to church, first the men, then the women, with bare feet, with loosened hair, beating their breasts, copiously watering their faces

---

[38] From the Latin 'quid de Cerepo?' This town, which was in 1114 on the border between the principality and Aleppo, seems to have been known by the Latins as Cerep. It was first conquered by Tancred in 1111. Albert of Aachen, XI.44; Kemal ed-Din, pp. 597-8.

[39] This phrase is a perfect example of Walter's laudatory attitude to Patriarch Bernard. See: Bernard of Valence, patriarch of Antioch, pp. 34-6.

[40] The First Crusaders had also followed this form of ritualized purification through three days of fasting during the sieges of Antioch and Jerusalem. J.S.C. Riley-Smith, *The First Crusade and the idea of crusading*, p. 85.

[41] The idea that bath houses were places of sin may be related to their connection to Eastern culture or because they encouraged baring of the flesh. See: The depiction of Islam and eastern Christendom, pp. 67-8.

[42] Matt. 11.21: 'in cilicio et cinere poenitentiam egissent'.

with tears; from day to day[43] with all their heart they repeat litanies to God; even by night they have time for vehement prayers, in churches as well as in their bedrooms. They call back the scattered citizens, they reform those in error, they are fully occupied bringing comfort to orphans and widows and remedying their need. Their hospitality also suffices: they strive with happy expressions to refresh the bodies of the poor, the needy and the destitute and to give them cheer by presenting them with gifts once they are refreshed. What more? Reformed by the benefit of penance, adorned by good works, they were kept safe from the danger of threatening earthquake for five months[44] and more not because of their own merits but through God's grace, and they gladly gave thanks to the Almighty in His church.

I.2   *The Antiochenes repair their defences and prepare for war against the Persians.*

Therefore the aforementioned Prince Roger visited his own demolished buildings in his castles and elsewhere and, having carefully sought out necessary supplies, he hastened to repair and fortify those which he knew to be most useful for the defence of his land and nearest to the enemy, even if he could not do it fully, nevertheless he would do it sufficiently for immediate protection.[45] When this was accomplished, as the summer weather returned, as is the custom of that region he made for the borderlands, where he would be able more swiftly to hear of the approach of the Persians and whence he might more swiftly meet the hordes of the enemy.[46] So they came to the bridge on the river Far, where he ordered in advance his army to meet

---

[43] This phrase is common in ecclesiastical Latin. Psalm 60 (61).89; 2 Cor. 4.16.

[44] From this comment we can assume that northern Syria experienced tremors and aftershocks until March 1115.

[45] Roger appears, at this point, to have visited sites outside the city of Antioch which had suffered earthquake damage. These probably included both fortified and un-fortified sites, but it is clear that Roger concentrated repairs at frontier settlements. Walter's use of the phrase 'his castles and elsewhere' may suggest that Roger was primarily concerned with lands within the princely domain at this point.

[46] Walter provides the interesting revelation that it was customary for the rulers of Antioch to make an annual tour of the frontiers of the principality in the early summer, on this occasion probably in May or June 1115. No other source from this period makes explicit mention of this custom in northern Syria, and it is not clear whether Walter refers to the customs of Latin settlers in the East or pre-existing Levantine customs.

him,[47] and in that place he discussed with his men matters of common utility,[48] and resolved to send scouts of different races[49] into those regions belonging to the Persians, the rulers of which, never deceived by rumours, were accustomed also through their own messengers to harass the garrisons of the Christian militia. The prince disbanded his army there, and returned with a few men to Antioch, where the Antiochene duke, Ralph of Acre, was summoned, a man experienced in council, and the prince decided with him above all what was to be done about putting the city to rights and about its entire condition; he also consulted him about those things which ought to be done with the lord and his warriors for the exigencies of war.[50]

Therefore the duke commanded the viscount[51] to be called before him, the viscount the magistrate,[52] the magistrate the herald, the herald the judge. When they had been summoned the matter was examined before them. The more important men were summoned by the lord prince's authorized command; the lesser were summoned too.[53] They assembled without delay. And so the duke addressed them eloquently and referred to the cause of the

---

[47] The 'Iron Bridge' crossed the Orontes River approximately 10 kilometres to the north-east of Antioch. It probably derives its name from a corruption of the local Arabic name for the Orontes 'Farfar' to 'Pons Ferreus'. Albert of Aachen, III.33, did, however, record that 'on each side of the bridge two towers overhung, indestructible by iron and perfectly adapted for defence'. The bridge was known in Arabic as Jisr al-Hadid. It was captured by the First Crusaders on 20 October 1097, during their approach on Antioch. *Gesta Francorum*, p. 28; Albert of Aachen, III.33-5. The relatively flat plains around the Iron Bridge would have made a suitable muster-point for the Antiochene forces.

[48] This example of the prince's consultation with his vassals correlates with other examples amongst Roger's predecessors. Bohemond I received advice about Melitene in 1100, while Tancred took 'advice from his men' about Apamea in 1106 and about the king of Jerusalem's summons in 1110. Ralph of Caen, p. 705; Albert of Aachen, X.22; XI.21.

[49] This explicit reference to the use of eastern Christian and perhaps even Muslim scouts is unusual in this period. See: The depiction of Islam and eastern Christendom, p. 68.

[50] The title duke was probably derived from the Byzantine office 'dux'. See: Walter and the early history of the principality of Antioch, p. 47.

[51] This may refer to 'Torold the viscount', who appeared in a charter issued by Roger of Salerno between 1113 and 1118. *Italia Sacra*, vol. 4, ed. Ughelli, pp. 847-8.

[52] From the Latin 'praetor'. This specific pattern of summoning implies a descending order of importance amongst these offices. The office described as 'judge' may have been derived from the Greek *krites*. The title of *praetor* certainly appears to have come from a Byzantine template.

[53] It seems that although the duke had the authority to initiate this call to council his power may have been derived from the prince.

matter in hand and to his lord's decree; moreover, he told them what was to be done, if he were not to be displeased by their advice. When they had heard the cause of the matter and received the prince's orders, they were all of the same opinion.[54] The extent of the destruction of the walls and towers was calculated and restoration works were offered to those who held lands and honours, more responsibility or less according to the size of their tenancy.[55]

Meanwhile the prince was very careful to place garrisons both in the citadel and in the city, with watchmen whom he knew were loyal to him, so that he could go forth to war. Then, having sent ahead weapons and other necessities of war and provisioning, he heard divine office, prayed in the churches of the blessed intercessors St Mary the Virgin, Peter and Paul, George and very many others,[56] received permission and patriarchal blessing, commending to God and the lord patriarch himself the city and all his possessions, then he bade farewell to all and set out on the expedition.[57]

From one direction the lord arrived in the army, from the other the scouts arrived. When questioned, they replied that there was official rejoicing in Persia on account of the ruin and destruction of Syria, and they reported that the sultan of Khorasan[58] had consulted the auguries of sun and moon[59] and

---

[54] Walter's two references to the 'orders' of the prince bring into the question the actual ability of this civil council to formulate policy.

[55] It appears that repairs were only organized within the city of Antioch itself.

[56] Those saints mentioned here are of course all universal, but the cults of St Peter, who was believed to have founded the Christian church in the city and St George, who was an important saint of the eastern church, were of particular importance in Antioch. M. Rheinheimer, 'Tankred und das Siegel Boemunds', pp. 75-93. See: Walter's attitude to religion and piety, pp. 69-70.

[57] The phrase 'permission and patriarchal blessing' is of particular interest as it suggests that Patriarch Bernard gave some form of licence to the forthcoming expedition. This might imply that he had the ability to either condone or condemn the military activities of the prince. It is also probable that Roger left Patriarch Bernard in control of Antioch as some form of regent. See: Bernard of Valence, patriarch of Antioch, pp. 36-7.

[58] The sultan of Baghdad, Ghiyah ad-Din Muhammad Shah, brother of Barkuraq. Ibn al-Athir, p. 217.

[59] Walter may here demonstrate his misunderstanding of Islam, suggesting that the Muslims revered solar and lunar portents, perhaps conflating ideas of astrology and religion. It is interesting that Walter goes on to suggest that the Muslim's consultation of auguries had led him to reach the same conclusion as the Christians, namely that the recent earthquakes indicated God's displeasure. See: The depiction of Islam and eastern Christendom, p. 61.

taken command of the army of all Persia,[60] asserting that Syria itself - deserted by God, as shown by the earthquake - along with whatever tiny remnant there was of its inhabitants, could really be easily subjected to his rule.[61] Moreover, once the scouts had been admitted they hastened to reveal new and more secret information to the prince alone, with his interpreter, in his privy apartments.[62]

When the envoys of the people had been heard, those who needed to be got rid of from the curtained apartment were sent away, so that they would not make a noise, while those who should be admitted for their wise counsel were admitted.[63] The prince, therefore, thought things over, and since javelins seen in advance do less harm and wise men have no regrets after taking advice,[64] he disclosed to his men in due order the envoys and the reasons for the envoys, and he consulted them as to what best should be done.[65] When the necessary reason for the council had been revealed, they led off in haste to worthy al-Atharib. For they had heard, by way of rumour, that the king of Damascans, Tughtegin,[66] had arrived at Aleppo with Il-ghazi, emir of the Turcomans,[67] accompanied by ten thousand soldiers,[68] on account of the fealty of Ridwan's son;[69] however, the fact of the matter was that, having

---

[60] In fact, as Walter subsequently related, the sultan's forces were commanded by Bursuq of Hamadan. Walter the Chancellor, I.3, p. 90.

[61] Walter seems to have believed that Bursuq's invasion of the principality was designed to completely expel the Latin presence in northern Syria.

[62] This passage confirms that these scouts were not Latins and indicates that Roger could not speak their foreign tongue, be it Arabic, Armenian or another eastern language.

[63] Walter may be indicating that Roger dismissed the scouts and perhaps also his interpreter before receiving his advisors.

[64] This may be a play on Cicero, *Tusc.* 5.117.

[65] Walter again portrays Roger asking the advice of his vassals, on this occasion making it clear that he views such consultation as shrewd.

[66] Tughtegin, atabeg to Dukak of Damascus, and ruler of the city after Dukak's death in 1104 until his own demise in 1128. Walter's use of the title of king may result from his misunderstanding of the title of atabeg, which actually meant a Mamluk military chief and regent. For a discussion of Walter's knowledge of the Muslim world see: The depiction of Islam and eastern Christendom, pp. 59-61.

[67] Il-ghazi ibn Artuk, brother of Soqman, ruler of Mardin, d. 1122.

[68] This is the first example of Walter's tendency to report Muslim numbers in multiples of 10,000. See: Walter as a military source, pp. 55-7.

[69] Ridwan ibn Tutush, emir of Aleppo (1095-1113) was succeeded by his two sons, first by Alp Arslan until his assassination in 1114 and then by Sultan-shah, whom Walter refers to here. Kemal ed-Din, p. 602.

made peace for the murder of Maudud,[70] they would strive to hand Aleppo over to the sultan, if they could.[71] For this reason our men had hurried, being eager to change utterly their fate by provoking trial by battle.

When the Turks heard that our men had reached their frontiers, they were brought low by fear and they concealed their state of mind by falsifying the evidence of their voice. For they said, by way of go-betweens sent to the prince, that they had come for the sake of confirming a treaty of friendship with him and against the conquered Persian enemy. Tughtegin, moreover, although he feared the formidable power of both of them, Christians and Persians, yet he preferred to be united with the Christians in a pretended peace, so that he might lead them to disaster, rather than to make an agreement with the Persians, whom he knew to be much more cruel towards him in peace than in war.[72]

So they assembled in the designated place, and there they confirmed agreements and became as if they were friends.[73] They arranged how they should best proceed against the hordes of the enemy, but in different ways. For the Damascene ordained that it was more advantageous for him and his

---

[70] Maudud, atabeg of Mosul (1108-1113). This former commander of the sultan of Baghdad's armies and ally of Tughtegin was assassinated in Damascus in 1113. Public opinion suspected Tughtegin of being involved. Ibn al-Qalanisi, pp. 137-42.

[71] In this passage Walter draws a distinction between the 'rumour' which Roger and his advisors believed - namely that Tughtegin and Il-ghazi travelled to Aleppo because of their allegiance to Sultan-shah - and what he believed to be 'the fact of the matter': that they intended to hand over the city to Ghiyah ad-Din, the Seldjuk Sultan of Baghdad. In fact the Arab sources record that Tughtegin and Il-ghazi brought their forces to Aleppo precisely because they hoped to prevent the city falling into the hands of the Sultan, probably in an attempt to preserve the existing balance of power in northern Syria. Ibn al-Athir, p. 296; Kemal ed-Din, p. 608. See: The depiction of Islam and eastern Christendom, p. 60.

[72] Walter is probably right to state that Tughtegin was prompted to seek an alliance by fear for his political future if the sultan of Baghdad gained a foothold in northern Syria. However, Walter uses the phrases 'pretended peace' and 'lead them to disaster' to make it clear from the start that he does not approve of this Latin-Muslim alliance. For a discussion of his attitudes and the other sources for these events see: The depiction of Islam and eastern Christendom, pp. 66-7. It is interesting that he focuses his attacks upon Tughtegin and not Il-ghazi, given the fact that it was the latter who led the subsequent attacks against the principality in 1119. For a discussion of how this affects the possible dating of composition of Books One and Two see: Our knowledge of Walter, p. 8.

[73] From subsequent events it would seem that an alliance between Roger, Tughtegin and Il-ghazi was arranged for the duration of the summer of 1115.

men to go to places of both sorts of fortune, while the Antiochene ordered his men to those places from which he could sooner attack the enemy head on. To cut a long story short: the opinion of the prince prevailed, to whom it had already been predicted that an army of barbarians would come through Salamyah[74] to Shaizar, which had formerly been tributary and served our men, but now had turned against us,[75] relying for approval on the Persians, by whose later action it suffered losses from both sides.

I.3 *Bursuq, the Persian general, invades Syria and Prince Roger summons his allies to resist.*

At length[76] our men, having sent out scouts against the enemy,[77] set out for Apamea[78] where they seemed to meet with a welcome, even a bond of complete love, like sons and parents in companionship, although they might differ in number or military worth.[79] For on the side of the prince no more than two thousand warriors were to be found, while the side of his counterpart was reckoned by many to equal ten thousand. Yet this side, which was greater

---

[74] A Muslim held town to the south east of Shaizar and Hamah.

[75] Shaizar lies on the banks of the Orontes, to the south of Apamea. Its formidable citadel survives to this day. The Banu Munqidh, the ruling family of Shaizar at this time, had begun paying tribute to Antioch in 1111, and had renewed this payment to Roger, upon his accession, in 1113. Ibn al-Qalanisi, p. 99, p. 132; Ibn al-Athir, p. 279. Shaizar had, however, co-operated with the sultan of Baghdad's armies, under the command of Maudud of Mosul, in 1111. Kemal ed-Din, pp. 600-1; Ibn al-Athir, pp. 282-3. The predicted course of the Persian approach, which was presumably made by Roger's advisors, proved to be accurate. It was perhaps based on the fact that in recent years Shaizar had been the sultan's main ally in northern Syria. The Muslim writer Usamah ibn Munqidh, a member of the Banu Munqidh, also recorded their participation in this campaign, pp. 101-5.

[76] The departure of the Latin army can be dated to June 1115 on the basis of Walter's subsequent statement that the army camped at Apamea for two months up to August.

[77] Even within the borders of the principality it seems to have been accepted practice to utilize scouts ahead of a marching army.

[78] The town of Apamea lies on the south western fringes of the Jabal as-Summaq. Also known as Femia, Afamyah or, in Arabic, Qal'at al-Mudiq. It was captured from the Muslim Abu l-Fath by Tancred in 1106. It was probably still part of the princely domain in 1115, perhaps held in castellany by Engelrand, who was named prefect of Apamea in 1111 by Albert of Aachen, XI.40.

[79] Again Walter reflects on the apparent friendship between Roger of Salerno and Tughtegin of Damascus. It is clear, however, that he believed Latin and Muslim forces joined in co-operation at Apamea as early as June 1115.

in number, was indeed less in worth. They camped before Apamea and stayed there two months, before the certain approach of the Persians was announced to them. In August it was reported that Bursuq, general of the Persians,[80] had massed his very powerful ranks of warriors beyond the Euphrates and now he had invaded and fiercely attacked the regions of Syria. When the prince realized this was true he notified, by means of messengers with sealed letters, the king of Jerusalem[81] and the count of Tripoli,[82] and he revealed the enemy's approach and that the place named was not far from our men at Salinas,[83] where, having taken drink and other pleasures, they were awaiting the augury of the crescent moon, and he urged them for the sake of his own forces to march towards the position of the Christian army with all speed.[84]

The king, therefore, who was always intent on valour, did not respond sluggishly, he sent ahead messengers to the count of Tripoli that very same day so that he would make no delay, and he himself followed as swiftly as possible.[85] Yet he warned the prince with an oath of Christianity and by the bond of brotherly affection, wherever they should go or wherever they stood firm, not to venture to attack the Persians now without the assistance of themselves.[86] Meanwhile the enemy, as rumour foretold, set out through Salamyah, taking on provisions there, and arrived at Hamah.[87] Since they

---

[80] Bursuq ibn Bursuq of Hamadan, commander of the sultan of Baghdad's army.

[81] Baldwin I king of Jerusalem (1100-1118). Also styled as Baldwin of Boulogne, count of Rethel. Baldwin had participated in the First Crusade and was count of Edessa (1098-1100). He succeeded his brother, Godfrey of Bouillon, as ruler of Jerusalem.

[82] Pons, count of Tripoli (1112-1137), son of Bertrand of Toulouse.

[83] This site is unidentifiable.

[84] In spite of frequent bickering, the Latin rulers of the Levant frequently cooperated in times of military crisis. The princes of Antioch had both given and received military assistance on a number of previous occasions. Fulcher of Chartres, II.27, p. 475; Albert of Aachen, XII.9.

[85] Although separate messages were sent by Roger to both Jerusalem and Tripoli, Walter records that King Baldwin sent word to Pons. This may be because the count of Tripoli was the king's vassal.

[86] There were precedents for Baldwin I's suggestion that Roger should perform a holding manoeuvre at Apamea. The combined armies of Antioch, Edessa, Tripoli and Jerusalem had forced a stalemate with Maudud of Mosul's army, camped at Shaizar, in 1111 by holding their position at Apamea. Albert of Aachen, XI.42; Fulcher of Chartres, II.45, pp. 557. See: Walter as a military source, p. 50.

[87] A town, to the south east of Shaizar, held by dependants of Tughtegin of Damascus at this point.

had demanded on behalf of the sultan that this town be handed over to him, and they had been unable to take it by threats or by entreaties, they surrounded it with a very powerful force of armed men and launched a vigorous assault, and after the assault from all sides, when many had been slaughtered, the enemy boldly forced an entry; this deed causing no slight terror to the inhabitants. Once in the town they immediately expelled its lord[88] and certain of the more powerful of the townspeople; some they killed and distributed their wealth among themselves, and they installed their own garrison there.[89]

When these things had been achieved, relying on the friendship of the emir of Shaizar[90] and wishing to billet themselves upon him, they marched on Shaizar. He, however, was not unmindful of the injury done to the people of Hamah, and he considered it more advantageous to offer them provisions while stationed outside, rather than to put up with the inconveniences of their entering Shaizar. For he was afraid that the enemy's savagery would overflow among his possessions, but much more he feared that he himself would be murdered. Therefore he sent out his brother,[91] so rumour reports, accompanied by horses bearing exotic gifts, by means of whom he might endow Bursuq in advance with the precious gifts, and the other magnates with other things, and they might make themselves agreeable to him, and with the brother as mediator a treaty of friendship might be confirmed between them, yet in this way, that while the lord of Shaizar stayed in the citadel of the town, his brother, as a native knowing the advances and retreats of their native land that were necessary for devastation in time of war, would set out with them as leader of their march and be of service to them;[92] but as I shall tell in the following chapters, with God's help, contrary to their hope the affair turned out against them. The brother, obeying his brother's orders, gladly undertook the business enjoined on him; however the army pitched

---

[88] Ali the Kurd. Ibn al-Athir, p. 279.

[89] Hamah was given into the possession of Kirkhan of Homs at this point. Sibt ibn al-Jauzi, 'Mir'at ez-Zeman', *Recueil des historiens des croisades. Historiens orientaux*, vol. 3 (Paris, 1884), p. 554; Kemal ed-Din, p. 608.

[90] Abu'l Asakir ibn-Munqidh, emir of Shaizar.

[91] Abu Salama Murschid ibn-Munqidh.

[92] Apparently Murschid ibn-Munqidh was to act both as a mediator and a military advisor to Bursuq's army, offering his superior knowledge of local geography in order to give him a strategic advantage against the Latins.

camp in the caves of Shaizar, and they once again took to drinking day after day, having posted the watch at a distance, tempting our men to join battle. The prince, indeed, who was joined with the king by a sacred Christian oath and by brotherly love, forbade all his men generally either to skirmish or even to wage war on pain of having their eyes torn out.[93] Hearing this, a part of the enemy army unexpectedly laid claim to Kafartab, a castle three leagues distant from our men,[94] and they reached it and attacked it again and again, but although the army inside was assaulted by frequent blows of arrows and stones[95] and by awful wounds, yet it could not be taken on that account, but, after one of their emirs was killed and many wounded, they returned to the main army, claiming that their own grief could be lessened by revenge.[96]

While they were doing their best to attack our men dreadfully, a rumour reached their ears announcing that the king's approach was very close. They, indeed, had confidence not in the power of the Holy Ghost but in the great numbers of the army,[97] so before the king came near they drew up marching columns and ordered those who were more skilled in skirmishing to the tents of our men. They determined the battle-lines, ordered according to their custom to follow one another at intervals,[98] while Bursuq, their general, assigned them a place, remaining with the greatest force of warriors in the camp. What more? They shook their spears, loosed their arrows and charged almost into our camp. When he saw this, the renowned prince, riding a swift horse, unsheathed his sword and rode around his men's encampment, declaiming: 'God's faith, by which we live, if anyone dares to ride out now, he will perish by my sword.' Indeed, on the contrary, he warned every one

---

[93] This harsh threat has parallels, particularly in the Byzantine empire, where blinding was a traditional method of removing someone from power or a punishment for treason. Anna Comnena, *The Alexiad*, ed. & trans. S.J. Leib (Paris, 1945), XII.6, p. 385.

[94] Kafartab, a fortified town in the Jabal as-Summaq. Occupied by the First Crusaders in 1099. Raymond of Aguilers, pp. 101-2. It was probably held by Bonable of Sarmin in 1115. See charter (b), p. 207.

[95] This suggests that the Muslims used catapults against Kafartab at this point. See: Walter as a military source, p. 58.

[96] This attack upon Kafartab was probably designed to lure Roger from the safety of Apamea. Although severely harried, however, Kafartab remained in Latin hands at this point.

[97] Walter is keen to highlight the differences between the Latins, who maintain their bravery by trusting in God, and the Muslims, who trusted not their faith but their military manpower.

[98] Walter suggests that it was Muslim practice to attack in successive waves of troops.

of them to stand before his camp, weapons in hand and mind alert, and yet not to venture in any way or to signal the start of the battle for themselves. Therefore the Persians marvelled that a race so ready for war and always intolerant of injury, who had been provoked so often by arrows, afflicted so often by jeers, was so long-suffering, because the Christians did not signal the start of battle and were already submitting as if conquered by fear of them.[99] Some of our men even considered it an act of cowardice; however some of greater perspicacity interpreted it as the purpose of the prince so that, when he was sure the time was right, they would be stronger to attack, not at the enemy's summoning, nor in anticipation of their forces, but by the prudent disposition and enormous experience of himself and the king,[100] whose arrival was very near. For, as experience shows, a handful of warriors with boldness and ingenuity will more often prevail in war than an ill-disciplined and unreliable multitude of armed men.[101]

I.4 *Bursuq feigns retreat and the Latins disperse; the Muslims then attack northern Syria and Roger rallies his forces.*

Meanwhile, as rumour travels faster than the deed is done, it was learnt that King Baldwin and Count Pons were hurrying manfully and swiftly. Bursuq, therefore, a general of deceitful cunning,[102] pretended to flee by turning back on himself, and by splitting up his forces through the territory of Shaizar as if he wanted to return to his homeland; he concealed his wickedness for the time being, so that with our men having retreated and separated he could with

---

[99] Walter heightens the impact of Roger's bravery and force of character by focusing upon the amazement of the Muslims. It is interesting to note that, in order to achieve this effect, Walter does acknowledge that the Latins had a reputation for being easily goaded into battle.

[100] Walter identifies Roger and King Baldwin I as the two most potent commanders, effectively ignoring Pons of Tripoli.

[101] In an interesting aside, to end this chapter, Walter reflects on, what he believes to be, the over-riding importance of strong and effective military leadership. See: Walter as a military source, p. 50.

[102] Although Walter here vilifies Bursuq for pursuing a strategy of feigned retreat, he goes on to congratulate the Latins for their attempts to prosecute a feigned attack upon Gistrum. See: Walter as a military source, p. 58.

more security destroy our maritime towns.[103] Meanwhile the king, in accordance with ancient custom, entered our men's camp with cymbals clashing and flutes and bugles blaring, and as soon as the king realized the enemy had retreated he complained bitterly that he had come too late. Nevertheless, after a short council of war, since they did not know where the enemy could be pursued or discovered, they decided in their turn to go and attack a certain castle, subdued by the Persians, called Gistrum,[104] thinking that the enemy could be recalled to battle by this deed.[105] They set about it at once: our men arrived there; all of a sudden, after appointing their battle-lines around the outside, the suburbs as well as the town, they were fully occupied in a most vigorous assault; at length the suburbs were partly destroyed by an attack with blows of the sword, partly consumed by fire. The Persians, indeed, although they realized from the evidence of the smoke-laden clouds, and by seeing with their own eyes, the conflagration made of that same town by our men in order to dishonour them, yet they feared to approach them, whom they had formerly attacked. For surely they considered this as evidence for a bold and worthy character, to the same extent as they had taken their behaviour for ignorance and cowardice before the camp.[106]

When, however, they neither came nor was any rumour heard as to where they were stationed, a discussion was held as to what should be done about it. Therefore that party which hoped rather to gain from war than to have been left at home suddenly confirmed that it was a good idea to pursue. Another party, whose mind was sweetly recalled by possessions, since the enemy was numerous and very strong, judged it more advantageous to return, every

---

[103] Walter here suggests that the primary aim of Bursuq's campaign was to destroy the principality's ports. In 1115 these included St Simeon, Latakia, Jabala and probably also Alexandretta. These ports did play an important role for the Latins, providing maritime connections with Byzantium and western Europe. It should be noted, however, that there is no evidence that Bursuq actually attacked any coastal towns during this campaign.

[104] This is unidentified. It may have been the citadel of Shaizar, or the fortification, known as Tall ibn-Ma'shar, which Tancred built near Shaizar in 1111, or even Jisr al-Shugur to the north on the Orontes. Kemal ed-Din, p. 599.

[105] Walter suggests that this attack was designed to lure Bursuq and his forces to battle rather than to actually capture Gistrum.

[106] Walter is keen to demonstrate that by these actions the Muslims were shown the 'reality' of Frankish bravery.

single one to his own, for the sake of protecting his townships.[107] Therefore the king returned with his men to Jerusalem, the Tripolitans to Tripoli, the Damascans to Damascus, the Antiochene prince to Antioch.[108] And we realize that this was not done by the power of these men, but no doubt by His influence who wished to break up the alliance of Belial with our people.[109]

Not long afterwards in the region of Shaizar the enemy one day made a dreadful attack, as was their tyrannical practice, on the castle of Kafartab, from which harm had already happened to them.[110] Here they attacked, there they battered with petraries[111] and other engines, in such a way, indeed, that the wall was demolished and a huge entrance was afforded to them. Soon they were inside, and once there they killed some of the inhabitants in revenge for their own men who had been slain and had died; others, more fortunate, they spared so that they could present them to the sultan in exchange for the victory palm.[112] But, thank God, their good fortune afterwards gave way to bad.

After the castle had been utterly destroyed, they marched through the borderlands laying waste and mutilating all they found, and arrived at Ma'arrat,[113] which they had formerly devastated, and there, as if they were

---

[107] Walter here appears to split opinion between a faction who were hungry for booty, and were perhaps largely landless, and another who wished to protect the lands they already held. In this passage Walter avoids passing judgement over these differing views, but in Book Two he returns to the re-examine the interests of the landed nobility. Walter the Chancellor, II.1, pp. 112-13.

[108] This is the first time that Walter actually mentions the presence of Muslim troops from Damascus. For an analysis of his narrative of these events see: The depiction of Islam and eastern Christendom, p. 66.

[109] Walter use of the term 'Belial' implies that this had been an alliance with the devil. Corinthians, 6.15.

[110] Usamah ibn-Munqidh, pp. 101-5, also recorded Bursuq's attack upon Kafartab, noting that the town fell on 5 September 1115.

[111] A form of catapult driven by either torsion or counter-weights.

[112] From the Latin 'pro victoriae palma'. Walter makes a number of other references to 'the palm of victory' in connection with both Muslims and Christians. I.7, p. 106. He may be alluding to the classical Roman concept that significant successes in battle might be commemorated by official public celebrations.

[113] Ma'arrat-an-Nu'man, was a major town in the Jabal as-Summaq, the plateau region to the south-east of Antioch. It was first captured by the crusaders in the winter of 1098-99. *Gesta Francorum*, pp. 79-80; Raymond of Aguilers, p. 98; Fulcher of Chartres, I.25, p. 4; Ralph of Caen, p. 679.

still on their own lands,[114] they painstakingly built siege-engines with which Zardana[115] could be taken. These things and others like them were swiftly reported to our lord, Prince Roger, who was still at Antioch; when he heard them he was stirred to manly boldness, and taking only the domestic members of his household[116] he withdrew to Rugia[117] and instructed all his men to make their way there without any delay or excuse.[118] Moreover, with utmost devotion he entreated the lord patriarch to join him there so that, empowered by his office and by his benediction, they could more freely and more safely fight in God's service.[119]

Therefore, in the month of September, on the Sunday before the feast day of the Exaltation of the Holy Cross,[120] the Antiochenes had assembled in the appointed place and the virtuous patriarch had hurried there, and he spoke clearly and plainly words more pleasing to God than to men. For he knew there was something reprehensible in them and something inimical to God, and in that place he did not keep silent, in fact, but, as befits a father, he instructed them by means of argument, entreaty, reproof what things they were to avoid and what they were to strive after.[121] What in particular? They did not feel ashamed to confess their sins to God and the lord patriarch; and it was enjoined on each of them by the lord patriarch, instead of a true penance, that each of them according to his ability was to defend full justice with God's help, in such a way, as I say, that those who would die in the war which was at hand would acquire salvation by his own absolution and also by

---

[114] The date of the previous Muslim attack upon Ma'arrat-an-Nu'man is unclear, but given the fact that Bursuq could afford to camp in the region with such confidence, it would appear that the town was in Muslim hands at this point.

[115] Also known as Zerdana or Zeredna, this town lay to the east of Antioch, on the border between the principality and Aleppo. It was first captured by Tancred in 1111 and was probably held by Robert fitz-Fulk the Leper in 1115. Ibn al-Athir, p. 278. See also charter (a) p. 205, n. 78.

[116] From the Latin 'comitatus domestica familia'.

[117] This settlement lay in the Ruj valley, to the south of Antioch, which acted as a major route between the city and the Jabal as-Summaq.

[118] This summons must represent a full levy of all of Roger's vassals.

[119] Walter contrasts Roger's authoritarian summons to his vassals with the supplicatory invitation to Patriarch Bernard. Once again the suggestion is that Bernard sanctioned Antiochene military activity.

[120] 12 September 1115.

[121] Given Walter's earlier discussion of specific sins, he is here rather evasive as to exactly what was 'reprehensible' about the Latins.

propitiation of the Lord, while those who returned should all meet at a council arranged for the next feast of All Saints,[122] where on the advice of the Antiochene church they would administer open justice both with regard to possessions and other matters, but with this addition, that if through ignorance or weakness they could not render justice fully, they should not refuse to accept the advice and judgment of those men who were more capable of truth in pursuing justice. Thus the matter was managed and enjoined on them and all agreed, and each of them placed his joined hands between the hands of the patriarch and gave their word to God and to him, through a truce and the Church's indulgence, that if perchance they erred they could be saved through the correction and reparation of the Church.[123]

I.5   *The Latins make physical and spiritual preparations for war.*

After these things were done, the reverend patriarch celebrated the ritual of Mass and, having pronounced absolution from their sins to the people entrusted to him, he strengthened them all with his patriarchal benediction, and he humbly commended them for the cure of souls to the bishop[124] of Jabala,[125] who was going off to war at the same time,[126] and, after farewells to all, he returned to Antioch, earnestly entreating the Lord and interceding with Him so that He, who brings low the haughty[127] and who destroys wars from the beginning,[128] might destroy the enemies by an

---

[122] 1 November 1115.

[123] In this rather confused passage Walter seems to suggest that the patriarch offered a remission of sins to those who died in the forthcoming battle and required those who survived to attend a special council on 1 November. The exact nature and purpose of this meeting is unclear.

[124] William, bishop of Jabala. See: Walter attitude to religion and piety, p. 70, n. 171.

[125] Jabala, also know as Gibel, a port on the coast to the south of Latakia, was probably occupied by the First Crusaders before the spring of 1099. Albert of Aachen, V.33.

[126] William appears to have been appointed as Bernard's representative or even legate at this point. Walter suggests that unlike the patriarch, whom he always distances from warfare, William might participate more fully in the forthcoming campaign. See: Bernard of Valence, patriarch of Antioch, p. 37.

[127] Psalm 17 (18).28: 'oculos superborum humiliabis'.

[128] Judith, 9.10: 'qui conteris bella ab initio'.

assault of His people.[129] Moreover, on the following day, after guards had been posted all around, the prince confidently ordered his columns to march and at a rapid pace to make for that place where, from the reports of people in the neighbourhood, he had heard that the Persians had even now arrived. They approached, all ready to rush upon the enemy in the appointed place, but since they did not find the people whom they already sought to destroy, they pitched camp outside Hab.[130]

In the morning, after he had performed the service of Mass of the life-giving Cross, whose exaltation was celebrated on that day,[131] William, bishop of Jabala, a man worthy of praise in every respect, instructed, advised and exhorted by way of words and examples appropriate for that same feast the people entrusted to him by God. What more? Everyone flocked to adore the most holy wood of that same Cross of Our Lord[132] before they went off on their journey, and, protected by the bishop's permission and blessing,[133] having sent scouts ahead to reconnoitre, so that the enemy would not attack them unexpectedly, after the marching column of the count of Edessa[134] was

---

[129] Walter appears to be making a strong allusion to the concept of 'just war', suggesting that the battle would be won through God's direct intervention on behalf of 'His people'.

[130] This small fortified settlement, also know as Hap, was on the fringes of the Jabal as-Summaq. It had been occupied by the Latins before 1105. Kemal ed-Din, p. 592.

[131] 14 September 1115.

[132] This is a reference to an Antiochene relic of the True Cross, a fragment of wood believed to have been part of the cross upon which Christ was crucified. See: Walter's attitude to religion and piety, p. 70. This relic may actually have been a segment of the Jerusalemite True Cross. According to Albert of Aachen, VII.48, King Baldwin I accused Patriarch Daimbert of chopping up and distributing pieces of this relic in 1101. If this story is true, then Daimbert may have given his ally Tancred, then regent of Antioch, one of these fragments.

[133] This suggests that, like the patriarch, William had the authority to proclaim a war as just.

[134] Baldwin of Le Bourcq, the cousin of Baldwin of Boulogne, participated in the First Crusade. He succeeded Baldwin I as count of Edessa from 1100 to 1118 and then as king of Jerusalem from 1118 to his death in 1131. Walter does not record that Roger called for military aid from Edessa in 1115. As we have seen, he earlier mentioned the appeal Roger made to Jerusalem and Tripoli while at Apamea, but no mention is made of Edessa. Walter the Chancellor, I.3, p. 90. Matthew of Edessa, III.70, pp. 218-19, did, however, note that Baldwin II was also present at Apamea. Perhaps Walter did not think that it was necessary to mention that the county provided the principality with military support because he viewed Antioch and Edessa as such close allies. On the other hand, he might have been implying that Antioch dominated Edessa to such an extent that Baldwin II would automatically owe Roger military service almost as a vassal.

drawn up, since the princes had bestowed on him the honour of striking the first blow in battle,[135] and the rest of the army was ranged in battle order, they took to the road.

Suddenly, Theoderic of Barneville,[136] one of the scouts, arrived at a gallop, and with a cheerful expression he spoke thus: 'Behold what we were seeking, behold what we desired, by grace of God's work, in the place where we had arranged to pitch our tents, around the springs in the valley of Sarmin,[137] in that very place the enemy are unfolding theirs, some already pitched and some yet to be pitched.' At his words the prince shouted: 'In God's name to arms, knights!' Then, confident in his manly boldness, he rode swiftly to and fro from line to line, telling them all that they should now rejoice, since the battle was at hand in which it was fitting for them to practise their knightly profession.[138] Therefore he commanded them to couch[139] their weapons and not to delay preparing for battle any further.[140]

In that very place the renowned bishop, bearing in a spirit of humility the Cross of holy wood in his reverend hands, circled the whole army; and while he showed it to all of them he affirmed that they would claim victory in the coming battle through its virtue, if they charged the enemy with resolute heart and fought trusting Lord Jesus. Immediately everyone shouted with heart and

---

[135] The position of vanguard in a march or battle carried with it considerable honour and responsibility. It is not clear whether the 'princes' who had allotted this position included only Prince Roger and Count Baldwin himself or a wider group of nobles.

[136] Theoderic was probably related to Roger of Barneville. This Norman family originally came from Barneville in the Cotentin, Dep. Manche. Roger, who had settled in Sicily, was a vassal of Count Roger of Sicily and had participated in the First Crusade. For further discussion see: E.M. Jamison, 'Some notes on the *Anonymi Gesta Francorum*, with special reference to the Norman contingent from south Italy and Sicily in the First Crusade', *Studies in French Language and Mediaeval Literature Presented to Professor Mildred K. Pope* (Manchester, 1939), pp. 207ff.

[137] This settlement, to the south-east of Antioch, had been occupied by the Latins before 1105. Kemal ed-Din, p. 592. It may have been held by a man named Bonable in 1115. Albert of Aachen, XI.40.

[138] Walter seems to have been interested in the concept of 'chivalric' behaviour, exploring both Roger's personal bravery and the his perception of correct knightly behaviour. See: Roger of Salerno, p. 20, and Walter as a military source, pp. 52-3.

[139] From the Latin 'baiulari', meaning to lower or prepare their weapons.

[140] Lucan, *Phars.* 1.281: 'differe paratis'.

voice:[141] 'Holy God! Holy and mighty, holy and immortal, have mercy on us!' They fell to their knees three times before the Lord's Cross, and, kissing it reverently, they entrusted themselves to Him. Protected by this consolation, marked by the sign of the cross, they saluted that same Cross again and again, then swiftly mounted their horses.[142]

I.6   *The battle of Tall Danith, in which the Latins were victorious.*

The prince, being undaunted in spirit, imposed silence on the rest by a gesture, and he himself spoke thus: 'Come, my brothers and fellow knights! And you, the infantry, let us now draw nearer. Remember with how much praise, how much honour - indeed, with how much written remembrance the deeds of good men are committed to memory by the whole world.[143] Behold, the time has come when your strength and virtue may be esteemed, when the name of your victory over the barbarians may shine brightly throughout the regions of the world. Strive, too, because the crown is already promised by the Lord to those who fight lawfully.[144] Therefore let us hasten to attack them and, when our lances are broken, let us approach closer as quickly as possible brandishing our unsheathed swords around their heads,[145] so that their pride[146] may be brought low by our constant blows and, by God's vengeance, their annihilation will not be delayed.' And when they proceeded in ordered columns, the prince warned them all generally not to give in to any greed for riches and allow themselves to plunder, but, as befits warriors, in order to protect their own safety they should strive to destroy the

---

[141] Rom. 10.8: 'verbum in ore tuo, et in corde tuo'. The quotation which follows is part of the Good Friday liturgy for the veneration of the Holy Cross.

[142] Walter's use of the term 'signed' by the cross bears some echoes of practice of individuals taking the cross for the First Crusade. Walter also seems to imply that these spiritual preparations were limited to the knights within the army, that is those who 'then swiftly mounted their horses'.

[143] Walter once again passes comment upon the importance of written historical record.

[144] This would appear to be an allusion to the Augustinian concept of 'right intention'.

[145] Walter makes frequent reference to this process of battle whereby knights attack first with their lances and then use their secondary weapon the sword. See: Walter as a military source, p. 53.

[146] Walter comments once again upon dangers of pride, but in this instance it is the Muslims, not Christians, who are guilty of the sin.

enemy's ferocity.[147] The aforementioned bishop, therefore, proclaimed that anyone resisting this worthwhile judgment deserved to be punished with revenge on his body, and, even more intolerable, he assured them, to suffer eternal damnation. Speaking thus, he armed every one of them more eagerly for the fray.

Meanwhile, the eyes of the Persians were dazzled by the scintillating light of the sun reflected from our men's weapons, so that the enemy thought and said that the prince was not in that place, but a common group of wandering soldiers protecting the borders. Bursuq, therefore, ordered them to be brought to him with their hands tied behind their backs with ropes. At once the prince's banners came into view,[148] and by God's guidance they were seen by the Persians spread out in such a way that they believed from the banners that the very land was clothed all around with white-clad knights.[149] Nevertheless, Bursuq and all his men, steeped in the rottenness of error, with his brother[150] and a very great force of warriors, made haste to climb the hill called Danith,[151] to withstand our men in that place, and on the top of this high ground they made calculations from the stars and summoned false gods to appear for them.[152] At length they were seen to have burdened that same hill not only with themselves, but truly also with manifold riches,[153]

---

[147] This prohibition against the distractions of plunder during battle is common in the accounts of warfare in the Latin East. Ralph of Caen, p. 666, for example, made use of this theme, praising Tancred for his lack of interest in booty after the battle of Antioch on 28 June 1098. The Latins do not appear to have condemned the concept of booty as a just reward for battle, rather the indiscipline which might result if troops stopped to collect wealth during combat.

[148] This bears comparison to Venantius Fortunatus' hymn to the Holy Cross, *Oxford Book of Medieval Latin Verse*, ed. F.J.E. Raby (Oxford, 1959), no. 55, p. 75. The metre of the hymn is the same as Walter's hymn below, and, given Walter's reverence for the Cross, he may well have imitated the 7th century hymn deliberately.

[149] The image of a host of white-clad knights bears close resemblance to that recorded by the anonymous author of the *Gesta Francorum*, p. 69, at the battle of Antioch on the 28 June 1098, during the First Crusade.

[150] Zengi ibn Bursuq, d. 1116-17. Ibn al-Athir, p. 298.

[151] Tall Danith, a hill in the vicinity of Sarmin and Hab.

[152] The 'rottenness of error' to which Walter makes reference is undoubtedly religious. He goes on, however, to demonstrate some of the common Latin misconceptions of Islam, namely that it was a polytheistic religion. See: The depiction of Islam and eastern Christendom, p. 61.

[153] Although he noted the prohibition against seeking booty before the end of the battle, Walter is still keen to demonstrate that the Muslims possessed considerable riches.

with Tamirek[154] in support hiding beyond the hill with his battle-array; the
rest indeed were detained in their tents and outside them by greed[155] for the
riches present, and were waiting arrogantly for their comrades, trusting very
greatly, moreover, in the forces of their princes, and they were not aided by
penitence, because it was too late, nor were they comforted by the protection
of their comrades, because it was lost.

For, as bugles were being sounded throughout the midst of the camp, Roger
was at hand, most fine prince of a Christian host, with his battle-array so
fierce towards the enemy, to deliver their captive comrades[156] and slaughter
the enemy, to treat their riches as ordure; he directed the march to the hill,
on which the enemy's standard and strength were assembled. The count of
Edessa and Guy Le Chevreuil,[157] positioned for the first attack, declared that
they were going to make the first advance from the left,[158] the one attacking
the enemy head on on the hill-side, the other from the side. Moreover,
Bursuq, wounded by the dart of divine terror, was coming down with his
brother and his household[159] as if he were about to join battle, and he
ordered them to fight manfully and defend the hill; he himself was resolved
to escape with whatever he could.[160]

---

[154] He can probably be identified with Tamirek of Sinjar. Ibn al-Athir, p. 288.

[155] This was a rather hackneyed Latin phrase. Vergil, *Aeneid*, 4.194: 'cupidine captos';
Ovid, *Metamorphoses*, 13.762: 'cupidine captus'. See also below, Walter the Chancellor, II.6,
pp. 130-31.

[156] These may well have been the prisoners taken after the fall of Kafartab. Walter the
Chancellor, I.4, p. 95.

[157] Guy was the ruler of the Latin holdings in Cilicia, to the north west of Antioch. Albert
of Aachen described him as the 'prince of the cities of Tarsus and Mamistra' when he was
called to arms by Tancred in 1111. Albert of Aachen, XI.40. Guy also issued an undated
charter granting land and revenues to the religious house of Our Lady of Josaphat, which was
subsequently confirmed in a document issued by Roger of Salerno in 1114. 'Chartes de
l'abbaye de Notre-Dame de Josaphat', pp. 115-16, no. 4; *Chartes de Terre Sainte provenant
de l'abbaye de N. D. de Josaphat*, pp. 26-7, no. 4. Guy was in fact the first Antiochene noble
to issue a surviving charter in his own name. His position within the principality is reflected
in *The Antiochene Wars* by his command of the vanguard alongside Count Baldwin II of
Edessa.

[158] It is interesting that Count Baldwin and Guy Le Chevreuil seem to have possessed
sufficient authority to declare their own intentions in the battle independently of Roger.

[159] Walter may here be imposing the Latin term of 'household' upon Bursuq's closest
followers.

[160] This indication of Bursuq's personal cowardice and materialism contrasts with Walter's
heroic image of Roger.

Meanwhile, from this side Count Baldwin, from that side Guy, having broken their lances in the first charge, struck the enemy with drawn swords. The din of this, the wailing and the clash of weapons on both sides so deafened the warriors that a friend could not recognize his friend, nor a brother his brother.[161] But our men were not terrified by the sounds nor overwhelmed by the exertion, and, recovering their strength, with equal boldness they put the enemy to flight, hacked them to pieces and killed them. When he saw this, Tamirek broke out from the left-hand side, accompanied by a magnificent battle-array of three hundred knights,[162] to gallop after the prince's battle-line,[163] and since they did not dare to attack it, and they could not use a constant bombardment of arrows to disrupt the charge,[164] at a swifter pace they caused the Turcopoles,[165] who were shooting arrows at them, to be swallowed up among our men. From this charge they met Robert fitz-Fulk's[166] cohort,[167] advancing from the right, head on; when they saw

---

[161] Walter frequently adds colour to his account by providing detailed descriptions of sounds.

[162] Walter may be imposing the Latin 'knights' upon Muslim cavalry. His use of 'magnificent' to characterize Tamirek's force was perhaps intended to heighten the impact Roger's military success.

[163] This demonstrates that Roger personally commanded a division of the army during this battle. See also: Walter the Chancellor, II.5, p. 127. For other examples of armies or divisions being led by princes of Antioch in this period see: Albert of Aachen, IX.43; X.19; Fulcher of Chartres, I.34, p. 342.

[164] In this period Muslim forces often used sustained volleys of arrows to disrupt Latin battle formations. R.C. Smail, *Crusading warfare*, pp. 80-82. See: Walter as a military source, p. 58.

[165] A generic term denoting troops recruited from the indigenous population of the Levant. They were often the product of mixed marriages. Usamah ibn Munqidh, p. 79, suggested that they were used as archers by the Latins. See also: R.C. Smail, *Crusading warfare*, pp. 111-12. Smail incorrectly ascribes Usamah's comment to the first battle of Tall Danith, which he calls Sarmin.

[166] Robert fitz-Fulk the Leper was a powerful Antiochene noble whose lordship included the frontier town of Zardana, the castle of Saone and the nearby settlement of Balatanos. He first appeared in the written record in 1108 as a witness to two of Tancred's charters making grants to the Pisans. *Carte dell'Archivio Capitolare di Pisa (1101-1120)*, vol. 4, pp. 80-83, n. 37-8. He played a prominent role in the events of 1115 and 1119. See also; Usamah ibn-Munqidh, p. 149; Kemal ed-Din, pp. 620-22; Walter the Chancellor, II.14, pp. 159-62.

[167] It is not clear whether Walter intended the use of 'battle-line' and 'cohort' to denote divisions of different size or composition.

this, Robert Sourdeval[168] and Bochard,[169] distinguished knights, were not afraid to seek out the savagery of that desperate race, and they conveyed themselves suddenly into the midst of the enemy, to slaughter the infidels, then they themselves were slaughtered and became martyrs of Christ.[170] Robert[171] did not hold back from avenging the blood of his men by fighting zealously, but after his horse's reins were cut through he was wounded by an arrow and died, while his cohort was utterly routed.

I.7   Prince Roger's victory over the Persians is followed by the division of spoils. He is welcomed in Antioch with thanksgiving and praise.

The young man Alan[172] and Guy Fresnel,[173] advancing at the same time,

---

[168] Robert was a Norman, whose family originally came from Sourdeval in the Cotentin, Dép. Manche, but who had settled in Sicily, where he achieved prominence under Count Roger. E.M. Jamison, 'Some notes on the *Anonymi Gesta Francorum*, with special reference to the Norman contingent from south Italy and Sicily in the First Crusade', p. 207. Robert participated in the First Crusade, travelling in Bohemond's contingent. *Gesta Francorum*, p. 7. He also appeared in two Antiochene charters in 1098 and 1114. *Liber Privilegiorum ecclesiae Januensis*, ed. D. Puncuh (Genoa, 1962), pp. 40-1, n. 23; *Chartes de Terre Sainte provenant de l'abbaye de N. D. de Josaphat*, pp. 26-7, no. 4. See also charter (a), pp. 205-6.

[169] This individual is unidentifiable. He was, however, probably not the same Bochard who later fought alongside Il-ghazi. Walter the Chancellor, II.11, p. 150.

[170] Once again this reference to slain Latins as martyrs bears comparison to the accounts of the First Crusade and perhaps suggests that Walter viewed this campaign as a Holy War. J.S.C. Riley-Smith, *The First Crusade and the idea of crusading*, pp. 115-18.

[171] Given the fact that Robert fitz-Fulk did not die until 1119, this must be a reference to Robert of Sourdeval. Walter's suggestion that Robert also commanded a 'cohort' of troops, which were routed after his death, does however cause some confusion.

[172] Probably the same Alan who was named as lord of al-Atharib, the fortified town on the eastern frontier of the principality, in 1119. Walter the Chancellor, II.2, p. 117. He was later to hold the fortified monastery of Hisn ad-Dair in the same region between 1121 and 1126. Kemal ed-Din, p. 628, p. 635, p. 639; Ibn al-Athir, pp. 166-7. Du Cange was probably wrong to identify Alan of al-Atharib with Alan of Gael, the son of Ralph of Gael, the former earl of Norfolk. C. Du Cange, *Les Familles d'Outremer*, ed. E.G. Rey (Paris, 1869), p. 273. Both father and son did travel in Robert of Normandy's contingent during the First Crusade. Orderic Vitalis, vol. 5, p. 35, p. 54, p. 58. Du Cange assumed that, as Ralph's son, Alan was quite young, and thus linked him with the 'youth' Alan mentioned by Walter the Chancellor in 1115. Given the fact that seventeen years had elapsed between these two appearances it is surely impossible that Alan of Gael would still have been described as 'a youth'.

announced this out loud: 'Our most esteemed comrades! Even now help must be brought to our men!' Soon reinforcements arrived, and after wielding their lances they protected our dead comrades by sword-blows and they defended the living of that battle-array. But from our side and theirs, in turn, there was immense bloodshed. Meanwhile our men's battle-array was regarding the host of Persians raging on all sides, both right and left, and, proclaiming of one accord, 'Jesus Christ!' they charged into the midst of the enemy. In the first attack, as the divine sword struck home, the din of the enemy, previously terrifying and very loud, was exchanged in different ways for the constant sobs of dying men.[174] What of the details? As a result of the different attacks some suffered the stuff of death; others, indeed, struck by the dart of divine vengeance, turned round and fled. Therefore the prince, faithful to God, seized victory that day through the virtue of the holy Cross;[175] by God's bounty the rich pickings of the battlefield were available to him.[176] And so he himself, as was proper, stayed on the field with his household[177] and the esteem of his men, to direct the rest forthwith to the pursuit;[178] in this pursuit the battle line of St Peter[179] gained a praiseworthy name before all others.

---

[173] Guy probably came form La Ferté-Fraisnel, on the borders of Perche. He was named in 1111 as 'Guy, known as Fresnel, who held the town of Harim'. Albert of Aachen, XI.40. Alongside Artah, Harim represented the last line of defence for the city of Antioch from eastern attack. Guy's importance is reflected by the fact that he appeared as the second witness to a charter issued by Roger of Salerno in 1118. *Cartulaire général de l'ordre des Hospitaliers de S. Jean de Jérusalem (1100-1310)*, vol. 1, p. 38, no. 45. See also charter (b), pp. 207-8. Guy also fought in the Battle of the Field of Blood in 1119. William of Tyre, XII.9, p. 557; Walter the Chancellor, II.5, p. 126.

[174] Walter once again plays with the theme of sound, here producing an evocative aural image to illustrate the Muslim defeat.

[175] Here Walter explicitly states that God's will manifested itself through the relic of the True Cross.

[176] Once the battle is over, Walter seems keen to comment on the plentiful booty gathered as a result of the victory. See Walter the Chancellor, I.6, p. 101, n, 147; p. 101, n. 153.

[177] Walter does not specifically state that Roger fought alongside his household during the battle of Tall Danith.

[178] The fact that Roger stayed behind while allowing the rest of his forces to pursue Bursuq's army reflects the fact that maintaining control of the field was an important criterion in determining victory in battle. See: Walter as a military source, p. 52.

[179] This group may have been a military confraternity or a proto-military order. Its connection with St Peter may even indicate that it was a body of 'fideles sancti Petri'; along the lines of those of other bishops, and particularly the pope, and thus linked to Patriarch Bernard. See also, Walter the Chancellor, II.5, p. 126.

In that place there was a certain plain partly covered by dead bodies, partly crammed by a mass of camels and other animals laden with riches, which were a hindrance to killing for our men, and a help to escape for those fleeing. Yet our men pursued the enemy less than two miles beyond Sarmit, running them through, wounding them and killing them.

Eventually the victors returned bearing, driving, leading various spoils, and laden with wealth; giving thanks to God the creator, they arrived rejoicing at their lord Prince Roger himself, who occupied the battlefield. What list of captured wealth shall I report, when neither its measure nor its variety is reckonable by anyone? What number of slaughtered enemies, when they are innumerable? Among us few casualties were counted. The prince, indeed, occupied the battlefield for three days and personally directed the wealth which was brought to him to be kept for him, as befitted so great a prince; the rest was to be shared out, as his sovereignty and the custom of that same court demanded.[180]

When this was finished, the prince sent ahead of him an abundance of different treasures and a multitude of prisoners, praying to God and giving thanks to Him with all his people; and because they had accomplished God's service courageously and wisely, he dismissed them all with the love of a good father;[181] moreover, he directed his nobles who were returning to their possessions that after they had visited their wives and children they were to return to Antioch to discuss what should be done for Christianity at a council of the Antiochene church, at an arranged time.[182] He himself, as he returned with the undisputed palm of victory, was happily received with hymns and songs by all the people throughout countryside and castles. And when he approached Antioch, the venerable city, the noise of his arrival resounded through the whole city. Therefore, as a series of holy relics led the way, the reverend patriarch, with his clergy adorned according to ecclesiastical custom, a multitude of men and women following, went out to meet him; they

---

[180] Walter here reveals that a customary law did exist to govern the distribution of booty taken in battle. Unfortunately he does not provide any further details of this process.

[181] Ralph of Caen, p. 636, used a similar phrase to characterize Tancred of Hauteville's treatment of Mamistra during the First Crusade.

[182] This is a reference to the council imposed by Patriarch Bernard upon those Latins who survived the first battle of Tall Danith. Walter the Chancellor, I.4, p. 97.

resounded with angelic voices, 'Fear God and keep His commandments,'[183]
and they received him, praised him highly and revered him.

In honour of the highest king
and for love of his flock
child, slave and maidservant
rejoice on that day.

Meanwhile, too, people
of different nations[184]
are bent upon garlanding
the town with flowers.

Whatever dear or rare
ornament a person may have
then he does not hide it, but reveals it
in order to please the victor.

They strew the streets and squares
with silken decorations,
they are adorned with gold and jewels
for the arrival of the prince.

So much perfume is poured
of different kinds,
that it could entirely be called
an earthly paradise.

The prince enters,
the populace resounds with hymns of praise;
they praise God,
they greet the prince with sublime voices.

Thus they arrive together

---

[183] Ecclesiastes, 12.13: 'Deum time, et mandata eius observa'.

[184] This comment again highlights the cultural and ethnic diversity of Antioch's population.

at the temple of St Peter[185]
where they render gladly
praises to God the father.

Therefore the prince bears to the altar
the triumphal banner[186]
and offers it as a special,
princely gift after these events.[187]

Having worshipped the true God
he gives thanks to all the clergy
by whose prayers he emerged
a distinguished and blessed victor.[188]

As he comes out of the doors
they all shout with all their heart:
Hail king!
Champion of truth!

The enemies of God fear you,
and may you have continuing
peace, prosperity and victory,
world without end! Amen!

.

---

[185] This must be a reference to the basilica of St Peter in Antioch.

[186] This may be a reference to a banner captured from Bursuq's forces, or an allusion to classical concept of triumph. See, p. 95, n. 112.

[187] Walter does not mention whether the relic of the True Cross was returned to Patriarch Bernard at this point. The movements of the Jerusalemite True Cross were, in contrast, closely tracked by Fulcher of Chartres, III.6, pp. 632-3.

[188] Walter appears to move away from his earlier insistence this victory was direct attributable to the relic of the True Cross, focusing instead upon the spiritual activity of the clergy.

The Second War

In this book Walter narrates how the very worthy Prince Roger of Antioch died.

Prologue

In earlier times, whatever the outcomes of wars, some historian would assuredly be put forward by his colleagues to relate for the minds of his listeners as best he could the occasion, whether of sorrow or of joy.[1] But this is the record of the grief of griefs and of complete unhappiness which by sudden disaster stole into the warlike part of Roger, prince of the Antiochenes, and, as a mass of offenses drove that prince,[2] utterly removed his joys and went beyond the limit and bounds of complete wretchedness to such an extent that it cannot be expressed in words or conceived in thoughts how many and what kind of torments and unheard of deaths were visited on our men in an enormity of destruction. For this reason we are compelled necessarily to speak, since there is no history-writer who can describe the succession of events in full, nor anyone else who might dare to say that it was other than divine vengeance.[3]

But nevertheless, lest it should seem entirely to slip the memory, and because it may be considered worthy of recital for the good of those who hear it, having changed the style I adopted for the first war, which went well, I myself, Walter the chancellor,[4] having experienced both sorts of fortune and knowing therefore that prosperity of the flesh is more harmful for the soul than adversity to the body, have taken pains to describe that part of the second

---

[1] This use of the word 'listeners' may suggest that Walter expected his work to be read aloud to his audience. This theory is supported by his comment, below, that his writing would be 'recited' for the benefit of 'those who hear it'.

[2] For a discussion of Walter's attitude to Roger's sins, see: Roger of Salerno, pp. 20-22.

[3] Walter demonstrates that he is consciously writing a history for posterity, one which he feels no other is qualified to write. It is not clear, from his use of the phrase 'other than divine vengeance' whether Walter thought it necessary to look beyond the power of God's will to explain the events of 1119. See: Our knowledge of Walter, p. 6; and Walter's purpose in writing *The Antiochene Wars*, pp. 11-12.

[4] See: Our knowledge of Walter, p. 5.

war as it gave way to contrary fortune with the aid of Himself, who inspires both faith and love of Himself by good deserts, whom none excels, so that we can fulfil those things which are pleasing to Him. Therefore first I warn those who wish to comply with divine law not to glory in malice nor to be powerful in iniquity,[5] but also not ever to take pride in their own good deeds.[6] For by this defect souls are cast down from the very pinnacle of perfection and by the same fault we are both ungrateful to God and unmindful of His kindness, and because we put the success of the earlier war down to the victory of our own forces, in the second detestable war some of us fell suddenly, having become the stuff of death, others indeed were kept alive for long and dreadful torture, just as we shall describe in the following treatise, commending it to the memory of posterity, to the utmost of our ability, dulled by the experience of the prison-cell.[7]

II.1   *Il-ghazi attacks and Roger prepares for war again, disregarding, however, the patriarch's advice.*

Perhaps by chance news arrived that Il-ghazi, prince of the delusion and dissent of the Turcomans,[8] had reached the borderlands of the Antiochene lordship in battle array. When he heard this Prince Roger gathered his men from all around and set off for Artah,[9] humbly asking Lord Bernard, the first

---

[5] Psalms, 51.3: 'quid gloriaris in malitia qui potens es in iniquitate'.

[6] As in Book One, Walter shows a particular interest in the sin of pride. Walter the Chancellor, I.Prologue, p. 77, n. 8. See: Walter's purpose in writing *The Antiochene Wars*, pp. 11-12, p. 21.

[7] This key statement suggests that Walter was amongst those taken prisoner by Il-ghazi after the Field of Blood, and helps to explain his extensive discussion of the fate of these captives. Walter the Chancellor, II.6-7, pp. 132-6; II.13-16, pp. 156-68.

[8] In Book Two Walter immediately vilifies Il-ghazi, while in Book One he described him briefly and in neutral terms. For a discussion of how this may have some bearing upon possible dates of composition for the two sections see: Our knowledge of Walter, p. 8.

[9] A town, containing a citadel, c. 15 kilometres to the east of Antioch. Also known as Artesium. Artah was perhaps the most important fortified site in close proximity to the city, acting as its last line of defence against attack from the east. It was first occupied by the Latins, during the First Crusade, in the autumn of 1098. Albert of Aachen, III.28-9; Ralph of Caen, pp. 639-40; Kemal ed-Din, p. 578. Ralph of Caen, p. 712, described Artah as 'the shield of Antioch' when in 1105 it was temporarily re-occupied by Ridwan of Aleppo. Ridwan's forces were, however, defeated by Tancred in a battle outside the town on c. 20 April 1105. Ralph of Caen, pp. 714-15; Kemal ed-Din, p. 593; Ibn al-Qalanisi, pp. 69-70;

Latin patriarch, to follow him to that place.[10] If he had wished faithfully to agree to his holy doctrine and advice, he could have consulted there Baldwin, called by the Lord to be king of Jerusalem,[11] by waiting cautiously for him and his men. For at that time the lie of the land was abundant and healthy with regard to food and drink, and offered open and safe approaches to our side; to the enemy quite the opposite. For the approach offered essentially a threat of great destruction to their side, both the site and its access, mountains being intermixed with the dense vegetation of valleys and the crags of every single one crowding in.[12]

When he had inspected how things were for both sides with the liveliness of his powerful mind, the patriarch, a man of venerable life[13] and most distinguished in demeanour, having discharged in no small measure the celebration of the divine work of prophecy, delivered a sermon to that same prince and to all the people, concerning deeds which were done and those which were to be done: concerning those done, he prayed for all of them with fatherly compassion, that they might reform their behaviour by his attention;

Albert of Aachen, IX.47;   Fulcher of Chartres, II.30, pp. 485-8.

[10] In his second book Walter quickly re-iterates Roger's deference to Patriarch Bernard by noting that he humbly asked him to come to Artah. See: Bernard of Valence, patriarch of Antioch, pp. 40-41.

[11] Baldwin of Le Bourcq, king of Jerusalem (1118-1131). It is interesting that Walter makes no mention of the question marks surrounding Baldwin's accession to the throne of Jerusalem, but maintains an aura of legitimacy by noting that he was 'Deo vocante Ierosolymorum regem'. For a discussion of whether Walter was here drawing upon Fulcher of Chartres, see: Our knowledge of Walter, p. 9. The succession was in fact contested by Eustace count of Boulogne. A. Murray, 'Baldwin II and his nobles: Baronial faction and dissent in the kingdom of Jerusalem, 1118-1134', *Nottingham Medieval Studies*, vol.38 (1994), pp. 60-85.

[12] The fortified town of Artah enjoyed the physical protection afforded by the low, rocky range of hills known as the Jabal Talat, to its east. For a further discussion of the significance of this range and its impact upon the battle of the Field of Blood see, T.S. Asbridge, 'The significance and causes of the battle of the Field of Blood', pp. 309-11. There was already a strong tradition amongst the Latins of avoiding full set-piece battles with invading forces. Instead the common practice was to apply indirect pressure upon the enemy force by holding one's army at a nearby well supplied and fortified site, thus enabling the Latins to police a region through retaliatory raiding while deterring a full enemy attack. See: Walter as a military source, pp. 50-51.

[13] Bernard died in 1135. By the estimate of Bernard Hamilton, *The Latin Church in the Crusader States*, p. 22, he would have been in his fifties at this point.

as to those deeds which were to be done,[14] he proclaimed those things that were going to happen and exhorted his listeners not to boast of their virtues, but to reform their behaviour, keeping the law of the churches, having returned or engaged to return at a suitable time. Thereby they would have the righteousness of the clergy and all the Christian people on their side, and by behaving well in these ways and others, by resisting sins and guilty passions,[15] they might begin to become warriors of God, so that indeed, fortified by the weapons of faith in the conflict against the infidels, they could be called both Christians and soldiers of Christ.[16]

But the prince at that time - oh woe! - venturing where he should not venture and daring to do what should not be done, even neglecting his own safety and that of his men,[17] disregarded the warnings of the fatherly priest in favour of his own temerity, and he did not seem to be inspired by fear of the enemy or in any way to be able to be prevailed upon, and though the performance of his duties had been neglected in a way which was harmful, and threatened to be so in the future, both to himself and to others of his subjects, to whom they were due, he did not delay to make amends. Even when many people, motivated by piety, asked and advised him to remain, he openly dissented, saying that no one should wait there any longer;[18] and when he was advised by certain barons, whose possessions the enemy were accustomed to lay waste every single year - and they were devastating them even at that time[19]- he called his courtiers to him and those of his people who had been designated,

---

[14] Walter is expressing the sentiment, rather than the words, of Cicero, *De divinatione*, 1.3.

[15] For a discussion of the sins committed by Roger and the Antiochene army, see: Roger of Salerno, pp. 20-22.

[16] The references to 'warriors of God', 'weapons of faith' and 'soldiers of Christ' suggest that Walter wanted this campaign to be viewed as a just war.

[17] Walter seems keen to stress that Roger was also placing himself, and not just his men, in danger.

[18] Roger here gives his reason for desiring to advance to Balat. Other evidence confirms that he had already called upon the king of Jerusalem and the count of Tripoli for assistance. Fulcher of Chartres, III.4, pp. 624-6. See also: Walter the Chancellor, II.5, p. 129. Walter takes pains to demonstrate that Roger rejected shrewd advice that was given for pure reasons of 'piety'.

[19] Walter appears to distance Roger from direct blame by claiming that he was finally persuaded to advance by men who held land on the eastern frontier of the principality. These might have included Alan of al-Atharib, Robert fitz-Fulk the Leper of Zardana and possibly Bonable of Sarmin. See: Roger of Salerno, p. 19.

rejoicing in his unadvised mind, and he decided to cross over with the tents from the suitable place to a useless position.[20]

The patriarch, realizing by the light of truth what was desirable for the common good, since he had plainly perceived that that same prince and many others who were not amenable to reason were going against his righteous advice, showed them with very clear reasons that where there was fear, they should not be anxious, and where there was no fear, they should be anxious, and that which he had preached before in figurative language, he pointed out openly to the prince with his finger:[21] woe! woe! just as happened to the prince and the majority of his men not long afterwards.[22]

Therefore the prince, frightened in every possible way by the voice of the holy man, did not blush to confess his sins, whereby he had lived steeped in worldliness, to these people being present: that is to say, the aforesaid father, the archdeacon and deacon and court chaplains, quite privately aloud in his tent, and would that it had saved him! In the presence of the same people he ordered his possessions to be written down there to be divided and disbursed according to his will, if it should befall him to die in battle. And would that this had saved him![23] The aforesaid father, therefore, having compassion for his weakness and that of all the people, acting on behalf of St Peter,[24] and only for true penitence, enjoined the prince and all his people generally to

---

[20] As a result of this decision Roger moved the Antiochene camp from Artah to a valley named Balat, near the town of Sarmada. Kemal ad-Din recorded a slightly different version of events, in which the Antiochene army marched straight to 'Balat, between two mountains near the Sarmada pass, north of al-Atharib', arriving at the site of battle of the Field of Blood on 20 June. Kemal ed-Din, pp. 619.

[21] Walter may be making a conscious reference to Quintilian, *Institutio oratoria*, where the use of fingers in oratorical delivery is discussed, e.g. 1, 10, 35.

[22] This statement is linked to Walter's suggestion above that Bernard had the power of prophecy.

[23] Thus, even before leaving Artah, Roger carried out a private confession and wrote a will. Unfortunately, Walter does not record what provision was made for the succession at this point. It is possible that, in the absence of any of his own offspring, Roger left the principality to Bohemond II. This might explain Walter's later comment that Antioch belonged to him 'by right'. Walter the Chancellor, II.10, p. 144. See: Roger of Salerno, p. 25.

[24] From the Latin 'vice beati Petri functus'. The use of this phrase stresses Bernard's authority and demonstrates the importance in Antioch of the Petrine cult. It may also suggest that Bernard considered himself to be the vicar of St Peter in the see of Antioch just as the pope considered himself the vicar of St Peter in the see of Rome.

lament their evil deeds, I say, and not to commit lamentable deeds, and in a friendly way he enjoined on his lord future good behaviour for the good of his life. And thus, after they had been signed with his patriarchal benediction, he said farewell to everyone, pouring forth tears and constant sobs from the depths of his heart, and he returned to the church to pray for God's people.

II.2   *A preliminary skirmish in which Robert of Vieux-Pont distinguishes himself.*

However, by some ill omen[25] we were snatched into danger, not waiting for the proud to be brought low according to their deserts and the humble to be exalted.[26] We, as if braver than lions[27] and more inexorable than tigers, forced our way to pitch camp at the Field of Blood[28] - the Field of Blood, I say, it is called by the populace, both in reality and in the name - and there we stayed for some time, under pressure day after day through lack of food and natural drink, which was not forced on us by the enemy's strength, but by the shortage of both in those parts, and we would send to wherever else we could, inside and outside the camp, so we could remove the want.[29]

Then also some of our men were sent to fortify the camp outside,[30] which did not escape the notice of enemy troops for long. For indeed spies had been

---

[25] Ovid, *Epist. Heroid.*, 13.49: 'a nobis omen remouete sinistrum'.

[26] Luke I.52: 'et exaltavit humiles'.

[27] 2 Samuel, 1.23: 'Aquilis velociores, leonibus fortiores'.

[28] From the Latin 'Ager Sanguinis'. For a discussion of the exact location of this site see: P. Deschamps, 'La défense du comté de Tripoli et de la principauté d'Antioche', *Les Châteaux des Croisés en Terre Sainte*, vol. III (Paris, 1973), p. 60, pp. 100-1. The decision to name this site 'The Field of Blood' may be linked to the fact that the Vulgate Bible used the name 'Ager Sanguinis' of the biblical site 'the potter's field', also known as Hakeldama, which was a burial ground purchased with the blood-money returned by Judas.   Acts 1.19; Matthew, 27.3. The Latins certainly had knowledge of this site during their occupation of Jerusalem as they built a charnel-house there, the ruins of which are still evident. D. Bahat, *The Illustrated Atlas of Jerusalem* (New York, 1990), p. 91. Our thanks to Professor Benjamin Arnold for his assistance with this matter.

[29] Walter re-emphasises the fact that the camp near Sarmada was poorly provisioned. The region is, today, characterized by relatively fertile valleys surrounded by arid and rocky foothills.

[30] For a discussion of Walter's descriptions of the techniques adopted by armies camped in the field, see: Walter as a military source, pp. 51-2.

sent out by the enemy in the guise of bird-sellers[31] to find out however they could what our position was. And when they returned and told their tale, both Il-ghazi and his nobles[32] clearly understood as if they had seen with their own eyes. Therefore those men of crafty cunning, to conceal what they were working at - that is to say, to attack us unexpectedly - openly organized their battle-lines and now sent ahead the more expert in preparation, as if they came to lay siege to excellent al-Atharib, expressly for the purpose of observing and being observed.[33] They would observe, I say, the outside parts of the paths and the approaches of the inside footpaths, by which they could attack the prince with greater safety for themselves and greater damage to our men; they would be observed, moreover, so that they might be considered powerful by the mass of the army and we might seem to fall short of our usual worth, driven back by fear of their great number. In short: what happened to us was not the result of that multitude's strength, but the just judgment of God for our sins and wickedness,[34] as in a little while I shall try to explain in detail, not on my own, but with God's will and assistance prompting me. First things first, however, lest in an abundance of words I should seem to have forgotten the order of events.[35]

The Turkish chieftains from all around[36] who were at al-Atharib for the deception suddenly saw the knights of al-Atharib and a band of infantry of that castle[37] and certain of our men, who had come there by night, arriving close

---

[31] Walter does not comment upon this seemingly unusual choice of disguise. This might suggest that the Latins were used to purchasing supplies from the local Muslim population.

[32] It is assumed that this is a reference to Il-ghazi.

[33] Walter may, here, be misinterpreting Il-ghazi's intentions. I have argued elsewhere that the Aleppan forces may have been making a serious attempt to capture al-Atharib, and not just an attack designed to inspire fear or divert attention from scouting activities. See T.S. Asbridge, 'The significance and causes of the battle of the Field of Blood', p. 313. It is worth noting, however, that Kemal ed-Din, p. 617, although writing much later, did state that at this point the Latins 'imagined that the Muslims were besieging al-Atharib and Zardana'.

[34] Although Walter stresses that God allowed the Latins to be defeated because of their sins, he does still emphasise that the Muslim force was numerically powerful.

[35] For a discussion of his attitude to divine inspiration and narrative continuity, see: Our knowledge of Walter, pp. 6-7.

[36] Kemal ed-Din, pp. 616-20, suggests that Tughtegin had not joined Il-ghazi at this point, but does mention the presence of the qadi Abu l-Fadl ibn al-Khashshab and Tughan Arslan ibn Dimlaj.

[37] Al-Atharib must have maintained its own garrison even when the Antiochene forces were gathered for this campaign. They were joined by troops from this main army on 27 June.

by in the manner of defenders as if to challenge them to battle. When they saw this, the enemy, although they seemed to be surrounded by sixty thousand soldiers or more, yet tightened their reins and took their bows from the hanging straps and their shields from their shoulders onto their arms, having drawn back their arms to their chests, holding themselves as if they were faltering in courage and as if they were afraid to offend, muttering about turning tail. But reality was disguised by deceit and deliberate artifice, so that our men could be drawn further away from the camp by these indications. This deed is often deemed dishonest by many wary observers of warriors, although many times it is confirmed to come about as a result of creative genius.[38]

Our men, relying on their courageous boldness and disregarding both the enemy's boldness and their ingenuity, drew their shields close to their sides, brandished their lances, sank in their spurs - all these at once as befits knights - and charged into the middle of the enemy.[39] Dealing violent blows in knightly fashion they cast some down to the ground, some again, with blood pouring forth, they drove down to hell with fatal wounds.[40] During these skirmishes Robert of Vieux-Pont,[41] fighting energetically and showing his

---

[38] Walter comes close to actually praising the Muslims' use of a feigned retreat on this occasion. See: Walter as a military source, p. 58.

[39] On this occasion Walter stresses the importance of Latin fortitude rather than piety. For a discussion of his attitudes to chivalry, see: Walter as a military source, pp. 52-3.

[40] Vergil, *Aeneid*, 12.750: 'letali vulnere'. In spite of the comparisons made between the military activity and attitudes of the Latins and Muslims, Walter stresses that ultimately the latter group were doomed to damnation.

[41] Robert was a member of a well known family from Vieux-Pont-sur-Dives, Calvados in Normandy, his ancestor Robert having been in the service of William the Conqueror. Having fought in Bohemond of Taranto's force during the siege of Durazzo in 1108, Robert must have travelled from the West to Antioch by 1111, when he was apparently amongst those called by Tancred to assist in campaign against Maudud. 'Anonymi Florinensis Brevis Narratio Belli Sacri', *Recueil des historiens des croisades. Historiens occidentaux*, vol. 5 (Paris, 1886), p. 361; 'Ex Historiae Francicae Fragmento', *Recueil des Historiens de Gaule et de la France*, vol. 12, ed. L. Delisle (Paris, 1877), p. 6; Albert of Aachen, XI.40, described him as 'an indefatigable soldier who often raided the gentiles' lands with his military following'. In 1114 his grant of a village named 'Burio' to Our Lady of Josaphat was confirmed in the charter issued by Roger of Salerno. *Cartulaire général de l'ordre des Hospitaliers de S. Jean de Jérusalem (1100-1310)*, vol.1, p. 38, no. 45. See charter (a), p. 205. This site has been identified as the village of Bouraya in the mountains near Jabala. P. Deschamps, 'La défense du comté de Tripoli et de la principauté d'Antioche', p. 55, no. 3. This would suggest that Robert's lordship was not in the region of al-Atharib and that he was

usual devotion to duty by the attack of his vigorous spirit and the speed of his bold horse, charged many of them as they rode in troops and struck them, and at once, after he had broken his lance on one of them he drew his sword and struck others of them again, and only when he himself had been struck in return by many, and his horse pierced by many different weapons, did he fall, brought down by irresistible force. But he did not forget the son of his mother and, although he was brought down to the ground by the constant blows of lances and arrows, yet he rose up and mustered his forces of courage with agility, and, brandishing his sword, he fought back, and when he saw his own men hurrying to assist him he stood fast, shouting eagerly: 'Here, comrades, here! Have faith in your knightly strength!' At once they came to him and brought him a second horse, which he mounted and, brandishing his sword, he said to his comrades that pain inflicted could be lessened by revenge.[42]

Soon after he joined them they charged the enemy together a second time. But the enemy had launched a similar attack on Robert first, and he hit the ground protected by his shield, and by God's help escaped death.[43] What of his comrades? Each in his place, they eagerly inflicted blows worthy of their knighthood on the dense ranks of the enemy; also from another part Alan, lord of that same castle,[44] accompanied by his household, was perceived to have performed manfully: for he delighted in resisting the enemy like a wall and is described as a lion in pursuit. What of the rest? The last came first in striving both to be seen and to exceed the first in knightly deeds. But, as I may truly declare, it was not the hangers-on, but the true-born knights[45] who by dealing blows and overthrowing the enemy were all of them kept busy with the enemy one by one, to do good and to become knights of Christ by this affair.[46] But many who had been called up gained strength in that battle, not

---

probably, therefore, amongst the troops who had come from the main Antiochene army. Orderic Vitalis, XI.25, pp. 106-8, noted that Robert fled the Field of Blood, bringing news of the defeat to Antioch.

[42] Ovid, *Amor.* I, *eleg.* 7.65: 'minuit vindicta dolorem'.

[43] Here Walter combines the concepts of chivalric fortitude and divine assistance.

[44] Alan can almost certainly be identified with the 'youth' Alan mentioned in 1115. Walter the Chancellor, I.7, p. 104. Alan is the only Antiochene landholder who is specifically stated to have had his own household in the first decades of the principality's history. See also, Walter the Chancellor, II.10, pp. 145. For references to Geoffrey the Monk's retinue see, Walter the Chancellor, II.5, p. 126. See: Walter and the early history of the principality of Antioch, p. 47.

[45] From the Latin 'naturales milites'. See: Walter as a military source, pp. 52-3.

[46] Once again, Walter makes use of the terminology of justified violence.

by fighting strongly, but by resisting with God's will; by that same will our men did not suffer the barbarity of the enemy, but as the sun inclined towards setting, people both in the castle and elsewhere welcomed a well earned rest after so much passion: for there the lesser harm was more than the greater harm, indeed the poor are believed to have been hurt by the least more than the rich by the greatest.[47]

II.3   *Reconnaissance and other preparations for battle. A lunatic woman prophesies.*

Therefore some of these were looked after in the castle, some returned to the army late and reported to the courtiers that the deeds of the past day had brought honour to their knighthood; as a consequence, as is the fixed habit of knights, everyone lamented who had not been there. After he heard them the prince ordered the nobles[48] to be summoned to him very quickly, in order to decide with them about the immediate business of bringing back those who were in the fight, and what should be done that same night or in the morning; those who were called came; the aforesaid matter was discussed. When the men had made their reports, as befits a knight of vigorous spirit,[49] their over-lord said: 'Let's march to al-Atharib tomorrow, and approach nearby, for if they should come, the knights' courage and love of God, which have moved us to come to revenge the blood of His servants,[50] will not fear the host of the heathen, but by battling courageously may strive to destroy the fierceness of tyrants; and if they don't come, we may take counsel on the following day and turn our march against their tents.'[51]

---

[47] This rather confused passage seems to imply that the infantry had suffered more damage than the cavalry during this skirmish.

[48] This group was presumably made up of the principality's most powerful landholders.

[49] In this context Walter does not criticize Roger's willingness to seek battle, as he presents him as an idealized 'knight' rather than as a 'prince'. See: Roger of Salerno, p. 20.

[50] Walter may here be supporting his presentation of the campaign as a 'just war' by making reference to 'revenge', an important theme in the concept of 'just cause'.

[51] Walter suggests that on the night of 27 June Roger decided to march to al-Atharib on the 28th, with the expectation of meeting the Aleppan army in battle, and that if this was not forthcoming the army would make a pre-emptive attack upon the Muslims on the 29th. This indicates that, although the Latins were surprised by the Muslim attack on 28 June, they were actively seeking battle in this period.

Some of the nobles persisted in resisting his words; some, however, considered that their tents should be moved from that position to one by the rock.[52] Some, indeed, declared the lord's advice to be sound and advised in its favour. After they had spoken thus, turning round and round what was right, what was wrong, what was honourable, what was dishonourable, what could usefully or uselessly be done quickly, or not, they agreed what was best for the present business, and they chose that same night to send both cavalry and infantry to the aforesaid castle, and decided that first thing in the morning Mauger of Hauteville[53] was to sortie with forty knights beyond the district and to direct ten knights as scouts to the tower situated on the top of the hill so that, if the enemy should approach al-Atharib once more, it might be announced to the prince by way of a swift horse and a shrewd knight. And on the advice of Peter the archbishop of Apamea[54] it was decreed that an edict should be made to all the army that they should all come together to the chapel[55] before first light, so that having amended their lives and behaviour

---

[52] This is presumably a reference to the foothills of the Jabal Talat.

[53] Mauger presumably came from the prominent southern Italian Norman de Hauteville line. The most famous member of this family in the context early Latin East was Tancred, nephew of Bohemond of Taranto, and ruler of Antioch between c.1105 and his death in 1112. The only other member of the line linked to the principality in this period was William de Hauteville, son of William de Hauteville, the count of San Nicandro in Puglia, and Maria of Conza-Salerno who, who witnessed a charter issued by Guy Carpenal, the lord of Tarsus and Mamistra, at some point before 1114. J.A. Stargardt, *Europäische Stammtafeln*, vol. 2 (Marburg, 1984), no. 205; 'Chartes de l'abbaye de Notre-Dame de Josaphat', pp. 115-16, no. 4.

[54] Listed simply as 'P.' in the Latin text, Peter of Narbonne, archbishop of Apamea, first came to prominence when he was chosen by Raymond IV count of Toulouse to be the first Latin bishop of Albara in 1098, during the First Crusade. Raymond of Aguilers, pp. 91-2. He was initially consecrated by the Greek Orthodox patriarch of Antioch, John IV. *Gesta Francorum*, p. 75. Then, soon after the elevation of Bernard of Valence as Latin patriarch of Antioch in 1100, Peter transferred his allegiance to the Latin church. William of Tyre, VII.8, p. 353. Peter rose to become one of the most prominent ecclesiastical figures in northern Syria after he was consecrated as the archbishop of the newly conquered Apamea at some point between 1106 and 1110. He continued to hold both sees simultaneously. *Cartulaire de Sainte-Sepulchre*, pp. 197-9, no. 86. Peter may also have exercised secular control Albara in this period. Albert of Aachen, IX.47; Kemal ed-Din, p. 637. Peter almost certainly enjoyed a close relationship with the patriarch of Antioch, having 'received the pallium directly from Bernard' when he became archbishop of Apamea. William of Tyre, VII.8, p. 353. It is more likely that he was appointed as the patriarch's representative during the 1119 campaign. See: Walter and the early history of the principality of Antioch, p. 48.

[55] Given Walter's later reference to this chapel being amongst the Latins' tents it can be assumed that it was some form of portable shrine.

there, and being restored by heavenly food and drink, they could live or die in the service of God and in His name, as befits knights;[56] and the edict was made directly.

While these things were being done there was a moon-struck woman outside, who uttered these sayings: 'Come on! Come on! You haven't got long! For tomorrow the enemy hand will prevail, heads will be cut off, and you will give me credit for my prophecies, which up to now you have discounted.' After the events of the following day we considered these words were consistent with the spirit of prophecy. When they heard them, some laughed from sheer terror, and some reckoned among themselves it was better to bewail in earnest the sins they had owned up to. What happened in detail? The barons[57] were given permission to refresh themselves with a night's rest, then the prince called the household[58] and ordered that what had been decided should be brought to its intended conclusion speedily, and he showed them what and where and how it should be done; he secretly called his chancellor and settled with him what should properly be done for the business in hand about those things which seemed burdensome to the warriors.[59]

Therefore from this side and that the emergency was broadcast, his chamberlain was called, and so were his household knights,[60] and it was decreed that the precious vessels and all burdensome goods[61] should be taken away by night to the tower of Artah[62] and entrusted to the bishop. Following

---

[56] Walter implies that after having received the Holy Communion the Latin army would be able to fight as soldiers of God.

[57] It is not clear if Walter intended to draw a distinction with the group earlier styled as 'nobles'. Walter the Chancellor, II.3, p. 119.

[58] This indicates that the prince's 'household' were responsible for implementing the decision of the council.

[59] It is not clear why, on this occasion, Walter refers to himself in the third-person. He may have stated that he was called secretly in order to stress the intimacy and importance of his relationship with Roger. On this occasion Roger and the chancellor seem to have discussed non-military matters. See: Walter and the early history of the principality of Antioch, pp. 45-6.

[60] This military group may have been distinct from Roger's domestic household. See: Walter and the early history of the principality of Antioch, pp. 43-4.

[61] This is presumably a reference to Roger's moveable wealth and his baggage train.

[62] This is probably a reference to the town's citadel. Bernard of Valence was consecrated as the first Latin bishop of Artah in December 1099. Ralph of Caen, p. 704. After Bernard's elevation to the patriarchate in 1100 the episcopal see was presumably filled, but its incumbent

this the Turcopoles were called, and the household was called; the lord ordered these men to do it at once; they were ready to obey his order immediately. The army, who had not forgotten the earlier edict, assembled before daybreak at the church, where matins was held and they watchfully worshipped God the highest with hearts and voices,[63] and when the service was over the archbishop, the finest man in either retinue,[64] preaching both of heavenly and of earthly things, taught the Christians that they should cleave to earthly things in such a way that in heavenly things they would earn the right to be crowned as God's knights by His kindness freely given.[65] When morning came, moreover, and divine office had been celebrated, all with one voice freely acknowledged in public confession and public lamentation that they had sinned against God's law, and one by one, renouncing all their faults, with which they had been afflicted, and confessing to God and the archbishop, they promised most faithfully that they would nevermore fall into those errors or similar ones, by the help and protection of God's grace.

After he heard this, the aforesaid archbishop, observing the mood of good will, in the name of and in response to true penitence, enjoined on everyone, if they should happen to engage in battle against the infidels, not to presume that success came of their own efforts, and to entrust entirely to God whether they should die or live. Therefore, encouraged by these words and blessed by the archbishop, refreshed by the Lord's body and blood, fortified by these weapons of faith,[66] and as yet ignorant of the coming battle, each returned to his own tent. The prince, sustained by the Holy Spirit, poured forth tears before the altar for all the sins he had committed against God by way of sight, hearing, taste, smell or touch, and he gave himself up to the Divine Majesty as guilty, and he confessed to the archbishop out loud all his sins individually, of whatever kind or number, and he received a like penance, after which he was invigorated by the Lord's viaticum and left. In front of the entrance to his tent he charitably paid out with his own hand to Christ's poor, who were seeking alms from him, pounds of gold as a princely gift, and he mounted his

---

in 1119 is unknown.

[63] Rom. 10.8. See above, Walter the Chancellor, I.5, p. 100, n. 141.

[64] It is not clear whether this refers to the retinues of Roger and Alan of al-Atharib.

[65] Walter seems to suggest that fighting would bring martyrdom.

[66] Walter frequently combines the concepts of spiritual and material warfare.

horse, ready to ride early as usual.[67] His birds were brought to him, his small hounds were brought, others were brought, hunting spears were taken, boys were sent ahead with the hunters; as befits a prince, he followed. Here he travelled through fields and valleys, there he went round mountains and hills; here he captured birds with his birds, there he destroyed wild beasts with his hounds.[68]

II.4 *Forty knights are sent out to ascertain the enemy's dispositions. Roger's speech of encouragement and the order of battle.*

Suddenly, however, his future appeared before him and he felt the urge to change course to the tower in order for a look-out, putting aside his recreation. As he was leaving it a messenger came up to him who had ridden at great speed, to whom the lord said: 'What is the matter?' The messenger said this to him: 'I observed the enemy hordes with these very eyes, all over the mountain slopes and inaccessible valleys, in places, I tell you, which are not even accessible to the tracks of wild beasts. I tell you truly they are approaching us quickly from three directions to wage a threefold war, and I firmly declare that innumerable columns, distinguished both by standards and by other displays of cyphers, are following the first ones.'[69] The prince replied to this: 'It is granted to us for Christ's sake not only that we may believe in Him, but even that we may suffer for Him,[70] and that we may now render to Him the debt which we owe, that is to say, that all our rational will may remain subject to His will, and we who have violated His honour in us, according to the breaking of the exhortation made towards this Our Saviour, that with His own support we shall reinstate ourselves and not sin in

---

[67] Walter re-emphasises the purified image of Roger just prior to the battle via this reference to the donation of alms.

[68] This hunting scene may have been intended to highlight Roger's 'chivalric' nature. See: Roger of Salerno, p. 20.

[69] It appears that one of the main reasons why the Latin army was surprised at the Field of Blood was because they underestimated the number of passable routes into the valley in which they were camped. With their greater knowledge of local geography the Aleppan forces were able to approach via paths which the Latins had thought not even animals could negotiate. Kemal ed-Din also noted that the Latin army was encircled stating that 'as dawn broke they saw the Muslim standards advancing to surround them completely'. Kemal ed-Din, p. 617.

[70] Phil. 1.29: 'pro illo patiamur'.

future, and as we have sinned through sweetness, let us make amends to Him through bitterness and not refuse to give ourselves up to death to honour Him.'[71]

After this, the prince summoned his marshal and the public criers, and at once commanded the entire army to prepare for battle and ordered it to be announced in a loud voice that at the first sound of the bugle everyone should make haste to put on arms and armour, and on the second, being ready with battle-lines drawn up, both knights and also foot-soldiers should all assemble and, hearing the third, individual battle-lines should advance, marching behind their standard-bearers, and present themselves at the sign of the Cross of Our Lord.[72] Without delay the criers carried out the prince's command in a loud voice and Roger, riding a swift horse before the tents, ordered weapons of war to be brought before him. When this had been done, while the earlier messenger was still there another arrived who interpreted the same signs of war in a different way, for he said: 'There they are on this side of the Sarmadan district, very close.' Therefore the prince ordered everyone to be warned by the sound of the bugle. There was no delay: at the first signal they were alerted, at the second they were made ready, at the third they assembled; they assembled and presented themselves to the prince in front of the chapel, where the Cross was. Therefore the bishop,[73] bearing the Cross of Our Lord in reverent hands, said: 'What more? Strengthened by the arms of faith, with this sign of the health-giving Cross going before, and not afraid to change completely the purpose of the heathens, let us advance into their midst.'

This said, the prince, by publicly renouncing pleasures of the body in the past, present and future in his confession to God and the bishop, surrendered himself as slave about to die for God's law, as befits a Christian, and had his helmet strapped on. The archbishop received him on behalf of blessed Peter, he absolved him of all his sins in the name of the Lord and in the name of true repentance, and he instructed him to go to this war and to do or receive what pleased the Divine Majesty, to die or to live. And so, happy and

---

[71] Walter suggests that Roger actually acknowledged his sinful state prior to the Field of Blood. See: Roger of Salerno, pp. 21-2.

[72] Walter provides a detailed description of the steps by which an army would be prepared for battle. See: Walter and the early history of the principality of Antioch, pp. 44-5.

[73] This must be a reference to Peter archbishop of Apamea.

uplifted, he asked for the symbol of the Cross of Our Lord to be carried before him in the hands of a priest,[74] so that he might humble himself before it, and it would be on the spot for his prayer. Meanwhile, Alberic, the deputy-steward,[75] not like a person fleeing but like an attacking soldier, who had been struck by a lance in his face and pierced by an arrow almost in his eye, appeared as the third messenger, to forewarn our men. He was questioned first about the forty knights sent out with whom he had gone, and he replied that some had had their heads cut off, that is to say, Jordan of Jordan[76] and Eudes of Forestmoutiers,[77] and many others had already fought their way from the mockery of this world to God, and Mauger was here, compelled by the enemy's intolerable strength. And so it suddenly was: Mauger was there, and another with him.

These men's horses, stuck with arrows, overpowered by leaden missiles, fell down dead; at once they seized others before the barons' eyes, and they said to the prince: 'A consultation is needed about these men who are threatening us, an urgent consultation. They come prepared: act quickly! Indeed, divided into three parts they are trying to destroy us with three-fold war.' At this, some of the nobles and of the rest who agreed with this sound advice, as it seemed, together praised all our men, placed as they were around the tents in ordered battle-lines, the infantry everywhere in the front line, and in doing thus they claimed they could wait for the enemy's barbarism more easily and more safely. On all these things, of course, it was for men to speak and discuss according to the events' outward appearance, but it was for God, to whom the entire heart is open[78] and all desires spoken, to judge. What next? Suddenly the flags and standards of the heathens appeared from the mountainsides among the olives. When he saw them the prince carried on in this way: 'Aha! Soldiers of Christ, let us not be put off by the many-sided contest of fighting men, but let us now play our parts, and we should thrive

---

[74] Given that Peter of Apamea was not killed at the Field of Blood, it would appear that the relic of the True Cross was carried into battle by an unnamed cleric rather than the Archbishop. See Walter the Chancellor, II.5, p. 128.

[75] See: Walter and the early history of the principality of Antioch, p. 45.

[76] *Galterii Cancellarii, Bella Antiochena*, ed. H. Hagenmeyer, pp. 229-30, n. 43, suggests that he was an ancestor Geoffrey Jordan, constable of Antioch in 1156.

[77] This individual, otherwise unknown, may well have come from Forest-Moutiers in the Somme region of Picardy.

[78] A liturgical reference to the collect from the Votive Mass for the Holy Spirit.

thereby; whether we end up alive or dead, let us fight today in a successful battle as soldiers for God, seeing that we have served the world as soldiers up to now.' When he had said this he commanded Rainald Mazoir[79] to be reinforced very quickly with a three-fold company so that they might go through the districts of Sarmada and Rainald might attack very visibly, and he claimed that with God's help he would very boldly strike at the strength of the impious princes, wherever he went or wherever he stood firm, on mountain or plain.[80]

II.5 *The battle of the Field of Blood, in which Roger of Antioch, fighting against overwhelming odds, at first inflicts much damage on the enemy, but finally is killed, having lost his entire army.*

What details of these things? Just as often before he had drawn up his battle-lines one by one, so then he also commanded them to march in ranks, but much better,[81] for he said: 'In the name of Our Lord Jesus Christ, as befits knights, set off eagerly for the sake of defending God's law and, when the place of battle is at hand, do not forget the blood shed by God's servants, and remember to bring down the pride of the evil-doers and to shed their blood by inflicting constant blows!'[82] After saying this he venerated the symbol of the Holy Cross and kissed it most reverently, then one by one the ranks raised their standards and set off in their assigned order, with bugles, flutes and trumpets blaring, and started their march eagerly in the name of God. Meanwhile, hither and thither messengers were sent from column to column, flying like javelins or even like arrows, as the custom of warriors

---

[79] Rainald founded a powerful Antiochene dynasty. His own career is, however, poorly chronicled. During his life he amassed a powerful lordship including Marqab and possibly Baniyas. C. Cahen, *La Syrie du Nord*, p. 543. By 1127 he had been appointed constable of Antioch, and went on to act as regent in the principality in 1132. William of Tyre, XIV.5, p. 637; 'Liber Jurium republicae Genuensis, I', *Monumenta Historiae Patriae*, vol. 7 (Augustae Taurinorum, 1853), pp. 30-31, no. 20.

[80] The intention seems to have been that Rainald would lead either a flanking or diversionary attack.

[81] Walter stresses that Roger has military experience, but highlights the added benefits of religious purpose and conviction in this instance.

[82] By using terms such as 'as befits knights', 'God's law' and 'God's servants' Walter is combining the elements of chivalry and just war. See: Walter as a military source, pp. 52-3.

requires.[83]

And so the battle-line of St Peter[84] took the lead from the right, whose prerogative it is both to advance first and to be first to strike the enemy,[85] giving their horses their heads, brandishing their lances as they made haste to strike the cohort in their path violently and quickly, and they scattered it almost totally, striking down many of the heathen. When he saw this, Geoffrey the Monk,[86] accompanied by a distinguished battle-line, trusting to his manly courage, sought out and attacked a cohort of the heathen, at least ten thousand soldiers massed together,[87] in such a way that he almost put to flight and defeated both the cohort and others positioned nearby. Equally, the battle-line of Guy Fresnel,[88] for its part, attacked and assaulted the enemy with all its might.

But because our men failed to carry through with force, as was necessary, many from both the one line and the other suffered destruction. For the heathen, with the Lord's assent,[89] re-mustered their forces and were not afraid to attack our men, but, falling upon them again with spears, lances and arrows tipped with lead and iron, and with constant blows of the sword, they assaulted them violently, as the bloodshed on both sides bore witness.

---

[83] This is a fairly uncommon acknowledgement of the importance of messengers. See: Walter as a military source, pp. 54-5.

[84] See Walter the Chancellor, I.7, p. 105, n. 179.

[85] This suggests that the battle-line of St Peter had gained in importance since 1115.

[86] For a discussion of Geoffrey's career see, G.T. Beech, 'The crusader lordship of Marash in Armenian Cilicia, 1104-1149', pp. 43-5. Beech claims that Geoffrey is first mentioned in William of Tyre, XII.9, p. 557. William was, however, almost certainly drawing from the evidence presented here by Walter. It is not clear whether Geoffrey was already associated with the lordship of Marash in 1119, and thus we cannot definitely state that the troops in his battle-line came from that town. Nevertheless, given that Arnulf the seneschal of Marash is mentioned by Walter, we can assume that troops from Marash were involved in the battle of the Field of Blood. Walter the Chancellor, II.15, p. 165.

[87] This would appear to be a numerical exaggeration. See: Walter as a military source, p. 56.

[88] See also, Walter the Chancellor, I.7, pp. 104-5. William of Tyre asserted that Guy was in joint command of a battle-line with Geoffrey the Monk. He may, however, simply have distorted Walter's account. William of Tyre, XII.9, p. 557.

[89] The idea that God allowed the Muslims to defeat Roger at the Field of Blood is a perfect illustration of Walter's belief that the events of 1119 can ultimately be explained through divine will rather than practical military considerations.

Meanwhile, Robert of St Lô's cohort,[90] advancing with the Turcopoles from the left, when they should have struck were unable to withstand the opposition of fate, as the Turcopoles were first to flee, and, driven by their own side's charge and the shouts of the heathen, they got in the way of the prince's battle-line as it rode against the strength of the impious, and they could not be called back from their headlong flight - not by reins, not by bridles, not by ropes, not even by any desire for safety; for, what was even worse, they carried along with them part of the prince's cohort as they scattered.[91]

Then as well, as one misfortune often follows a worse, a whirlwind sprang up from the north, and it held all who saw it fast to the ground in the middle of the battle-field and, creeping along the ground, it snatched up dust, which got into the eyes of the warriors so they could not fight and, twisting itself upwards like an enormous jar on the potter's wheel, burnt up by sulphurous fires, it reached as if to the stars;[92] when they saw this an immense and dreadful clamour arose from the sinners on all sides.

The prince was nevertheless keeping up the struggle with steadfast mind, though his men lay cut down and dead on all sides, and he never retreated nor looked back, but, accompanied also by a few of his men,[93] he was obeying the command of God and the bishop by fighting energetically against the entire military might.[94] He was struck by a knight's sword through the middle of his nose right into his brain, and settling his debt to death in the name of the Lord, in the presence of the symbol of the Holy Cross he gave up his body to the earth and his soul to heaven.[95]

---

[90] Robert appeared in three charters issued in the principality before 1119. *Carte dell'Archivio Capitolare di Pisa (1101-1120)*, vol. 4, pp. 80-83, no. 37-8; *Chartes de Terre Sainte provenant de l'abbaye de N. D. de Josaphat*, pp. 26-7, no. 4; *Cartulaire général de l'ordre des Hospitaliers de S. Jean de Jérusalem (1100-1310)*, vol.1, p. 38, no. 45. See also: William of Tyre, XII.9, p. 557.

[91] Walter indicates that, at this key moment, it was the indiscipline of Turcopole troops which broke the formation of Roger's forces, and contributed to the loss of the battle.

[92] If factual this whirlwind, and the dust storm it caused, would presumably have affected both Latins and Muslims equally.

[93] From the Latin 'paucis etiam comitatus'.

[94] At the moment of Roger's death, Walter stresses his personal bravery and the fact that, by fighting, he was obeying the will of God and the clergy, and was thus waging a 'just war'.

[95] Walter obviously wants his audience to be in no doubt that Roger achieved salvation after death.

After this attack, the priest was killed who was carrying that same Cross in his hands, and indeed many of the heathen were possessed by greed for the gold and precious stones,[96] and knowing nothing of the strength of God's power hidden in the Cross, they came to swift blows amongst themselves, and thus they were made the fodder of death, and they passed away to the lower regions, never to return, for burning by the fires of hell.[97]

And at once, all together, as the hundred thousand fighting men had been detailed, they attacked our men very fiercely from the four corners of the world. Therefore, compelled now by divine revenge with the agreement of the highest judge, as the shouts of the heathens swelled again and again and the enemy's swords prevailed, some of our men, of whom there were reputed to be seven hundred knights and three thousand foot-soldiers,[98] with many others who had gone to battle for the sake of pay or on account of greed for enemy wealth, were wounded, some were killed, and some who were mutilated with different injuries were brought out for destruction on that same battle-field and not far off, while some were put in the bonds of most wretched captivity by judgment of the just God.

While these things were happening in our ranks, Rainald Mazoir also, waging war courageously on his side, destroyed and conquered a considerable number of the enemy as they came in through the district of Sarmada, in such a way that in the opinion of both sides in the battle our men were thought to be the winners and the enemy defeated.[99] However, it pleased the Divine Majesty, whom nothing pleases unless it is right and fitting, that the defeated re-mustered their forces and became the victors and the earlier glory of our men was not held from the enemy's hand, but the ultimate power of God was at work. Indeed, destroyed and defeated, some were ceasing to be mortals in that place, and some were escaping in the same headlong flight, from which still others were slain. Moreover, it happened that Rainald Mazoir, who was

---

[96] This probably indicates that the relic of the True Cross was held in a reliquary. See: Walter's attitude to religion and piety, pp. 70-71.

[97] Walter not only interprets this as a miracle of the True Cross, but also juxtaposes the fate of the Muslims damned to hell with that of Roger who ascended to heaven.

[98] This would appear to be a more realistic estimate than those associated with Muslim forces. See: 'Walter as a military source', p. 56.

[99] The fact that some sections of the Antiochene forces believed they had won the battle indicates how chaotic the fighting was at the Field of Blood.

seriously wounded, entered the tower of Sarmada[100] with a few of his men, in order to take possession of it as a refuge for himself and the others escaping and, if he could, to wait there for Baldwin, king of Jerusalem, who was hurrying to the aid of Christianity.[101]

II.6 *Those who died or were captured in battle, and those who deserted without putting up a fight.*

But the weakness of the tower and the lack of food and, most of all, Il-ghazi's arrival there were good reasons why he could not remain there and should give himself up as prisoner to the victorious enemy. Nevertheless, he used his cunning to fortify his position, and as if he could defend himself in the tower he spoke guardedly; for he said to the victorious enemy: 'I shall never surrender to you, unless you first promise me on your honour and oath according to your law the defence of your protection and your assistance in escaping.'[102] Therefore Il-ghazi replied to the cunning man as one even more astute: 'What? While you were in the battle, you and others had to be treated as enemies, but now I feel as a man does and I recall that you are men, and lest you suspect me, you shall take my ring as a sign of my good faith and oath according to our blessed law, so that by this token at the end of one month you shall receive your freedom from me.'[103] Therefore Rainald, who had thought he could live no longer than a single day, heard the end of the month and, feeling sad inside, yet he accepted the ring as if he were happy on the outside and he surrendered himself captive.[104]

---

[100] This is probably a reference to a partially hidden sixth century Byzantine fortified tower over-looking the town of Sarmada, which one of the authors, Thomas Asbridge, was lucky enough to discover while visiting the region in 1993.

[101] Walter's admission that the king was already travelling north demonstrates that Roger sent a call for aid to Baldwin prior to the battle of the Field of Blood.

[102] Walter suggests that Rainald might actually expect Il-ghazi to treat prisoners with honour and according to Muslim 'law'. See: The depiction of Islam and eastern Christendom, p. 64.

[103] It is not known whether Il-ghazi kept his word and released Rainald in late July, but he certainly survived these events. See p. 64, n. 138.

[104] Although Rainald willingly surrendered to Il-ghazi Walter does not criticize him, nor accuse him of cowardice. Condemnation is reserved for those who fled the Field of Blood before the battle was decided.

However, some of the nobles, who had seemed estimable for their vigour and abilities and their noble blood, who also did not sustain the first assault, abandoned their prince alive on the battle-field, deserted their kin and friends, and set out at some speed, before the field of battle and the approach to the mountains could be closed to them by the enemy's ferocity, to return to Antioch, though they would have preferred the port. Yet before them others entered: as usual, last into battle, first through the gates.

However, lest I should seem to be indulging in too great a digression in speaking of those who deserted, I should first describe deeds on the battle-field, so that by recounting step by step the part played by evil men during the two battles in question, I shall also add to it and recount how the Promoter of Supreme Justice, by the agency of Baldwin, second king of the Latins of Jerusalem,[105] delivered from the lion's mouth[106] the people of the Antiochene lordship when they were almost destroyed by the enemy's devastation, and how their glorious name, lost in the prince's war, was restored to those same people by virtue of the Holy Cross in the king's war;[107] and so I shall return and stick to the order of the narrative.[108]

It goes as follows: after the prince was slain on the field and a considerable multitude was killed by enemies who came from the four corners of the world, in addition to those who raged against our men with swords from within the region, the battlefield was so hemmed in and access and paths to the mountains and valleys so observed, that not a single person trying to escape was able to get through unscathed. And so our men, all those who were still in the field with their swords, became obsessed by the hope of fighting their way out or cautiously indulging in flight back to the tents. But they did not find the tents, for they had already been carried off by the hands of the unrighteous, except for those of the prince and the chapel, to which very wicked men had hurried eagerly with their swords, possessed by greed

---

[105] This implies that Baldwin was acting as the tool of God. See: Baldwin of Le Bourcq, pp. 27-8.

[106] 2 Tim. 4.17: 'liberatus sum de ore leonum'.

[107] The implication is that God's will was manifested within Baldwin's army through the relic of the True Cross. See: Walter's attitude to religion and piety, p. 71.

[108] In this passage Walter sets out his agenda for the second half of Book Two, while again asserting his desire to write a flowing narrative history of events. See: Our knowledge of Walter, pp. 6-7.

for gold and silver and the prince's jewels.[109]

Seeing this, Euterpius arrived, most worthy knight in physical and mental strife, asking these men who were hurrying in front of the chapel and delivering blows: 'Has Christ's fellowship gone to the devil?[110] You are dividing the spoils, but the share-out is not equal.' With these words he pierced to the heart with his lance an emir clad in gold who was in front of the entrance of the chapel, and in attacking the rest, in accordance with God's appointed purpose, which he could not escape, he laid aside his humanity for martyrdom, and he passed over happily to the blessedness of peace.[111]

During these disputes an assembly of our armed force, with the equipment of the entire army, positioned itself on a certain hill which was nearby, thinking they could wait there either for the assistance of approaching soldiers, or in some way to take refuge in an escape from that point. So what happened? Not long afterwards individuals who were escaping from the battle-field, seeing our men positioned on the mountain, and feeling that death was rather close, weighed it up and sought the comfort of living. For they were deceived by vain hope, and they flocked together from here and there to cling tightly to the mountain, which in a moment was so blockaded by the infidels that those under siege preferred to die a quick death rather than to suffer their spears.

Rightly indeed: there was such a barrage of spears and arrows from all sides that even the infidels who were on the outside suffered severely from their clashing together with rebounding blows, while our men, indeed, suffered even worse:

For as the golden hour
shortly gives way to heavy showers,
and as the dried hay

---

[109] This suggests that Roger's moveable wealth was not transported to Artah in accordance with the instructions given on the night of the 27 June. Walter the Chancellor, II.3, p. 120.

[110] 2 Cor. 6.15: 'conventio Christi ad Belial'.

[111] Euterpius is unknown, but his name may indicate an Armenian or Greek origin. It is interesting that Walter uses the term 'martyr' of what appears to be a relatively obscure figure, but did not describe Roger in the same fashion. Walter the Chancellor, II.5, p. 127. Our thanks to Corun Johnson and Kin Quen-Chiu for this observation.

is damaged by hailstorms:
so our people soon, injured,
give way to constant blows.
And yet a part escaped
led by the Supreme Judge,
and a part was captured by ill fate,
and brought to its knees,
it was led out to the standard
of the prince of the impious.[112]

The punishment of sinners follows:[113] there in fact next to the battle-field five hundred or more prisoners were held, their hands twisted behind their backs and their feet bound with iron chains and other torments very tightly, in the manner of dogs tied together two by two by the neck, waiting in a circle bent over to the ground before the master criminal to undergo the death sentence. Moreover, the wicked leader, driven by destructive rage, ordered the prisoners' wounds to be examined in the death tent by the death squad and those men afflicted by severe wounds to be dragged out of the tent by the hair, using rods, for immediate execution, and the rest to suffer a night's torture and be kept for slaughter the following day. And so the wicked men joyfully obeyed the wicked command of their lord.

II.7   *The tortures and torments and martyrdoms of the prisoners.*

Moreover, this wicked command was followed by a worse: for, led to execution, the badly wounded and the others, they fell at the hands of the heathen not only with their heads cut off but they even suffered agonizing death with the skin flayed from the living and half-severed head. Also the rest, knowing they were to be tortured, spent that dark night in outrage and dread, desiring death with their minds, they raged at death, which was often called on again and again, not to come to them in their unhappiness. Yet then

---

[112] From this point in his narrative onwards, Walter uses a range of similar phrases to vilify Il-ghazi. See: The depiction of Islam and eastern Christendom, pp. 64-6.

[113] Even though Walter provides an extremely graphic and emotive account of the treatment of the prisoners taken at the Field of Blood, perhaps because he was amongst them, he still refers to them as 'sinners'. See: Our knowledge of Walter, pp. 5-6.

again they remembered among themselves under the pressure of their present circumstances what had happened to them, and they said that the very bad things happened to them justly and deservedly, and such things and the like belonged not to man's pure nature but to his corrupt, for by the latter he was worthy of wretchedness, by the former of blessedness.

Therefore, after a night squashed together in fetters, as soon as the sun rose on the following day - sun, I say, which was blacker for them than the dark night - they were ordered to be presented in the tents so that the prince of wickedness could decide what in his opinion could adequately be done to them. And this was the abominable prince's pleasure: at the third hour of the day the naked prisoners, some two or three hundred all tied together by the neck with rope, were led out for a distance of a mile under swords and cudgels, whips and ropes through the fields planted with thistles and brambles into the vineyard next to Sarmada, newly harvested, where human piety deprived of natural law was turned into sacrilegious frenzy, with the tyrant Il-ghazi wielding his tyranny there towards the Christians, and in this way:[114]

It was hot, of course, not only for the wounded and ailing prisoners but also it was entirely intolerable for the healthy, the enemy and free men, so that not a single one of the prisoners would have refused to offer even one of his limbs or life itself for a cup of cold water. In that place certain prisoners, seeing the grapes of the vineyard sticking to the earth, vied with one another to fall face downwards, and they even gathered the dirt-covered grapes and those trampled by feet eagerly into their mouths. When the juice ran from their mouths as they bit on the grapes, no matter how, it was caught in the mouth of another, and frequently, thinking to hold the dribbled juice and driven by frenzy they would bite their own tongues with their teeth, and some were raging wretchedly and holding on to others' beards having seen a little drop of juice, and more then were thirsty and drank urine for the first time.

Moreover the minister of death saw this, and, needing a cold drink for his very own use, he ordered water to be brought by horse and cart from distant regions. When it was brought he ordered the better part of it to be reserved

---

[114] The intensity of the following description suggests that Walter may have been an eye-witness to these events. See: Our knowledge of Walter, pp. 5-6.

for himself and his men, and the muddy dregs to be offered to the prisoners, and he decreed that they should be led out two by two to the water-skins, and if any approached who was not led, he commanded that that man should lose his head on the spot. When the water had been put out in the middle, those who wished to trade their lives for a single taste did not think twice, but lots and lots of them ran to the water through the midst of the swords. There some were struck down with stones, some pierced by javelins and many were mutilated in different ways.

Watching this, the wicked man was delighted by their torments and he laughed at them as if he were refreshed by some food to fuel his cruelty. And yet he was not satisfied and he was thinking up crueller things. He commanded everyone at once, however many there were, to be brought into the middle of the field so that, as their blood shed one by one was of little account to him, he might at least savour to the full in every possible way a universal sacrifice of destruction for the increase of his enjoyment. And so they were brought into the middle: at his order a thousand or more soldiers were ready, carrying naked swords in their hands so that by striking out they could at the same time tear the prisoners to pieces and delight the unholy one.

When the soldiers were ready to attack with a charge a certain very powerful emir approached and he spoke to the lord of the slaughter in these words: 'Aha, the star of law![115] What are you losing by letting your enjoyment of these tortures be finished so quickly? Once these men are dead, what glory shall you show to kings and princes of other countries under our law? Stop handing them over to death in this way and be willing to trust me to look after your honour. For I shall have regard for nothing except that which agrees with our law and befits your honour. I approve, therefore, and I recommend to your highness that you give instructions for the richer, more powerful and more noble of these dogs to be singled out to be kept for you, either to escape death by ransom of their heads or to be put to death by the infliction of various tortures in your astrological rituals,[116] or to be sent to the sultan[117]

---

[115] Walter contrasts alternative images of Il-ghazi: in Latin eyes he is the cruel 'lord of death', while in this reported speech he is moved by an appeal to uphold Muslim law and protect his own honour.

[116] From the Latin 'sollemnitatibus mathematicis'. This superstitious mention of 'science' is typical of Walter's presentation of the Islamic faith. See: The depiction of Islam and eastern Christendom, p. 61.

and the other lords and leaders to represent with living voice glorious announcements of your name and victory and add to your reputation, and, when they have been singled out, the remainder may be cut to pieces by your swords and suffer death, because and to the degree that they and their kin and compatriots have sinned against our most holy law.'[118]

This wicked man's advice pleased his wicked lord and he gave instructions for things to be arranged in this way: those chosen were therefore put to one side for torture, the rest were left in the field for immediate destruction. For the most wicked one said: 'Come on, soldiers! Guardians and agents of the supreme law! Here is a sacrifice of dogs ready for your swords,' and he shouted, 'Hey! Hey! Run at them readily and quickly!' And so in one attack the impious soldiers struck the condemned men with death-dealing swords, and they did not cease from killing until there was no part of the prisoners' parts left whole; and there they rolled in the spilt blood as a pig wallows in mud; not yet sated with the slaughter of men, they entreated the power of the judge, Il-ghazi, on bended knee, begging to be able to destroy the chosen prisoners with a like slaughter at his command. However, his divine majesty[119] refused, so that the enormity of his cruelty would prevail in all things; therefore he ordered the chosen prisoners to be handed over to his son[120] who had them brought into captivity in Aleppo to be tortured there.

In accomplishment the son did not lack the authority of his wicked father, for he received the chosen prisoners and on the first night he handed them over to the tender mercies of stones mixed with thorns and thistles. And he also gave them flints for food and hard blows for drink, for a bed he caused halters to be bound on their feet and necks. Alas! That night was counted among the worst of hellish nights! On the following day they were led to the pillory in Aleppo, where they suffered constant blows and different sorts of torture. Some were killed and some, by God's appeasement, were ransomed, as I shall

---

[117] The Seldjuk sultan of Baghdad, Muhammad, d. 1131, son and successor to Ghiyah ad-Din Muhammad Shah. See: Walter the Chancellor, I.2, p. 86, n. 58.

[118] Walter implies that there was an Islamic religious justification for Il-ghazi's actions, that he was in effect fighting a Holy War.

[119] Walter perhaps made this strange comment in order to contrast Il-ghazi ironically with his 'swinish' soldiers.

[120] This was probably Sulaiman, the son of Il-ghazi who temporarily overthrew his father's power in Aleppo in 1121. Kemal ed-Din, p. 629.

explain in detail at the end of my account of the king's war, and this is why:
for it concerns many of the king's men involved with these in their wretched
fate, concerning whom I shall explain just as I saw and heard with my own
eyes.[121]

II.8 *Il-ghazi inflicts further damage after his victory, while Patriarch
Bernard organizes the defence of Antioch.*

But so as not to neglect the proper order of the narrative I have begun, I shall
return to what Il-ghazi did nearby after the battle and recount his tyranny.
After he had seen how things stood at al-Atharib,[122] he set out with the army
for Artah, where after a truce was agreed he brought the bishop's tower[123]
under his control in this way: he agreed to allow the bishop with all his men,
both clergy and others, to go to Antioch, freely, without restraint and in
peace. He partly kept this promise and partly broke it: for whatever gold and
silver and ornaments he ascertained the clergy were carrying off, he stole in
their entirety by sending robbers instead of escorts.[124] But he returned
openly their stolen priestly garments, and sent them after the priests as they
went away, so that he might conceal his own wickedness with them.[125] And
he arranged to spend a few days there where the tents had been pitched before

---

[121] This provides further confirmation that Walter was himself a captive in Aleppo at this
time. His comments also indicate that the prisoners mentioned later in his account included
Jerusalemites captured at the second battle of Tall Danith. See: Our knowledge of Walter, pp.
5-6.

[122] Given that al-Atharib was still in Latin hands after the Field of Blood, this statement
probably indicates that Il-ghazi decided that the town was too strongly defended to attack at
this point. He returned once Alan and his men had travelled to Antioch. Walter the
Chancellor, II.10, pp. 145-6.

[123] It is not known whether this tower was linked to the main citadel of Artah, but given
Walter's comments below it appears that Il-ghazi took possession of only part of the town's
fortifications at this point.

[124] These precious goods may have included at least some of the princely wealth sent back
to Artah from the Field of Blood. Walter the Chancellor, II.3, p. 120.

[125] Walter was not prepared to praise Il-ghazi for this minor leniency, but explained it by
a selfish desire to protect reputation. Later in the twelfth century the Muslim ruler Saladin was
to develop a formidable reputation for clemency and honour, and, in the aftermath of the
battle of Hattin in 1187, this enabled him to secure the rapid capitulation of many Latin
strongholds. H.E. Mayer, *The Crusades*, pp. 135-6.

Artah so that he could first take Artah[126] and from there set out to attack Antioch.[127] However it was God's pleasure and arrangement that he should be detained there by the words of a certain man, called Joseph,[128] a very wise individual. When Il-ghazi himself sought the citadel's[129] surrender, Joseph, fore-armed by wisdom, replied in this way, not rejecting but as if assenting:

'We know that everything belonging to this principality besides Antioch is subject to your swords and your authority;[130] therefore, if you obtain Antioch, with it both this and the other castles will immediately yield to you, and lest you believe that I am mocking you with my words, in the meantime you shall assign to me one of your men, Sahenas,[131] who will look after your affairs with me on your behalf and take possession as your lordship's proxy. For truly if I were to receive you yourself into the castle, for certain when it became known my son, who is in Antioch, would suffer a shameful

---

[126] The main citadel was evidently still in Latin hands.

[127] This indicates that, in Walter's mind, Il-ghazi's primary aim after the Field of Blood was to seize the city of Antioch itself. Later references to the defensive measures taken by Patriarch Bernard in the city indicate that a Muslim attack was expected. Walter the Chancellor, II.8, pp. 139-40. Strategically it was sound policy to secure control of Artah prior to an attack upon Antioch, as it was the city's closest fortified site and controlled the approach to the Iron Bridge. The First Crusaders took the town before besieging Antioch in 1097, while in 1105 Ridwan of Aleppo posed a significant threat to the city when he took control of Artah. Albert of Aachen, III.28-31; Ralph of Caen, pp. 640-41, p. 712; Kemal ed-Din, p. 593; Ibn al-Qalanisi, p. 69. I have argued elsewhere, however, that Il-ghazi's primary aim in 1119 was to secure Aleppan control of the fortified sites of al-Atharib and Zardana, to the east of the Jabal Talat, and that he may have seen a direct attack upon Antioch as unfeasible. T.S. Asbridge, 'The significance and causes of the battle of the Field of Blood', pp. 315-16. This might indicate that Walter used the actions of Joseph and Sahenas to explain what he saw as Il-ghazi's puzzling failure to attack Antioch directly.

[128] Joseph is unknown, but his name may suggest an eastern Christian, possibly Armenian origin. Given Artah's strategic importance and the fact that no individual is specifically associated with the town in this period, it is likely that it remained within the princely domain in 1119. Joseph may, therefore, have been its castellan. Although he did surrender the castle he is not criticized, but twice described as wise, presumably because he managed to maintain a foothold within the town and later returned his allegiance to the Latins. See: The depiction of Islam and eastern Christendom, p. 68.

[129] This must refer to the town's main citadel.

[130] This is an exaggeration, given that at this point Il-ghazi only held Artah.

[131] This individual is unknown, but the word 'sahenas' may actually have denoted a Muslim title equivalent to viscount.

death, and I, an old man and full of years,[132] if I do this will be considered the most wicked of traitors, which I do not want to happen.[133] And it is more fitting that you should consider me innocent than guilty.' Deceived by these words, Il-ghazi left the castle intact and placed there a certain Sahenas. But he was keen on drink and by God's will, forgetting about Antioch,[134] he often sent thousands of soldiers throughout regions far and near who returned to him day after day refreshed and laden with spoils both of men and of other things.

Meanwhile, as to the evils and misfortunes which were perceived to have happened previously and to threaten from the impending loss of the city of Antioch: every care, labour, fear, terror or harm to Christendom could happen, now that Antioch was deprived of military service and almost the entire military force of Frankish citizens was lost; in its place, of necessity, all came down to the clergy, in such a way, as I say, that they feared much more intensely being deceived by the betrayal of enemies within the city than being in any way vulnerable to pressure upon them from external forces. Nor was it remarkable if the Antiochenes wanted to return evil for evil,[135] and at that period of time they could greatly oppress our people by betrayal or in some other way, because that is how the scales of justice change; for indeed the people of Antioch had been deprived of their goods by the force and deviousness of our people and were devoted to bad habits and often overcome by despair.[136]

---

[132] Jer. 6.11: 'Senex cum plenum dierum'.

[133] The fact that Joseph could claim that his son might act as a form of hostage might also indicate that he was a non-Latin.

[134] Walter feels the need to explain Il-ghazi's decision not to attack Antioch, attributing it to his drunkenness and the will of God. A number of contemporary writers commented upon Il-ghazi's penchant for alcoholic consumption. Indeed, Usamah ibn-Munqidh claimed that Il-ghazi was 'so constituted that whenever he drank wine he would feel drunk for twenty days.' Usamah ibn-Munqidh, p. 149; Ibn al-Qalanisi, pp. 149-50. For further discussion of the traditions surrounding Il-ghazi's drunkenness and the aims of his 1119 campaign see, T.S. Asbridge, 'The significance and causes of the battle of the Field of Blood', pp. 314-16.

[135] Rom. 12.17: 'Nulli malum pro malo reddentes'.

[136] Walter sees the 'Franks' and 'the people of Antioch', namely its indigenous population, as distinct groups. He does not specify whether this indigenous group was made up of Greeks, Armenians or even Muslims, but does highlight the dangers of having a high proportion of potentially restless non-Latins within the principality. Walter's acknowledgment that the Latins treated the indigenous population unjustly is remarkable for this period. See: The depiction of Islam and eastern Christendom, p. 68.

The patriarch was acting wisely about these and other things, and he called the Franks to him; strengthened by God's power and surrounded by the worthy protection of his clergy, he decided with them about the situation, that the people, if they wanted to act treacherously, could not do so, and that he himself would take charge of the entire city for himself and the clergy with only the Franks, and he decreed that the peoples of different nations, wherever they were in the city and wherever they came from, except the Franks, should all remain unarmed and should never venture out of their houses at night without a light. And this was carried out, so that they would not in any way seem to be undone by any act of treachery and so that they could not be considered suspect in any way at all; and he decreed that where the entire city was evidently weakest, there his own tents should be placed, which was necessary for the protection of Christianity, and that every single tower, as many as there were, should be garrisoned at once by monks and clerics[137] mixed with laymen according to the power and number of the Christian inhabitants.[138] All the citizens carefully obeyed as one the orders of this wisest of fathers and teachers.[139]

And so, with the towers defended inside and out, guards were added to guards, and that same patriarch, preferring to fight with prayers rather than weapons, constantly beseeched God from the heart for the safety and defence of the Christian people;[140] and moreover he did not cease during those hours to visit in turn, night and day, with his armed clergy and knights, in the manner of warriors, the gates, ramparts and towers and walls all around the circuit, and their guards, and to comfort them and encourage them, so that they would add the care of Christian protection to their watchful minds and from a good beginning would not be deterred by any enemy disturbance. What happened in detail? The clergy, with the other faithful, acted the part of

---

[137] There is known to have been a monastery dedicated to St Paul in Antioch by the time of Bohemond II's reign. *Le Cartulaire de chapitre du Saint-Sépulchre de Jérusalem*, pp. 178-83, no. 77.

[138] At this point Walter's does not distinguish between Latins and Eastern Christians.

[139] See: Bernard of Valence, patriarch of Antioch, p. 34.

[140] Even though Walter praises the clerical defence of Antioch, he distanced Bernard from direct involvement, probably because canon law prohibited the clergy from carrying out acts of warfare. The reference to fighting with prayer rather than weapons has direct resonance with St Augustine's concept of spiritual warfare. See: Bernard of Valence, patriarch of Antioch, pp. 37-8.

military service wisely and vigorously, inside and outside, and with God's strength kept the city intact from the enemy so that it could be protected by Baldwin the king when he made his long-desired appearance.[141]

Among all these dangers, as we have learnt from reliable intermediaries,[142] it reached Il-ghazi's ears that King Baldwin, and with him Pons count of Tripoli, was hurrying at a rapid pace to Antioch. Therefore he decided at once to send against them ten thousand soldiers and he ordered the same number or more to follow after them at speed;[143] and once the decision was made, whom he would send and whom keep with him, he told those going to lie in wait carefully for the king's approach and to be watchful for any chance whatsoever of destroying Christianity.

II.9   *King Baldwin arrives at Antioch and takes charge of the defence.*

And so the infidels were mobilized at their lord's command, drawing up their battle-lines in their customary way, and they set out by night towards Latakia[144] and the hills of Mount Parlerius,[145] in order to be able both to plunder and to ambush the king's cavalry. When they reached those regions they separated into three parts so that some of them could intercept the king and some go and seize plunder, while the rest made their way to the port of

---

[141] The phrases 'wisely and vigorously' and 'with God's strength' demonstrate that Walter viewed these defensive measures in a very positive light

[142] Walter is keen to stress the credibility of his sources. See: Our knowledge of Walter, p. 7.

[143] It is unlikely that Il-ghazi's army was so large that he could dispatch 20,000 troops to intercept Baldwin and still maintain a force in the region of Antioch. See: Walter as a military source, pp. 55-7.

[144] From the Latin 'Laodiceam'. Lying on the coastline to the south of Antioch, Latakia was the principality's most important port. Although used as a foraging centre by the First Crusaders during the siege of Antioch, possession of the city was contested by the principality and the Byzantine empire during the first decade of Latin settlement. Albert of Aachen, XI.40, described a man named Martin as being 'count of Latakia' in 1111, but he must been castellan of the port as it remained within the princely domain until 1126. Ralph of Caen, p. 649, pp. 706-9, p. 712, pp. 715-6;   Raymond of Aguilers, p. 134;   Albert of Aachen, III.59; VI.55-59;   Anna Comnena, XI.11, pp. 47-9; XII.2, p. 92. *Cartulaire général de l'ordre des Hospitaliers de S. Jean de Jérusalem (1100-1310)*, vol.1, pp. 92-3, no. 109.

[145] The Jabal Akra. P. Deschamps, 'La défense du comté de Tripoli et de la principauté d'Antioche', p. 5, p.73.

St Simeon[146] on the coast. The king himself unexpectedly met those who had set out against him at Mount Hingro;[147] he therefore destroyed them with a vigorous assault and scattered them over the steep mountain slopes in such a way that comrade could not find comrade, nor friend find friend to bring him future assistance. After this the king ordered camp to be made before Laitor[148] and he set out from there early in the morning, being careful to arrange that he himself would go first, so that he would find the enemy first, and ordering the count with his Provençals to follow up and guard his rear so that if by chance he should see the enemy, he could at once let the king know by way of a messenger, and he might attack them.[149] As they marched along ordered thus, the Provençals happened to see some of the enemy driving before them a very great deal of plunder, and they wasted no time in attacking them very quickly and vigorously, in such a way that they seized that same plunder from them. But by wretched misfortune the heathens re-mustered their forces and by attacking the Provençals they brought them to such a condition that they were unable to return to the king that day.

Truly, with some of them destroyed and some scattered in the mountains, the rest marched on raggedly, and at night they found the king already quartered at Casabella;[150] they reported to him exactly what had happened to them, and the king found sure signs of the enemy there: for the camp of four thousand soldiers recently there lay exposed, still foully polluted with dead men and the limbs of animals which they had eaten. When he heard this, moreover, the king, thinking that they could be pursued, complained loudly that he, who pitied those killed in the past and the present, and whose

---

[146] Also known as Souwaidiya. This was Antioch's nearest port, lying approximately fourteen kilometres to the west of the city. Used by the First Crusaders from 1097 onwards, it was almost certainly part of the princely domain in 1119. The man named as 'Robert of St Simeon' by Albert of Aachen may have been its castellan. Raymond of Aguilers, p. 49; Albert of Aachen, XI.40.

[147] H. Hagenmeyer was probably wrong to identify this with the Jabal Akra. *Galterii Cancellarii, Bella Antiochena*, p. 238, n. 5.

[148] A small settlement in the Jabal as-Summaq. It was probably held by the descendants of Robert of Sourdeval. See charter (a), pp. 205-6, n. 85.

[149] This careful description shows that Walter was aware of the significance of the vanguard and rearguard during a march, and that he wished to portray Baldwin as militarily competent. See: Walter as a military source, pp. 54-5.

[150] This town, to the north of Latakia, is also known as Kessab and Ras al-Basit. R. Burns, *Monuments of Syria: a historical guide*, (London, 1992), p. 201.

prerogative it was to protect the fatherland,[151] did not know how he could most surely follow them; nevertheless he thought to himself that it would be better to go to Antioch for two reasons: namely, so that he could both comfort the desperate people of Antioch, and so that he might hear the rumours of that place, take counsel with the patriarch, and pursue the enemy.[152] Meanwhile, three thousand or more set out by night for the port of St Simeon,[153] and as dawn appeared they suddenly attacked them with the sword as they slept; the rest indeed, escaped by ship.[154] Moreover, the heathen had gathered together the plunder of men and other things and escaped by way of the mountain slopes, and now the sun had moved a distance of two hours, they appeared not far from Antioch with their banners held high, and as a result when the enemy were seen, as human nature compels, an immense clamour arose all around.

For this reason the clergy and knights, who had come to Antioch from the war, and the citizens and everyone else who was there, seized their weapons and sallied forth as if they were going to fight, and at once they sent some of them against the enemy to reconnoitre the numbers and strength of those enemy forces. However it came about that two of those sent died on the plain and the rest were driven back by an enemy charge and rapidly returned; when they saw this, our men who were waiting not far from the city, saw the unarmed crowd, which had gone with them, put to flight, and they began to move and to fidget. Immediately the enemy, who were pursuing the first, did not rein in their horses, but spurred them on, charging our men at the same time in such a way that some of them, even though they were mailed, were forced into the river, and they did not cease from pursuing the rest, striking them all the while, right onto the bridge.[155] In this charge thirty-seven of our men were killed. Nevertheless our men stood firm on the bridge, having sent away their horses and drawn their swords, and gradually they recovered their strength and drove off the enemy. And so those driven off and the rest who

---

[151] This implies that Baldwin II had a legal right to act as a form of overlord for all the Latin settlements in the East. See: Baldwin of Le Bourcq, pp. 27-8.

[152] Walter contrasts this cautious behaviour, and willingness to consult Patriarch Bernard, with Roger's hasty policy in June.

[153] These were Muslim troops sent to attack the Latin forces at St Simeon.

[154] Walter's Latin is ambiguous in this passage, but, as the Muslim were at this point in possession of plunder and escaping overland, Walter must be indicating that it was the Latins who were rescued by ship.

[155] This must refer to the bridge before the Bridge Gate of Antioch.

were burdened with plunder marched together beyond Corbara[156] where they rested for a short time between two stretches of water.

Not long afterwards Baldwin arrived,[157] the renowned king; to all the Christian people he was great in prospect, greater in arrival, greatest in the protection he brought. When he realized how the infidels' tyranny had burned into our men, penetrating beneath their skin and flesh and to the very marrow, and the Turks had not been held back by any knight, but only by the yawning waters of the sea,[158] he was stricken by very great sorrow,[159] and hurried to enter the city, not to rest, but first to seek God's kingdom and, since he was about to fight for his fatherland, to pray devoutly to God, as befits a king, in the church of St Peter in order that, strengthened by the Church's counsel to undertake the expedition freely and after absolution, he could confidently take on the infidels.[160] And he did not delay, but after making a speech and being invigorated by the patriarch's advice,[161] he was also motivated by a two-fold ardour: inwardly of his soul panting for revenge, and outwardly of his knightly station inspiring him to chivalry. He sent out scouts in advance, quickened the pace and drew up the battle-lines, then he hurried on his way in pursuit; but when he fully realized, from the reports of messengers, that the Turks were a long way off and not halting in any place for sure, but riding more rapidly than usual, as if impelled by fear, and he perceived that his own men were tired from the journey, to the approval of the clergy and the entire nobility,[162] he reconsidered and returned to Antioch. There he was called by God and elevated by His gift and assumed the rank of prince, by right indeed:[163] for truly it was by his hand that Divine Providence took care to return citizens to the ramparts and the city to

---

[156] This site is unidentified.

[157] Baldwin II probably reached Antioch in mid to late July.

[158] Vergil, *Aeneid*, 1.110: 'his unda dehiscens terram inter fluctus aperit'.

[159] Vergil, *Aeneid*, 9.139: 'nec solos tangit Atridas iste dolor'.

[160] In this passage Walter introduces the central theme of his depiction of Baldwin II: as the saviour of Antioch. His choice of language is obviously designed to portray the king as an idealized hero. See: Baldwin of Le Bourcq, pp. 27-31.

[161] Walter perhaps wishes to contrast Baldwin's interest in Bernard's 'advice' with Roger's actions.

[162] Walter uses yet another word to describe the nobility of Antioch.

[163] At the end of this laudatory description of Baldwin's arrival Walter actually asserts that the king assumed the title of prince. It is worth noting, however, that Walter was probably a prisoner in Aleppo when these events took place. See: Baldwin of Le Bourcq, pp. 33-4.

the citizens, of whom it had been deprived by wretched fate.

II.10 *The arrangements made for the principality of Antioch. Al-Atharib is taken and the king prepares to advance from Antioch against the enemy.*

And so the necessity for immediate action was broadcast, since the enemy were strong in number and were powerful in malice,[164] and the patriarch and the clerical order, whose right it is to advise, to do and to teach good things, supported by the strength of their inner being, said that the infidels and unbelievers could easily be overcome and destroyed, even by bands of few Christians, if they fought lawfully with true righteousness on their side,[165] and so that this would be the case, the king and the rest busied themselves amending their behaviour on their advice and being watchful over other good things. And so, after a council was appointed in the court of St Peter,[166] of great necessity it was decreed that the king, to whom the just and supreme Judge had subjected nearly all the kingdom of the eastern Christians,[167] for the love of justice and the common good, would hand over the principality of Antioch, to Bohemond's son, to whom it belonged of right, along with his own daughter, if he would come and marry her and protect the land of that very principality by his counsel and assistance.[168] This was also considered

---

[164] Psalms, 51 (52).3: 'Quid gloriaris in malitia, Qui potens es in iniquitate'.

[165] Walter seems to imply that a just war could be won if the concept of 'right intention' was upheld.

[166] It is not known whether this term denoted the princely or patriarchal court of Antioch.

[167] This bears some similarity to Fulcher's comment that in 1119 God made Baldwin the ruler of the 'land far and wide, from Egypt to Mesopotamia'. Fulcher of Chartres, III.7, p. 635. See: Baldwin of Le Bourcq, p. 33.

[168] This passage demonstrates the Antiochene succession was resolved in the summer of 1119, perhaps, if Walter's chronology is correct, even before the second battle of Tall Danith. The council concluded that Bohemond II, the son of Bohemond of Taranto, prince of Antioch from 1098-c.1105, and Constance of France, daughter of King Philip I of France, should be designated as successor. Orderic Vitalis, XI.12, p. 70. Upon his accession he was to marry Alice, Baldwin II's second daughter. Walter's statement that the principality belonged to Bohemond II by right, from the Latin 'cuius juris erat' must be reconciled with his description of Roger as prince of Antioch. See: Walter's purpose in writing *The Antiochene Wars*, pp. 23-6, and: pp. 33-4. Bohemond was probably eight or nine years old in 1119, and was living with his mother in Apulia, in southern Italy. It was clearly expected that Bohemond II would bring sufficient forces to defend the principality and commit himself to its upkeep. This was to be in keeping with future appeals for long term aid and heirs from western Europe. J.

and it was decreed with the guidance of justice that those men who had acquired lands and honours in a foreign country by the gift of lords and by many injuries and alarms, even by the shedding of their own blood and that of their kin in the defence of Christendom, should not lose their homes and belongings by any change of Christian lordship, but should possess them by hereditary right.[169] And this was enacted and confirmed by his words and the royal hand.[170]

When these things had been accomplished, the king, being at Antioch, swiftly assembled his people in the name of war, from regions far and near and wherever possible, and was busy arming himself and his men with weapons of war and other warlike equipment, as befits a king.[171] When he heard this, Il-ghazi left the castle of Artah and 'Imm[172] intact and set out to besiege al-Atharib. For he had heard, from many circumstantial rumours, that Alan, lord of that castle, with his knights, and also Edessene soldiers[173] and almost everyone from the other castles, were approaching Antioch at the king's

---

Phillips, *Defenders of the Holy Land*, pp. 14-43. The provision of binding Antioch and Jerusalem though the marriage to Alice was also accepted practice in the Levant. Bohemond I encouraged the allegiance of his nephew Tancred by arranging his marriage to Cecilia of France, the younger half sister of Constance, in 1106. William of Tyre, XI.1, p. 495. On Tancred's death in 1112 Cecilia married Pons, the new count of Tripoli, while in 1113 Tancred's successor Roger wed Cecilia of Le Bourcq, the sister of Baldwin of Le Bourcq, then count of Edessa (1100-1118) and future king of Jerusalem (1118-1131). Albert of Aachen, XII, 19; William of Tyre, XI.18, p. 522; XI.22, p. 527. Bohemond II did duly arrive in the Levant in 1126, at which point he took possession of the principality and married Alice. Fulcher of Chartres, III.61, pp. 820-22; Orderic Vitalis, XI.29, p. 134; William of Tyre, XIII.21, p. 613; Michael the Syrian, XVI.2, p. 224; Usamah ibn-Munqidh, p. 150; Matthew of Edessa, III.105, p. 237.

[169] These legal clauses, designed to prevent Bohemond II from altering the pattern of lay landholding within the principality, represent a significant proviso to his acknowledgement as the Antiochene heir.

[170] This must mean that the decisions of this council were set down in a charter witnessed by the king. Given the specificity of Walter's description it is possible that he had access to this document, although no extant copy has been discovered to date.

[171] The fact that Baldwin was able successfully to muster Antioch's remaining forces demonstrates that his authority was readily acknowledged within the principality.

[172] 'Imm was a smaller town to the southeast of Artah, occupied by the First Crusaders in 1098, and perhaps held by Tancred during the siege of Antioch. Kemal ed-Din, p. 582; Ralph of Caen, p. 650.

[173] Baldwin may well have still been count of Edessa in 1119. It is notable that there were no Edessene troops mentioned at the Field of Blood.

command, so that they could advance from the city and wage war on him there or wherever else he was.[174] Nor did he lack effectiveness[175] in this matter or others, because the king of heaven and earth[176] wanted it to be. Since Il-ghazi was unable to take the castle by storm, he sent men from different sides to dig out a cave made underground, and he prepared fuses by grafting together dry pieces of wood so that when they reached the towers and put in that same kindling they would collapse, being supported by posts.[177] In addition three or four times every day they both deprived the towers of their defences and destroyed the defenders with savage blows by way of petraries and the apparatus of various engines,[178] with an assault of armed men attacking in three ranks, shooting in arrows with a huge number of javelins.

Eventually the townspeople, some of them intimidated by these attacks, some of them compelled by the fire sent in to undermine the towers, preferring still to live in the world rather than to be afflicted by daily dread in the castle or to achieve martyrdom, were persuaded to the unfortunate and shameful decision that they could escape safe and sound and so, having received the infidels' word, they surrendered the castle and embarked on the journey to the king from there, tearful and shamefaced.[179] The infidels, indeed, having put in a garrison and other things necessary for the defence of the castle, set out to besiege Zardana. Meanwhile the king, thinking the wicked ones could be found at al-Atharib, got everything ready which for now he was able to command in the way of men and other necessities of war, and, in a spirit of

---

[174] In the short term Baldwin's decision to rally the principality's forces at Antioch weakened local garrisons and enabled Il-ghazi to capture al-Atharib and Zardana, and prompted the Banu-Munqidh of Shaizar to attack Ma'arrat-an-Nu'man, Kafaruma, Kafartab, Sarmin, Ma'arrat Misrin and Apamea. Usamah ibn-Munqidh, pp. 67-8. It did, however, provide a field army capable of challenging Il-ghazi in a set piece battle.

[175] Ovid, *Amor. eleg.* 2, 3, 15: 'non caret effectu'.

[176] Where this phrase is used in the Bible in the genitive, as in this passage, it always refers to God. e.g. Gen, 24.3; Matt. 11.25.

[177] Walter's understanding of military matters is demonstrated by his concise description of the process of undermining a wall, an important medieval siege technique. See: Walter as a military source, pp. 58-9.

[178] This refers to a variety of catapult devices.

[179] Walter criticizes the populace of al-Atharib for surrendering to Il-ghazi, even though their lord and garrison had travelled to Antioch.

humility and with a contrite heart,[180] he put on a woollen garment and marched barefoot,[181] hastening to entreat the Almighty in the churches of His blessed intercessors and to pray to Him from the bottom of his heart that, since it was with His assent that the king had taken on the governance of the realm, he would begin and finish to the honour and praise of His name, and by the power of the Holy Cross[182] put down and overthrow the tyrants and assailants of Christianity from their presumptuous elevation and from their strength, by which they thought they would conquer, and making no false claim of victory or human praise for himself, but entrusting all to God.

At length, when the clergy and people of the whole town had gathered in the church of St Peter, after the patriarch celebrated the divine office, as befits a father he instructed in the Lord's bidding his sons who were going to war and those remaining at home in God's service, advised them and prepared them for battle and signed them with his heavenly patriarchal benediction;[183] and after taking the mysteries of the divine service, all together bent their heads towards the altar with its shrines and symbols of holy relics, then with the Lord's Cross[184] going first, the order of clergy decked out according to the custom of the Church, and all the people following with humility and compliance,[185] beseeching with the litany and other prayers to God, both those going to war and those staying at home, all of them wearing wool and setting out barefoot outside the town,[186] they came devoutly to the point of separation. In that place the patriarch once again took up the Holy Cross in his consecrated hands and once again signed them all with its power and commended them to God from his heart in this way: 'He who ransomed you

---

[180] A liturgical reference from the Offertory of the Mass.

[181] This form of ritual purification can be compared to Raymond of St Gilles' decision to continue his march to Jerusalem barefoot in 1099 and the barefooted procession made by the First Crusaders during the subsequent siege of the city. J.S.C. Riley-Smith, *The First Crusade and the idea of crusading*, p. 84.

[182] The Jerusalemite relic of the True Cross played a major role in Walter's forthcoming account of the battle of Tall Danith. See: Walter's attitude to religion and piety, p. 71.

[183] Bernard seems to have given his spiritual license to Baldwin's campaign.

[184] It is known that Baldwin II brought the Jerusalemite relic of the True Cross with him to northern Syria in 1119. See: Walter's attitude to religion and piety, p. 71.

[185] Eph. 4.1-2: 'obsecro vos, ut digne ambuletis vocatione, qua vocati estis cum omni humilitate et mansuetudine'.

[186] According to Walter the entire populace now followed Baldwin's example of going forth barefoot.

at the cost of His own blood, may He be merciful towards you and be the gracious leader of your journey and the provider of advantage! Whether you are going or staying, absolved from sins[187] may you serve Him freely and fully in such a way that, having obtained His gift of consolation and the triumph of victory, you may rejoice in Him and through Him.' After this was said, from this side and that tears poured forth, and with the sign of the Holy Cross going before the king returned to war, the clergy to the church, the people to their homes, entreating and praying earnestly that the Author of supreme justice, who destroyed wars from their foundation,[188] would destroy their adversaries by a charge of His people, who were heaping praise on His name.[189]

II.11 *The king sets out with his army.*

On this same day and the following night, as the king was riding to al-Atharib he was met by those men who had been forced by wretched circumstances to surrender the castle. When he had seen and heard them, the king was overcome by inner grief and he was stunned and saddened. For he realized and it was proved by that same event that two contrasting injuries threatened the Christians now and in the future from the surrender of the castle, one with God's assent was recoverable in time, the other never reparable: the loss of the castle was recoverable; the disgrace of its surrender was irreparable.[190] And so he was fired to zeal by this realization, and he swiftly took counsel, then made his way to Rugia so that by riding from there through Hab he might pitch camp at the mountain called Danith;[191] for there he hoped he might see or hear sure signs of the enemy. Nor did he lack effectiveness,

---

[187] This may indicate that some form of indulgence was being offered by the patriarch in return for support or participation in the campaign against Il-ghazi.

[188] Walter is implying that through this one violent confrontation God would end further conflict.

[189] Judith, 9.10.

[190] Walter seems to show a slightly ambivalent attitude to the inhabitants of al-Atharib. He states that they were 'forced' to surrender the town, but noted that they still suffered 'irreparable' shame as a result of their capitulation.

[191] Tall Danith. It is strange that Walter makes no comment about the fact Baldwin was camping at the same spot at which the battle against Bursuq was fought in 1115. Walter the Chancellor, I.6, p. 101, n, 151.

because it was the nature of his mind to anticipate. On that very day, indeed, when he lay up on the mountain, having pitched camp, he gained certain information that the enemy were not far off. For he understood clearly from the report of people who had heard and seen them that the infidels had besieged Zardana,[192] and he learnt from a trusted messenger that on that same day or the following he might see some of them. For on the following day, very early in the morning, as the quicker and more skilful of the knights were skirmishing here and there, letting off arrows all around, it happened that the enemy attacked our men and in this way they spent the day two by two, a few with a few, many with many, from this side and that, from the rear and from the front, trying to throw part of our army into confusion or to strike them in every way.[193]

The king, however, relying on the vigour of his manly good sense, when he perceived that they were not conducting themselves in the manner of warriors, and were not marching in properly drawn up battle lines,[194] urged on his men and ordered everyone to come forth sensibly before their camp and to stand to attention with steadfast mind until he could have all of them gathered in one place or marching at the same time. In the evening the enemy, full of crafty cunning, also avoided retiring to their quarters at the same time, but in the darkness of night they rested up here and there around the army, each holding his horse in his hand; servant and master were the same that night. Meanwhile, since Il-ghazi had sought to have the castle at Zardana surrender to him, whether by threats or coaxing, fears or promises, and he had been unable to obtain it, he did not let up from attacking the castle by assault and using the earlier engine with like violence three or four times in the day, also by night.[195] Moreover, since in that place there was a lack of vegetation and crops, even of water which was needful to feed men and horses, on the pretext of procuring supplies and subsistence the infidels brought together

---

[192] Walter does not comment on the fact that Baldwin made no attempt to relieve the besieged populace of Zardana, even though he had earlier written of the shame caused by the loss of al-Atharib. See: Baldwin of Le Bourcq, p. 29.

[193] Given the comment below this rather confused description must refer to skirmishing near the camp on Tall Danith. It would appear, therefore, that none of the troops under Baldwin's command attempted to engage Il-ghazi's forces at Zardana.

[194] Once again Walter combines an observation on military practice with praise for Baldwin II.

[195] This presumably refers to the same siege-engines used against al-Atharib.

thousands of Turcomans and Arabs in swarms from throughout different regions, and they marched with them, like ravening wolves[196] seizing on and devouring prey and taking away with them as much as they could of that which they had seized, and set about taking it home.[197] Also the king of the Arabs himself, whose name was Dubais,[198] and Bochard,[199] a very renowned prince of his people, and very many princes who had fought alongside Il-ghazi in the battle, set out in a similar way after the first had withdrawn.

When he saw this, and before the king arrived, Il-ghazi pressed for the capture of the castle with his forces; however he strove more to deceive the townspeople by his deceitful cunning: he even promised them on his honour and on an oath binding in his law,[200] that if they surrendered the fortress to his lordship they would be conveyed safe and sound under his benevolent command to the boundary from which they could safely escape, with everyone's possessions safe and intact. When they heard this, they were partly persuaded by their wounds, partly by the powerlessness of bodies deprived of strength, and they accepted the prince's apparent good faith, assenting to the abominable petition by this agreement, and unwittingly they placed themselves in the hands of butchers instead of escorts to lead them, having abandoned the town on the orders of the unholy prince. And so, happily and with a happy heart he took the town, and even more happily he ordered his armies to put to death savagely the Christians as they departed. What details of these things? Almost all became the prey of death in a moment. But this had not yet reached the king's ears. On that night, when he camped at Danith, he found out from the account of a certain priest of Robert fitz-Fulk[201] that it had

---

[196] Horace, *Epod.* 16.20: 'apris reliquit et rapacibus lupis'.

[197] This passage highlights the difficulties associated with maintaining a Muslim army in the field. At this stage in events Baldwin seems to have pursued a cautious policy, holding a defensible position at Tall Danith, hoping that the extended siege of Zardana would force Il-ghazi's forces to break up into foraging parties.

[198] Dubais ibn-Sadaka, ruler of a Bedouin tribe.

[199] This is probably a distortion of an Arabic name, and was almost certainly not the same Bochard mentioned in Book One. Walter the Chancellor, I.6, p. 104, n. 169.

[200] This reference to Islamic law is presumably designed to further discredit Il-ghazi, as, according to Walter, he even contravened his own customs after Zardana surrendered. See: The depiction of Islam and eastern Christendom, p. 64.

[201] Walter provides a lengthy description of Robert's own fate later in the text. See: Walter the Chancellor, II.14, pp. 159-62.

happened thus. And then it was no wonder if the king, who was second only to the Lord as lord and defender of Christendom,[202] suffered greatly once more on account of the damage and disgrace to Christians; yet he was comforted by the power of the Holy Cross, and prepared himself manfully to fight against the enemy on the following morning.[203]

Il-ghazi already knew that the king was lingering at Danith from the report of those men who had been skirmishing around our army, so he garrisoned Zardana, and in the evening he and Tughtegin[204] with all his own army and with those soldiers whom they had sent on before, were joined together with those who were on watch and lying in wait around our men, so that in the morning they could launch a sudden attack while our men were asleep; for this tactic had often served many of them well.[205]

The king, however, was not sleepy, but even on that very day,[206] when the enemies mentioned earlier came, the Provider of advantage, protected by the venerable symbol by which both kings reign and enemies are conquered,[207] ensured that he who had often experienced the enemy's existence and wars,[208] with the archbishop of Caesarea[209] and other followers of the true

---

[202] This remarkable statement represents the height of Walter's praise for Baldwin II. See: Baldwin of Le Bourcq, p. 27.

[203] This must date the fall of Zardana to 13 August 1119.

[204] This is the first time that Walter mentions the presence of Tughtegin, atabeg of Damascus, amongst the Muslim forces. Arab sources inform us that Il-ghazi had made a military pact with Tughtegin in June 1119. When the Damascene forces failed to appear at Qinnasrin, the appointed site, Il-ghazi proceeded to al-Atharib without them, and it was only in early August that Tughtegin's forces actually united with those of Aleppo. Kemal ed-Din, p. 620. The Damascene writer Ibn al-Qalanisi, p. 159, provides a slightly different version of events, asserting that Tughtegin joined Il-ghazi at the start of the campaign against Antioch. He may be distorting events, however, in order to maintain Tughtegin's position at the forefront of his account.

[205] A surprise dawn attack had brought Il-ghazi victory at the Field of Blood. Walter the Chancellor, II.4, p. 124. Walter appears to be encouraging his audience to compare Roger and Baldwin II.

[206] 14 August 1119. See: Walter the Chancellor, II.12, p. 155, n. 223.

[207] The Jerusalemite relic of the True Cross.

[208] Walter stresses Baldwin's long military experience, combined with the aid of God, to explain his coming success.

[209] Evremar, archbishop of Caesarea (1108-1129), the former patriarch of Jerusalem. B. Hamilton, *The Latin Church in the Crusader States*, pp. 56-7.

religion, arranged for their tents to be gathered up by night, the soldiers to be
put on alert and all things needful for warriors to be settled thus, so that if the
enemy launched a surprise attack on them they would find nothing sluggish
and nothing disordered, but would discover that by God's power and His sign
the Christians thrived in trading blows and destroying the enemy; but in case
it should rather happen that he could take them on en masse, he arranged
himself with his entire army, battle-lines drawn up, as dawn was breaking
over the land, to ride towards Hab; truly only then he welcomed war, and it
was inevitable.[210]

II.12   *The battle against Il-ghazi and the king's victory through the power of the invincible Holy Cross.*

In the morning, therefore, the health-giving symbol[211] was sent ahead, nine
battle-lines were drawn up at the royal command, and the Christians, having
committed themselves to God and the power of the Holy Cross in the manner
of warriors everywhere, set out enthusiastically on the march, proceeding in
this order: three lines were placed in the vanguard and the infantry was
positioned to the rear, so that they could protect them and be protected by
them; the royal force, prepared for the protection of the former and the latter,
fell in in the necessary order for all; the line of the count of Tripoli, a very
vigorous knight, was placed on the right, with the barons' lines on the
left,[212] and after the king's command everybody was put in his rightful
place.[213] The enemy, positioned all around them[214] in the faint light of

---

[210] Walter stresses that Baldwin avoided battle as long as possible and was thus neither incautious nor overly zealous to act the aggressor in battle.

[211] The True Cross.

[212] This may indicate that the Antiochene nobility held the left flank. This was certainly the opinion of William of Tyre, XII.12, p. 561. See: Walter as a military source, p. 55.

[213] Walter stresses that Baldwin II was in overall command of all the Latin forces, including those of Tripoli. From Walter's account the forthcoming battle appears to have taken place on, or in close proximity, to Tall Danith itself. Although he did note that Baldwin had decided 'to ride towards Hab' to seek battle this conflict does not appear to have taken place outside that town, because Walter noted that in its aftermath some Latins 'escaped to Hab' while Baldwin himself was forced to seek supplies in Hab, setting out for the town in the evening of 14 August and only 'returning to the battle-field in the morning'. Even though he was almost certainly not an eye-witness to these events, Walter's evidence is probably more accurate than that of Fulcher of Chartres, III.4, p. 627, who located the battle at Zardana, as

dawn, made a loud din with drums and trumpets: they made a din and shouted, shouted and barked, barked and boasted. And since by these noises they expected to put off the Christians from their first step and to force them to scatter, they persevered eagerly with twice as much shouting, from here and there often inflicting savage blows with arrows and javelins.[215] And when they were unable to achieve in this way what they were attempting and they had realized that our men were falling in boldly and fighting back manfully, they took courage from the proud persistence of the multitude of warriors, being very keen to destroy the large infantry, which was seriously holding them back, since they saw that it was being protected by the battle-lines in the vanguard and the lines were protected by it, inspired to zeal after the blows inflicted by lances and arrows, they slung their bows on their arms, took out their swords and they assaulted our men with all their might, in such a way that many were now scattered, and they even made that very splendid battle-line of the count become mixed up with the royal battle-line.

There it was certainly evident that the count's knightly nature did not go astray: for truly his men were scattered and entirely put to flight, and the three battle-lines were scattered; he alone or with a few committed soldiers, dealing blows in turn and receiving blows in turn, was withstanding the enemy, and he set himself with steadfast heart to die or live with the Lord's Cross and the king.[216] Meanwhile the aforesaid battle-lines had been put to flight, and the greater part of our infantry, struck by the Lord's leave, fell to the enemy's sword, and at once from right and left, from the rear and from the front the enemy assaulted our men with a heavy charge. In this battle the archbishop of Caesarea, a man of venerable life, called Evremar, who was

---

Walter is supported by Kemal ed-Din, pp. 620-21. Thus, although it is historiographically inconvenient, it is probably more accurate to describe this conflict as the second battle of Tall Danith, rather than the battle of Hab as most historians have to date. R.C. Smail, *Crusading warfare*, pp. 180-81.

[214] This statement, when combined with the later description of the battle, suggests that the Latin forces were actually surrounded by Il-ghazi's army.

[215] This Muslim tactic of an initial missile attack was probably designed to break up the Latin battle formation.

[216] Walter does not criticize Pons in any way for allowing his forces to be pushed back into those of the king, but focuses upon his individual heroism.

wearing his priestly surplice, not a hauberk,[217] was carrying the Lord's Cross in his venerable hands; by its protection, even though he was struck by an arrow, as many bear witness, he remained unharmed, only a drop of his blood being visible as testimony. In that place the king's horse was wounded in the neck. When the archbishop perceived this and realized that the infidels were prevailing over our men, he turned the Lord's Cross towards them and proclaimed loudly: 'May you be cursed by the holy power of this Cross, most wicked men, and may you be scattered and put to flight by divine vengeance and perish very soon!'[218]

The king, therefore, relying on his manly courage, found out for sure which side the hordes of the enemy were stronger against our men by force of warriors, and there, calling upon the protection and assistance of the Holy Cross, he charged at great speed, overthrew the infidels and forced them to scatter; in such a way, I tell you, that he put to flight by his attack first the vanguard then the rearguard;[219] and it was enacted thus, in that battle through the agency of God's providence, that both sides considered they were both vanquished and victors.[220] But not in the same way: for indeed our men who were defeated escaped to Hab, to Antioch and even further away to Tripoli, where they announced that our men had been taken away to die. From elsewhere as well the Turks had fled to Aleppo with a charge of certain of our men, and they claimed that Il-ghazi and Tughtegin had been taken away with all the army of Turcomans to destruction. The Author and Examiner of

---

[217] A 'superpellicium' or surplice is a linen vestment worn by the clergy when carrying out many religious functions, with the exception of Mass. Walter seems keen to indicate that he was not dressed for combat and was, therefore, presumably not participating actively in battle.

[218] Walter depicts a miracle of the True Cross and implies that the tide of the battle was turned by Evremar's use of the relic. See: Walter's attitude to religion and piety, p. 71.

[219] Walter connects the Latin success at Tall Danith with Baldwin's personal bravery and prowess. This is in contrast to the account of Roger of Salerno's victory in 1115, in which Walter described the military achievements of a large number of individuals. Walter the Chancellor, I.6-7, pp. 102-5. See: Baldwin of Le Bourcq, p. 31.

[220] Most sources depict the battle of Tall Danith as inconclusive. See: Baldwin of Le Bourcq, pp. 29-30; and Walter as a military source, p. 55. Walter goes on to explain why the outcome of the battle was so confused. Troops from both sides fled from the field carrying tidings of defeat back to Antioch, Tripoli and Aleppo. More importantly either side could make claim to victory by the conventions of warfare, as Baldwin was able to claim possession of the battlefield, while Il-ghazi captured one of the king's banners. In reality the battle did at least put an end to Il-ghazi's 1119 campaign against the principality.

supreme justice granted this to King Baldwin through the power of the Holy Cross and as the piety of his life required, because both the enemy fled and with a few men he even obtained the field of battle freely and absolutely with the triumph of God's victory. Moreover it happened that a part of the enemy met a part of our army away from the rest as they returned weary from the charge, their failing horses with a groom who was carrying one of the king's banners; and when by ill-luck the infidels spotted the exhausted men, they destroyed the horses easily by shooting arrows at them, and the soldiers were compelled to submit by the force of their weapons; some were handed over to death and some were captured and put in chains and taken to Aleppo without the king's knowledge.

The king, claiming the battle-field, heard from a messenger that some of his men had fled to Hab and were still there, so he hastened to send the victory announcements for them two or three times. Although they knew very well from this sure sign and these sure indications that the king had won the field with the triumph of victory, yet they were afraid to approach him, partly as a result of fear and partly because they were overcome by shame, and yet they did not want not to return, lest they should seem utterly to have deserted. Therefore the king was forced by shortage of food and drink to set out in the evening for Hab, returning to the battle-field in the morning;[221] as was fitting, he ordered that both those wounded on the field and the dead to be brought from there and all around, whatever remained left over from the battle; he himself took charge of sending his men to look after what he had seen while riding. He even remained on the battle-field long enough to be certain from sure announcements and sure signs that the infidels had been defeated. In that battle, it is thought, five or seven hundred of our infantry and a hundred of our knights died; as they themselves claimed, of the Turks who escaped two or three thousand fell to the swords of the Christians.[222] This victory was won on the eve of the Assumption of the Blessed Virgin Mary by the power of the Holy Cross.[223]

---

[221] Baldwin may in fact have been forced to seek safety at Hab because of a lack of troops remaining on the battlefield. Walter stresses, however, that Baldwin clearly held the field and therefore achieved victory.

[222] Walter claims to have some first hand knowledge of the Muslims' own estimates of losses. See: Walter as a military source, p. 57.

[223] 14 August 1119.

Therefore the renowned king rejoiced and he ordered the ring from his own finger,[224] which was well known to the patriarch and to his sister the princess,[225] to be taken to Antioch, so that he might proclaim by this sign the victory of the Holy Cross and announce that the king had won the field of battle. And so the messenger set off swiftly, proclaiming these things to all the people of Antioch, who were plunged in grief, and he presented the ring to the patriarch on behalf of the king as a sign of the Christian victory. What then? All unanimously, once they had recovered their strength, reformed their behaviour and way of life, and joyfully offered up thanksgiving in their church. After this, moreover, when the triumph of Christianity had been regained by the life-giving power of the Holy Cross, the king returned to Antioch and, as was fitting, he was given a victor's welcome, further than usual outside the city,[226] by all the people and clergy with hymns and religious songs, and he was led happily and joyfully by a procession of the life-giving Cross to the church of St Peter, from where he had undertaken the journey and the beginning of the successful expedition, to the praise and glory of the Highest King and the Highest Lord, whom no one else can please except out of that which he himself will grant,[227] God who lives and reigns, blessed for ever and ever.[228] Amen.[229]

II.13 *The false joy of the enemy at Aleppo, who pretend that victory has fallen to them, and the true joy of the prisoners there, who have secretly been told about the king's victory.*

Now, moreover, I shall explain in orderly fashion so that people may see and

---

[224] Walter once again depicts a ring as a significant token. Walter the Chancellor, II.6, p. 129.

[225] Cecilia of Le Bourcq, widow of Roger of Salerno. William of Tyre, XI.22, p. 527. She was probably endowed with land in Cilicia in the aftermath of the Field of Blood, as in 1126 she issued a charter as Lady of Tarsus making grants to the religious house of Our Lady of Josaphat. 'Chartes de l'abbaye de Notre-Dame de Josaphat', p. 123, no. 13. Orderic Vitalis, XI.25, p. 108, probably confused her with Cecilia of France.

[226] Walter perhaps implies a further comparison between Baldwin's victory in 1119 and Roger's in 1115. Walter the Chancellor, I.7, p. 106.

[227] Romans. 12.1; Psalm. 51.18-19.

[228] A liturgical reference, the conclusion of certain prayers.

[229] Walter seems to draw his narrative to a conclusion at this point. For a discussion of whether chapters 13-16 were written at a later date see: Our knowledge of Walter, p. 8.

hear certain of those things which need explaining and which I experienced earlier concerning the destruction of the Christian prisoners.[230] For on that day when Tughtegin, king of Damascus, and Il-ghazi, prince of the Turks, were conquered by the power of the Holy Cross and the royal hand and were put to flight and scattered, it was announced to Il-ghazi's son, who was castellan of Aleppo in his place,[231] that the nobles themselves had fallen to the Christians' swords along with the greater part of their army. When they heard this, certain of the more powerful men of Aleppo who had earlier been ransomed by the hand and command of the wicked prince, and certain men who had been deprived of their homes and other public honours, those same things having been forfeited to the Turks, while appearing in public to grieve and protest, privately rejoiced, and they endeavoured to hinder by various sorts of destruction those who had escaped and were fleeing. For indeed they cunningly sent soldiers and other predators after the vanquished, so that as they plundered they would cut down the fugitives and in return for the losses inflicted on them by the Aleppans, would destroy them in vengeful rage. And it was done in such a way that those escaping outside the town were punished in different directions in different ways, and mournful lamentations were brought forth for the dead inside the city with some true tears and some false, in such a way that that the very town resounded on the surface and at the foundations of the walls and towers and various buildings just as if the whole was struck by lightning and thunder and was collapsing in pieces and being overturned from the foundations.[232]

And thus it was carried out, as their custom dictates: for when they have been conquered an edict goes out, and they announce that they have won and with pretended victory rejoicings, lest the minds of the desolate should despair, they rouse them to rejoicings by musical instruments: drums, flutes and blaring bugles. Now they were getting on with these things more joyfully and boldly than usual, in such a way that the Christian prisoners, who were then being held bound at Aleppo and subject to various kinds of tortures, would hear them and their minds be tormented more and more and they would lose faith in every way. They indeed were forearmed with the weapons of faith,

---

[230] In confirmation of his earlier statements Walter indicates that he was an eye-witness to the treatment of the Latin captives. See: Our knowledge of Walter, pp. 5-6.

[231] Sulaiman ibn-Il-ghazi.

[232] This confused passage may be intended to indicate a degree of disunity within Aleppo.

although they were thought to have suffered heartache and much harm for this reason, which they had heard from the report of the infidels, that their king and his men had fallen in battle;[233] yet they never wavered from the worship of the true faith, but much more zealously than usual from the bottom of their hearts they prayed to God with vigils and prayers for the safety of the Christian army and for themselves. Moreover, it happened that they had heard from a secret message of certain faithful and even infidels, that the rejoicings and various celebrations which were carried out in public were in fact full of sorrow and utmost grief over the destruction of the wicked and the victory of the Christians, which were clearly due to the remarkable power of the Holy Cross and the presence of King Baldwin who gained the field of battle. They even heard that Tughtegin had come to grief with Il-ghazi. So what happened? Whatever bitterness and sorrow they had earlier suffered, when they heard this are said to have been[234] entirely turned to sweetness, and they prayed without cease to Him from whom all good things proceed,[235] devoutly and with the desires of a pure heart.

Refreshed by this joy, they spent the day until the third part or middle of the night rejoicing, celebrating the sure hope of victory, then unexpectedly they heard from different sides shouts of men which were different from the earlier ones, rejoicings more intense than the others, instruments, drums bolder than they were played before, sending out noise and tumult. Therefore the prisoners were amazed and wondered what new thing their change might mean and what unusual thing the people of the whole town all around were predicting by kindling lights with loud shouts. Moreover, it had happened that Tughtegin and Il-ghazi, who had been put to flight from the battle into the region of Berroia,[236] weaponless and weary, had returned with a few men to Aleppo and because of this the aforesaid proclamation of triumph swelled marvellously among the Aleppans inside and outside. Then once again that which had been welcome and sweet to the prisoners gave way by most wretched fate to the opposite when they realized what had happened. In fact,

---

[233] This exchange of information would indicate a shared language between the Latins and their Aleppan captors.

[234] The use of this phrase almost seems to contradict Walter's earlier intimation that he experienced these events personally. See: Our knowledge of Walter, pp. 5-6.

[235] A liturgical reference to the collect for the fifth Sunday after Easter and Vigil of Ascension.

[236] This was the Greek name for the region around Aleppo.

very early the next day, while they were spending their time at prayer, messengers arrived from the accursed princes, and a considerable crowd of Aleppans came with them, bringing the heads of seven soldiers, knocking and hammering on the iron-clad door of the prison with their naked swords, as was their custom, this being the way they used to drag out the prisoners day after day for beheading, and they entered the prison shouting these words: 'We are bringing a message to you from the victor Il-ghazi, that your king and the rest of the Christian rabble have fallen to his sword in battle,' and they showed the heads to the prisoners, saying, 'The star of law himself has sent here these dishes to be a meal for you. And not long afterwards, when you have seen the head and banner of your king himself, you will certainly feel the nature and magnitude of the power of our excellent law, which henceforth you do not consider opposing.' After speaking thus, concealing the course of events, the messengers returned as if happy to their masters who were lying in tents outside the gate, trying to lessen their dishonour and disgrace by drinking wine. Moreover the prisoners, by listening at a small crack in the wall, where they would frequently hear the deeds of the accursed princes from the reports of the faithful,[237] then also found out the truth, that very great losses had occurred on both sides, and so, I say, the heathens with pretended rejoicing on the outside were tormented inside in their hearts by the loss of their triumph, while the Christians, who had recovered their triumph, celebrated their certain and complete victory in Christ.[238]

II.14 *The martyrdom of Robert fitz-Fulk, which is distinguished not so much by its piety as by its cruelty.*

On the fifth day[239] Robert fitz-Fulk,[240] who had been dragged away and

---

[237] This is probably a reference to eastern Christians,

[238] Although Walter reports the uncertainty at Aleppo in exhaustive length, he is still keen to stress that in 'reality' the Latins were victorious at the battle of Tall Danith. See: Baldwin of Le Bourcq, pp. 29-30.

[239] This may refer to the fifth day after the battle at Tall Danith, namely 19 August 1119, or possibly the five days after the arrival of Il-ghazi and Tughtegin at Aleppo.

[240] Robert fitz-Fulk the Leper, lord of Zardana, had presumably been captured when that town fell. This would suggest that he did not answer Baldwin II's call to arms prior to the battle of Tall Danith. Walter the Chancellor, II.10;   Kemal ed-Din, pp. 620-22;   Usamah ibn-Munqidh, p. 149.

torn apart by the hands of the impious, was presented to Il-ghazi at Aleppo;
on account of this there was two-fold happiness and incredible declarations of
praises, all unanimously, applauding him with their hands, flocking to him as
if to see a monster, not to redeem him from his punishment, but so that they
could mock him by their marvelling, and by mocking him they could torture
him, and by torturing him they could tear him limb from limb, and by this
savage kind of vengeance they might rejoice to lessen the pain inflicted on
themselves by him a long time since; but as their lord forbade it, they dared
not touch him.[241] So what happened about this? Since the people were
unable to do it, he turned upon himself and plucked ceaselessly at his hair and
beard. Moreover it pleased the wicked prince to send him for punishment to
Tughtegin, the investigator and discoverer of various tortures;[242] and so he
was sent, bound very tightly with iron chains on his neck and hands. When
he saw him, Tughtegin, instead of showing his pleasure, put on an
exaggerated expression, with a bestial grin, and with a piercing gaze he
goggled at that very knight, at whose hands and by whose ingenuity, with the
rest of the faithful, he had often incurred losses to his possessions and very
many injuries to his body when he was evading him.[243] What more? He
received Robert when he was presented to him, having received him he
examined him, having examined him he condemned him, having condemned
him he decreed that he should be put to death as he deserved, speaking in this
way: 'Ha, Robert! Ha! Look how much use your law is to you, look where
error and unbelief have brought you. Whence have you been led to this, that
you have striven to corrupt our law with your law and the better one with all

---

[241] Walter makes no direct mention of Robert's leprosy although the reference to him as
a 'monster' and the fact that the Muslim's feared to touch him may be related to his illness.
Usamah called him 'Robert the Leper' (rubart al-abras), while Kemal ed-Din noted that he
was known as 'the leper count'. Usamah ibn-Munqidh, p. 149; Kemal ed-Din, pp. 621-2.

[242] Usamah recorded a slightly different version of this meeting between Robert and
Tughtegin. He first observed that the two had become friends during the Latin/Muslim alliance
of 1115. Then, after Robert was captured during the battle of Tall Danith, he attempted to set
his own ransom at 10,000 dinars. In response Il-ghazi sent him to Tughtegin, saying 'perhaps
the latter will scare him and we shall get a higher ransom for him.' When Robert arrived
before Tughtegin, however, his former friend proceeded to behead him with his own hand.
This anecdote fits well with Usamah's interest in unusual twists of fate. Usamah ibn-Munqidh,
pp. 149-50. For the alliance, see, Walter the Chancellor, I.2, pp. 87-8.

[243] This familiarity with Robert must have come not only as a result of the alliance in
1115, but also because he held the fortified town of Zardana, on the border between Antioch
and Aleppo.

others? For what reason has your hand, your hand, I say, as trivial as a worm creeping upon the earth, raised itself against the power and dominion of our men? Behold, hitherto, as our destiny compels, we have proceeded by falling and rising again; only by that same change of fortunes do we believe that our justice is restored to us by God's gift. Moreover, I remind you that in the past you paid tribute to me from your possessions,[244] and so for this reason I cannot find it in me to kill you.'

And he sent him back to Il-ghazi, saying by way of an intermediary's words: 'I prefer this man to die by your sword rather than mine.' And he did not put off inflicting death on him for any reason other than for Robert to feel that he was being mocked by both of them in turn, and so that the dread and might of both of them could work upon him. Therefore, having been mocked in the presence of Il-ghazi, the wretched Robert was once more presented to Tughtegin, who drew his sword and said to him: 'Renounce your law, or die!' Robert replied to this: 'I renounce all the works of Satan and his vices, I do not renounce dying for Christ.' At these words the impious one, overcome by rage, separated the Christian's head from his body by a stroke of his sword, and he handed it over to the judiciary herald[245] to be put on public show; he granted the body to the clamouring crowd to tear to pieces as their chosen gift. And so what happened? The man bore the head through the squares and districts of the town, showing it and presenting it to the wealthy, he received from them five hundred bezants and various gifts and returned rejoicing to his wicked lord, thanking him for his generosity towards him, and on bended knees he prayed from his heart and returned the head. That wicked man ordered a drinking vessel to be made for him very soon from the skull by a craftsman of impious skill, fashioned from purest gold and precious jewels and wonderfully decorated, which could be exhibited as a symbol of his courage and victory for him to drink from, and his descendants, during festive celebrations. At once Tughtegin, having selected chiefs of his people, requested of Il-ghazi, through messengers, that by way of repayment of true friendship, since he had accepted from him sixty thousand Saracen bezants,

---

[244] There is fairly abundant evidence that Aleppo and other nearby Muslim settlements made regular tribute payments to Antioch in this period. This is, however, the first reference to Latin payments to a Muslim power. Kemal ed-Din, pp. 596-8; Ibn al-Qalanisi, p. 99, p. 106, p. 132; Ibn al-Athir, p. 279, p. 298; Usamah ibn-Munqidh, p. 150.

[245] Walter may have invented this office or transposed it from Latin practice.

he would allow him to enter the prison of the Franks so that when he had beheaded all who were in that prison with his own hand he could revel in the bloodshed instead of taking a bath and be restored to youth like an eagle.[246]

Il-ghazi, indeed, heard his plan and replied to his nobles in this way: 'I declare that the petition of this very great man is right, fitting and most just. However, there is another thing which I consider should be done first for the good of our law and to our advantage, and when it is carried out I shall entirely comply both in these things and in others with the wishes and authority of so great a friend. Moreover, lest the outcome of my plan should be unknown to you and to him, you should prudently understand what you should give heed to and what should be related to him: we are not yet able to hold the castle of 'Azaz,[247] which is reckoned to be the gate of entry and exit for Aleppo. For, because the Franks have re-mustered their forces and grown strong against us, this is too great a hindrance both to recovering the aforesaid castle and keeping the castles already recovered intact from their ingenuity and power. Because if we should allow the prisoners of their race whom we are holding, both noble and of lesser birth, to be put to death in this way, we shall surely suffer, both in recovering the castles and in other things, losses more severe than usual. And the plan is for us to see if by some exchange of prisoners, in whatever guise, or by surrendering a castle or in other ways we can deceive their clever and prudent king.[248] For truly while he lives it goes without saying that we can in no way, except by force or by

---

[246] Psalms, 102 (103).5: 'qui replet in bonis desiderium tuum: renovabitur ut aquilae iuuentus tua'. The suggestion that Tughtegin wished to bathe in human blood as a ritual designed to perpetuate immortality is probably fantastical.

[247] 'Azaz lay on the Roman road between Antioch and Edessa. Along with al-Atharib and Zardana it lay on the borderline between the principality and Aleppo. In 1098, during the First Crusade's sojourn in northern Syria, Omar, then ruler of 'Azaz, sought to throw off Aleppan rule by forming a temporary alliance with Godfrey of Bouillon. Albert of Aachen, V.7-12; Raymond of Aguilers, pp. 88-9; Kemal ed-Din, p. 586. Kemal ed-Din suggests that Tancred of Hauteville occupied the town shortly before his death in 1112, but if this were the case any Latin presence was short-lived as 'Azaz was again in Muslim hands in 1114. Kemal ed-Din, p. 601, p. 607. In 1118, however, Roger of Salerno did conquer the town with the assistance of the Armenian Leo, the son of Constantine. Walter suggests that Il-ghazi placed considerable strategic value upon possession of 'Azaz. This would support the theory that Il-ghazi's primary aim in 1119 was to recapture the line of fortified sites made up by Zardana, al-Atharib and 'Azaz.

[248] Walter's laudatory depiction of Baldwin II even extends to compliments from his enemies.

ingenuity, regain that castle, nor any of the land which is subject to his authority. Therefore the prisoners have to be allowed still to live, so that first their princes and lords are oppressed by an avenging hand, then afterwards Tughtegin himself may satisfy his bloodthirsty soul by torturing them again in whatever way he chooses.' The messengers heard this, then they returned and reported what they had heard to their lord, and they praised what the star of law advised as being fitting and profitable; when he had heard them Tughtegin, although unwillingly, yet consented and submitted.

II.15 *The martyrdom of other prisoners of all ranks.*

Moreover both of them were frightened by the flight and destruction which had happened to them, and, having put the cavalry out of their minds along with the rest of their concerns for the good of the state, they were paying attention only to drinking, during which, in the desperate hours of night and day, they sent their executioners to bring the prisoners in flocks like sheep and they made them stand before them. Some of them were hanged by ropes from a post, with their heads turned downwards, their feet upwards, and exposed to constant blows of arrows as the stuff of dreadful slaughter. Some were buried up to the groin, some up to the navel and some up to the chin in a pit in the ground, as the hands of the wicked ones brandished spears, and they underwent for Christ the end of a life full of sorrow. Several of them, indeed, were thrown with every single limb cut off into the squares and districts, as a spectacle of wonderful justice for the passers-by, and the more the infidels' drunkenness raged, the more the perversity of their tortures increased. This was made known to many as the result of drinking in the master's palace; for indeed on that day when Il-ghazi lay drunk by the madness of wine in his palace after the battle, all of the distinguished Christian prisoners,[249] as many as were in Aleppo, were brought before him together on his own orders. There, indeed, in front of the palace entrance where almost the entire population of the town had assembled, as those same people shouted out and longed for the desired outcome of the execution of the prisoners, thirty-seven

---

[249] If Walter was indeed a captive in Aleppo at this time it can be assumed that he would have been amongst those taken before Il-ghazi.

knights and footsoldiers[250] were handed over to a most wretched slaughter, to be executed with equal torment. Their bodies were beheaded in a moment, and a wave of blood flowed forth and spattered all the pavement of the entrance hall of the royal palace.[251]

At length the others besides these, soldiers of both battles, as many nobles as others, bound painfully tightly, were brought before the infidel in his exuberance from horrific drinking, onto the pavement where they were mocked by the bystanders and afflicted by insults and fears, and driven by many cuffs and goads of affliction, disfigured by the plucking of their beards and hair, embarrassed by their shameful nakedness, their teeth chattered,[252] their bowels trembled and they gaped heavenwards; in place of heaven, on earth nothing was more certain for them than the threatening blows of the sword, and they were tormented in mind and body. Individually, indeed, one after another they were called into the presence of the wicked one and were required by him, through an interpreter's words, to say which they preferred: either to forswear the Christians' law or to be painfully beheaded at once by a blow of his own sword. However, he was unable to wring from them any word or deed contrary to the true faith.

So when he heard the nobles' reply, full of faith, hope and charity,[253] and since they did not dread his threats and to suffer for Christ,[254] he sprang up, drew his sword and set out into their midst, to walk around in a circle and fix each in turn with staring eyes, and he ordered a certain soldier to be seized, thinking that he was a priest who was there with the prisoners, and he cut off his head with his own hand and sword, then he returned into the circle, drawing his sword in the midst of the prisoners in view of each of them, and he demanded bezants to be offered to him immediately, not that he wanted

---

[250] This level of precision would support the premise that Walter was an eye-witness to these events.

[251] It is unlikely that the palace at Aleppo was referred to as a royal residence in Islamic tradition.

[252] A common biblical phrase, e.g. Matt. 8.12: 'dentibus stridere'.

[253] A reference to St Paul, I Cor. 13.13.

[254] There is some inconsistency in Walter's account at this point. He is keen to highlight the atrocious treatment of the Latins and the extreme fear it inspired, while still maintaining that because of their Christian conviction they felt no 'dread' when Il-ghazi gave them the option of apostasy or death.

them to be ransomed with the money, but because under the influence of drunkenness he wanted to ruin them. Suddenly he ordered another of them to be seized, called Arnulf, seneschal of Marash,[255] a man of great piety, and he gave the sword to the patriarch of Damascus,[256] saying: 'Strike, strike! It is certainly fitting!' The *archadius* took the sword, conscience-stricken,[257] and said to a certain great emir: 'You carry out this act of respect for our law in my place! So great a man should lose his head at the hand of a great knight.'

After the man was beheaded, Il-ghazi, taking back his sword once more, came into the middle with the one purpose that all should be slain in the same way. But the Author of supreme piety granted to the prisoners that whatever Il-ghazi's wickedness intended to do, it should be changed by God's agreement to protect them. For it came about that at that moment there arrived there as a gift from Dubais, king of the Arabs, a horse of amazing beauty, adorned with bridle and saddle and trappings of rare and precious craftsmanship, decorated from its ears to its trimmed hooves with Arabian gold and precious jewels; when he saw it Il-ghazi threw aside his sword and was transformed by joy; he entered the inner chamber with his nobles and decked himself with very special ornaments of marvellous worth and craftsmanship. He commanded the nobles at once to call the prisoners to account, so that they heard from each of them how much someone could afford as ransom for his life. Having spoken thus, he mounted the horse and went off to Tughtegin, the minister of the Antichrist. So the nobles inquired of each of the prisoners, in place of their master, for how much they could be ransomed. When they had heard the price of each one, they wrote it all down on paper according to whether the price was more or less and, when this was done, the prisoners were sent back to their prisons.

And so with the different kinds of tortures by which the prisoners were worn

---

[255] The seneschal, or steward, was probably one of the highest officers within the lordship of Marash. See: Walter the Chancellor, II.5, p. 126, n. 86.

[256] From the Latin 'patriarchae Damasceno'. There was no Christian patriarch of Damascus, so Walter was wrongly attributing this title to some form of Islamic imam. In the next sentence he styles him as 'archadius', which may be an attempt to render the Arabic 'al-qadi', 'the judge'.

[257] Walter suggests that an Islamic holy man might feel the same unease as a Christian priest at the prospect of carrying out physical violence.

down in the Saracens' prisons I had much indeed which was amazing and astounding to describe and put into words;[258] but since kings, princes and other powerful people of the world, and even powerless men of the same condition and of the same faith as these men were themselves, inflict many different punishments on their prisoners to extort money when they capture them justly and when they capture them unjustly[259] and since nearly all kinds of mortals, inspired by the devil, are accustomed to take their examples rather from evil than from good things, I think it is better for me to keep quiet about the kind and quantity of their tortures than to express them, lest Christians bring the same to bear on Christians and turn them into accustomed usage.[260] But that miraculous thing which happened to the prisoners in prison I am spreading abroad for the compassion of people living now and as a written memorial for people in the future.

II.16 *One of the knights, Sanson, has a vision foretelling his own martyrdom. Il-ghazi's last battles and his disgraceful death.*

One night, when the prisoners had relaxed their limbs in sleep – such sleep, I say, as could be had in their wretched circumstances – a vision appeared to a certain knight, Sanson of Bruera by name,[261] in which he saw the heavens open and from them our Lord Jesus Christ, with the adornment and magnificence of his powers, sank from the height of heaven down upon the prison, and he called that very Sanson, commanding him three times to come to Him with his companions, and as they came to Him He stretched out His right arm from the top of the prison to where they were and with His right thumb, dipped in oil and chrism, He marked the sign of the Holy Cross on the

---

[258] Walter strongly implies that these are his first-hand experiences. See: Our knowledge of Walter, pp. 5-6.

[259] Walter suggests that there were customs governing the capture and treatment of prisoners.

[260] In this remarkable passage Walter qualifies much of his previous criticism of Muslim practice by observing that Christians also had the potential to carry out such acts of torture and abuse. See: The depiction of Islam and eastern Christendom, p. 63.

[261] This individual is unidentified. See, *Galterii Cancellarii, Bella Antiochena*, ed. H. Hagenmeyer, p. 298, n. 1.

forehead of each of them.[262] Among those singled out by name in the vision there were some whom the Lord did not mark in the same way, and when He was asked by Sanson why he would leave them out, it is reported He replied to him thus: 'I do not want more; at another time, when it pleases me, I shall mark the rest.' Sanson was awoken from this vision, and when as usual he awoke his brother prisoners in the middle of the night to pray,[263] after their early morning worship was completed he mentioned to them this vision.[264] What happened in detail? That same day all those who had been marked and others with them were led outside the gate to the gallows, where the prince of wickedness was intent upon celebratory drinking with leading members of Aleppo's entire nobility. When he saw them the master-criminal rejoiced and said to the nobles: 'Look how I wish the knights to return free from ransom or reward to their lord and king, and, so that each one may receive his gift from my very own hand, let them come now, led forward one after another, as is fitting.'

And so Sanson was brought to him first, and suffered capital punishment at the hand of that very Il-ghazi, and he was adorned with the name of martyr and presented to the Lord to reign with the saints,[265] and truly the same end was sanctioned with regard to the other twenty-four marked men. And there is something I consider should not be kept quiet: among those men there was a certain youth who was beheaded, son of the viscount of Acre,[266] and in the presence of all who were there, by the power and a miracle of the Lord, his body transported itself to another place from the place where it lay;[267] and when this happened the wicked one lost his powers, foaming with blood which

---

[262] Walter may be alluding to the signing with the cross of individuals intending to participate in a crusade. The primary accounts of the First Crusade make frequent references to participants' visions of Christ and the apostles. Perhaps the most famous examples are Peter Bartholomew's visions of St Andrew in relation to the Holy Lance. J.S.C. Riley-Smith, *The First Crusade and the Idea of Crusading*, p. 95.

[263] This reference to Sanson regularly leading prayers serves to reinforce the image of his piety.

[264] Walter may well have been amongst this group of prisoners who heard of Sanson's vision first-hand.

[265] This is the most specific description of salvation in Walter's text.

[266] *Galterii Cancellarii, Bella Antiochena*, ed. H. Hagenmeyer, p. 299, n. 18, identifies this individual with 'Petrus Hugonis'.

[267] For a discussion of Walter's attitude to these 'miraculous' occurrences, see: Walter's attitude to religion and piety, p. 72.

poured out, he was crushed and fell, harshly disfigured by a savage kind of passion so that, I tell you, his mouth seemed to form a horrible shapeless mass with his ears and his ears with his nostrils. Therefore the remainder, who had not been marked, were savagely driven and whipped and dragged away back to their prison by gangs of infidels.

Il-ghazi[268] himself was placed in his tent by gangs of his own men, overcome by wine as was his custom, and he lay as if dead in the stink of his own ordure for a period of fifteen days.[269] And he was very often exhausted by this kind of disgraceful passion. Moreover, after this, since he was unable to trick the king and the Christians by force or by ingenuity straight away, he took counsel with Tughtegin and his nobles, slighted the castle of Zardana and garrisoned his own towns, then Il-ghazi ordered the captured nobles and certain others to be ransomed from his land and price of the ransom to be assigned to the knights and serjeants who were to defend the land, then he himself set out for Mardin, a particular castle in his own territory,[270] to assemble a horde of Turcomans greater than usual, on account of the damage done by the Christians, and to return.

What happened in detail? He set out, he assembled an enormous horde of Turcomans as well as Arabs[271] and, when they were assembled and he saw so great a multitude, he was carried away by a feeling of immense arrogance, and he decided to ride against King David[272] in Iberia[273] with one of the sultans of Khorasan,[274] so that once he had been killed or disinherited, Il-ghazi would be able to kill the Christians and subjugate Jerusalem and Antioch

---

[268] The remaining sections of Walter's account are focused upon Il-ghazi's fate. He seems keen to demonstrate that after the 'evil' actions of 1119 Il-ghazi's power waned. Walter also refers to his physical infirmity and unpleasant death, which were presumably linked to the 'miracle' at Aleppo. See: The depiction of Islam and eastern Christendom, pp. 65-6.

[269] Walter does not make it clear whether this infirmity was the result of drunkenness or divine intervention.

[270] Il-ghazi had, in 1105, succeeded his brother Soqman as ruler of Mardin, to the far east of Aleppo, in the Jazireh. P.M. Holt, The Age of the Crusades, p. 28.

[271] Walter made an accurate distinction between Seldjuk Turks and the longer established Arab population of the Near East. See: The depiction of Islam and eastern Christendom, p. 59.

[272] King David II of Georgia (1089-1125), a Georgian Christian.

[273] A Levantine name for Georgia.

[274] This is probably a reference to Tughrul of Arran, Il-ghazi's ally in this campaign.

freely and absolutely to his authority.[275] But as he rode out in arrogance he met the wrath of God: for on that day when the sultan and Il-ghazi himself entered the king's lands with six hundred thousand[276] to wage war, that very same King David, forearmed with the sign of the Holy Cross,[277] and having between Medes and Christians eighty thousand warriors,[278] drew up his battle-lines between two mountains planted with very thick woodlands, holding fast in the valley where, as rumour had it, the enemy was daring to advance against him. He stood firm and spoke thus: 'Come, soldiers of Christ! If we fight lawfully to protect God's law[279] we shall easily overcome not only the countless attendants of demons, we shall indeed overcome even the demons themselves. Moreover, this is the plan which, if you approve, I consider best for our honour and our advantage, that is to say, we raise our hands to heaven and promise to Almighty God that for His love we shall die on this field of battle before we flee, and so that we cannot flee even if we want to, we shall block the open approaches of this valley, by which we entered it, with very thick heaps of wood, and we shall strike keenly with steadfast courage the enemy who are daring to fight against us at close quarters.'

What happened in detail? The resolution of so great a king, a true and perfect Christian,[280] was praised, approved and carried through to completion. There was no delay: individual battle-lines were deployed, the king positioned two hundred Frankish soldiers which he had in the front line to bear the first blows;[281] and at once on the other side or front of the valley, blocked with

---

[275] For other sources and further discussion of Il-ghazi's campaign against Georgia see: Matthew of Edessa, III.83-4, pp. 226-8; Ibn al-Qalanisi, p. 164; Kemal ed-Din, pp. 628-9; Ibn al-Athir, pp. 330-32; Michael the Syrian, III, p. 206; S. Runciman, *A History of the Crusades*, vol. 2, pp. 159-60.

[276] This manpower estimate seems uncharacteristically extreme, but Matthew of Edessa also reckoned the total number of Muslim troops in this war to be 560,000. Matthew of Edessa, III.83-4, pp. 226-7.

[277] This reference to the Cross emphasises David's Christian faith.

[278] The term 'Medes' is probably intended to indicate inhabitants of Mesopotamia.

[279] This perhaps implies that David's campaign constituted a just war in the same way as the earlier Latin wars described by Walter.

[280] Walter may be emphasising David's Christian perfection in order to make him a suitable punisher of Il-ghazi.

[281] This reference to 'Franks' indicates a Latin presence in this battle, but it is not clear whether these were mercenary troops. Matthew of Edessa mentions the presence of 'one hundred Franks'. Matthew of Edessa, III.84, p. 227.

a great shouting and din of horses and weapons, the fierce banners of the wicked came forth and, as they approached, the mountains and valleys on all sides resounded with the noise of different instruments. However, King David most humbly waited for the fierce attack of so many and urged on his men with manly courage and encouraged them, asserting that the insolent horde of infidels could soon be destroyed by a small band, with the help of the strength of the Holy Cross.[282] Not long afterwards the countless multitude saw the Christians and their spirit of arrogance was stirred up, and they attacked them with a clamorous din; but by the power of the Lord they were blinded in the first assault and fell at the hands of the Franks, put to flight and scattered. What else happened? By God's grace the infidels became as one the stuff of slaughter for the Christians and the Medes together and, as we have learnt in all seriousness from those who took part in the battle, in a flight which lasted for three days four hundred thousand fell to the royal sword.[283] And that same Il-ghazi, who had been wounded in the head, after almost all his men had been killed, was permitted by the Lord to escape with a few men, and, escorted by the king of the Arabs,[284] he reached his homeland half-dead, unarmed and famished.

The following year[285] he was regaining his strength and in the month of July, having gathered together as many battle-lines of knights and infantry as possible, he returned to besiege Zardana, which had been refortified by the king's hand.[286] When he heard this, Joscelin, count of Edessa,[287] took

---

[282] It is not clear whether this is a reference to a relic of the True Cross.

[283] This must represent a considerable exaggeration of manpower losses.

[284] This is a reference to Dubais ibn Sadaka who was allied with Il-ghazi during this campaign. Matthew of Edessa, III.83, p. 227.

[285] 1122, the year of Il-ghazi's death. The preceding campaign against David II of Georgia took place in 1121.

[286] Walter neglects to inform us that Sulaiman ibn-Il-ghazi revolted against his father in 1121, temporarily seizing power in Aleppo. In the period between the summer of 1121 and that of 1122 the Latins took the opportunity to recapture Zardana. At the time of Il-ghazi's offensive it was held by William, the son of Robert fitz-Fulk the Leper. Kemal ed-Din, p. 629, p. 631.

[287] This is Walter's only reference to Joscelin of Courtenay, one of the most prominent figures amongst the early settlers in the Levant. As cousin of Baldwin of Le Bourcq, Joscelin came to prominence in the county of Edessa after 1100. By 1104 he held the town of Marash. Ralph of Caen, p. 710. From c.1108 he transferred his lordship to one of the county's most important towns, Tall Bashir, on the Roman road between Antioch and Edessa. Albert of Aachen, XI.40; Matthew of Edessa, III.43, p. 202; William of Tyre, X.24, p. 483. In c.

advice from the patriarch of Antioch and set out with his own men and Antiochene warriors to Sarmada, to disperse the blockade of Zardana by battle; and when he heard this, the king of Jerusalem, bringing the Jerusalemites, arrived there at a rapid pace, and in front of his tents skirmishing soldiers arrived from the ranks of the infidels to see the Christians' army.[288] What happened in the end? When they saw the Christians the enemy's boldness was subdued by fear, and in the night they gathered up their tents and sent them in advance, and gave up their attempt to damage the castle, and Il-ghazi himself, afflicted by a kind of paralytic illness,[289] returned with his men to Aleppo; but since he did not want to give up the siege, he pretended he was going to go and that he would soon bring there a very great horde both of Arabs and of Parthians; because a man of his religion was ardently intent on the destruction of the Christians. However, it happened that on his litter, on which he was carried about on account of his rank and his infirmity, his filthy soul issued forth from his anus along with a flux of dung from his belly, and it was dragged away by the claws of infernal scorpions to tumble into the halls of deepest hell,[290] which are full of dreadful fires burning without end, blazing and inextinguishable, from which may we be delivered by the grace and mercy of our Lord Himself, Jesus Christ, whose authority is obeyed by all things in heaven, on earth and in hell, world without end. Amen.

The end of the Antiochene wars waged by Prince Roger.

1113, however, he fell out with Count Baldwin, and travelled to the kingdom of Jerusalem, where he was given the lordship of Tiberias by King Baldwin I. William of Tyre, XI.22. It was only after the death of Baldwin I that Joscelin returned to prominence in northern Syria. In return for his support of Baldwin of Le Bourcq's claim to Jerusalem Joscelin was appointed as successor to the county of Edessa, probably taking possession of the city in late 1119. William of Tyre, XII.4, p. 551. After the death of Roger of Salerno and Baldwin II's appointment as regent of Antioch, Joscelin became the only permanent Latin ruler in northern Syria. Walter's suggestion that he was closely involved in the principality's affairs in 1122 is not unique. He was also to command Antiochene troops in 1123 and 1124. Fulcher of Chartres, III.25, pp. 687-9; III.31, pp. 723-6; Kemal ed-Din, pp. 637-8.

[288] See also: Fulcher of Chartres, III.11, p. 649; Kemal ed-Din, pp. 631-2.

[289] Walter may be suggesting that this affliction was linked to the miracle at Aleppo. See Walter the Chancellor, II.16, pp. 65-6.

[290] On his death in 1122 Il-ghazi was succeeded at Aleppo by his nephew Badr ad-Daulah Sulaiman. Ibn al-Qalanisi, p. 166; Kemal ed-Din, pp. 632-4; Matthew of Edessa, III.88, p. 229.

Other Sources

A range of other sources which comment upon the events recorded by Walter the Chancellor are here translated in order to facilitate comparison. Two charters issued by Roger of Salerno are also included.[1]

Fulcher of Chartres

Fulcher wrote a narrative account, 'Historia Hierosolymitana', of the First Crusade and the history of the kingdom of Jerusalem and the Latin East down to 1127. He was King Baldwin I of Jerusalem's chaplain and continued to reside in Jerusalem during Baldwin II's reign until his death in c. 1128. The extracts given below are translated from H. Hagenmeyer's edition of 1913.[2]

II.52
In 1114 a countless multitude of locusts swarmed out of the region of Arabia, flying into the land of Jerusalem, and for some days in the months of April and May they totally laid waste our crops. Then on the feast day of St Laurence there was an earthquake. Moreover, in the following season, on the Ides of November, an earthquake at Mamistra overthrew part of the town. Another great and unbelievable earthquake struck places throughout the region of Antioch in such a way that it overthrew many towns either completely or partially, and brought to the ground both homes and defences, and in the ruins some of the people were suffocated and died. They say that the quake in

---

[1] Three Arabic sources for these events are also available in translations into English. Ibn al Qalanisi, *The Damascus Chronicle of the Crusades*, trans. H.A.R. Gibb (London, 1932), pp. 141-61. Usamah ibn-Munqidh, *Memoirs of an Arab-Syrian gentleman and warrior in the period of the crusades*, trans. P. K. Hitti (Beirut, 1964), pp. 101-5, pp. 148-50. A short extract from Kemal ed-Din's *Chronicle of Aleppo* appears in F. Gabrieli, *Arab Historians of the Crusades* (London, 1969), pp. 36-8.

[2] Fulcher of Chartres, *Historia Hierosolymitana*, ed. H. Hagenmeyer (Heidelberg, 1913), pp. II.52-4, pp. 578-91; III.3-7, pp. 620-42; III.9, pp. 638-42. A full translation of the text is available: Fulcher of Chartres, *A History of the expedition to Jerusalem 1095-1127*, trans. F.R. Ryan, ed. H.S. Fink (Knoxville, 1969). See also: V. Epp, *Fulcher von Chartres: Studien zur Geschichtsschreibung des ersten Kreuzzuges* (Dusseldorf, 1990); D.C. Munro, 'A Crusader', *Speculum*, vol. 7 (1932), pp. 321-35.

Marash, a city which is sixty miles south of Antioch, I think,[3] was so great that it completely destroyed homes and defences and - alas - killed the entire population. Another town as well, which they call Trialeth, near the River Euphrates, was destroyed no less completely.

II.53

In 1115 the Turks forsook their usual openness and boldness, and in the month of June they stealthily crossed the River Euphrates and entered Syria and pitched camp between Antioch and Damascus, that is to say before the town of Shaizar, where they had similarly taken up position four years before, as I have written earlier. When he realized and appreciated this, Tughtegin, the king of Damascus, notwithstanding that he was as hateful to them as we Christians are (on account of Maudud, commander-in-chief of his army, whom he had wickedly conspired to kill in the previous year, as may be read above), made a truce with King Baldwin and Prince Roger of Antioch, so that by joining his third to their two-thirds they might form a three-fold rope which then would not be easily broken by the Turks.[4] For he feared that if he remained on his own he and his kingdom would be utterly destroyed. In this emergency and in response to the Antiochenes' summons, the king came thinking there would be a battle. But when the Turks heard that the king, whom the Antiochenes and Damascans had been expecting for about three months, was already drawing close to them, they feared the danger of death if they waged war on so great an army, although theirs was much bigger, and they retreated, moving very quietly, and went down into some caves which were, however, not far from our men. And when they had done this, the king and the others thought that the Turks had completely withdrawn from our regions. For this reason the king went back to Tripoli.
[The Egyptians invade and besiege Jaffa]

II.54

Moreover, when the Turks mentioned above ascertained that our army had turned back, they returned to their former position and rampaged through the regions of Syria, capturing as many castles as they could, and plundering

---

[3] Fulcher is in error here, as Marash lay to the north of Antioch. See, p. 82, n, 32.

[4] Fulcher's account differs from Walter's here, in that Tughtegin is described making an alliance with both Baldwin I and Roger and that Il-ghazi is not mentioned. Walter the Chancellor, I.2, pp. 87-8.

estates and devastating our land, carrying off with them male and female prisoners. But when this was announced to the Antiochenes, who had already withdrawn, they hastily retraced their path back to the Turks. And when they approached them and spotted their tents closer than they thought, at once they drew up their battle-lines and went down onto the plain, riding against them with banners unfurled. This battle was next to the town of Sarmin. And when the Turks saw them, one division of their archers boldly stood firm in that place. But our Franks were stirred by a strong hatred and they chose either to defeat them if God granted, or to be defeated if He allowed it, rather than to be destroyed by them in this way every single year, and so, marvellously, they sought them out wherever they saw that the press was denser. The Turks, moreover, resisted somewhat at first, but then they quickly turned tail and fled from both the attackers and those who were falling. It is estimated that three thousand of them were killed, many captured. And those who escaped being killed saved themselves by flight. They lost their tents, in which a great deal of money and equipment was found. The worth of the money was thought to be three hundred thousand bezants. They abandoned prisoners from our side there, as many Syrians as Franks, their own women and maidservants, very many camels. Thousands of mules and horses were counted. Truly God is wonderful in all His wonders. For while the Jerusalemites, together with the Antiochenes and Damascans, were ready to do battle, they accomplished nothing at all. Does the victory of warriors depend on the size of their army? Remember the victories of the Maccabees and Gideon and very many others, who did not put their faith in their own strength but that of the Lord, and with only a few men destroyed many thousands.

These things have been written down thus, as a note for posterity.
Three nights went by, so that the Virgin's star might go away,
when false fortune cruelly deceived the Turks:[5]
whence it was perfectly clear to everyone they should beware
never to believe anything before the matter is finished.

In that very year the city of Mamistra was once more overthrown by an earthquake. At another time there was an equally bad quake in the region of Antioch.

---

[5] 14 September 1115. This date concurs with that given by Walter the Chancellor, I.5, p. 98, n. 131.

III.3

In the year 1119 of the Lord's incarnation Gelasius the pope, Paschal's successor, died on 29 January and he was buried in Cluny. After him Calixtus took his place, who had been archbishop of the city of Vienne. We shall shun the prolixity in our writing which would result from wanting to relate all the wretched events which occurred in this year in the Antiochene region. How Roger, prince of Antioch, rode out with his nobles and his people to fight against the Turks and was killed in battle near the town of Artah, where seven thousand of the Antiochenes were killed, but of the Turks not even twenty. Nor is it surprising if God allowed them to be destroyed, since they were very wealthy in all sorts of riches and in the way they sinned they neither feared Him nor respected men. For according to his own wife the prince himself shamelessly committed adultery with many others. He disinherited his lord, the son of Bohemond, when he was still in Apulia with his mother, and both he and his nobles did many other things, living in pride and excess. It is appropriate for this verse of David's to be said of them: 'Their iniquity hath come forth, as it were from fatness.' For a sense of moderation was scarcely preserved among these lavish pleasures.

III.4

However, after this slaughter of the Antiochenes there followed a fortunate enough victory which, by God's favour, fell wonderfully to the people of Jerusalem. For when the aforesaid Roger notified the king of Jerusalem by means of envoys that he should make haste to rescue him, because the Turks were attacking him with a great army, the king left off his other business, for which he had gone with his men not far from the Jordan to fight with the Damascans, taking with him the patriarch with the Lord's Cross, and when he had forcefully evicted the Damascans from the plains where they were positioned, he immediately rushed to the assistance of the Antiochenes, taking with him the bishop of Caesarea, who afterwards bore the Lord's Cross most inspiringly into battle against the enemy. The king also took with him on the expedition the count of Tripoli, and there were also two hundred and fifty knights with them. And when they reached Antioch the king sent a legation to the Edessenes, instructing them to hasten by a forced march to the war which they were committed to waging on the Turks.

When these were assembled with the king and those Antiochenes who had either fled from the first battle or had escaped death by some chance, battle was joined near a town they call Zardana, twenty-four miles away from Antioch.[6] We had seven hundred soldiers, the Turks had twenty thousand. Their commander was called Il-ghazi. I do not think I should fail to reveal that a certain Turk who observed that one of our knights knew Persian spoke to him, saying, 'I say to you, Frank: why are you so foolish as to labour thus in vain? For indeed there is no way you can prevail against us; for you are few, we are many. On the contrary: your God has forsaken you, seeing that you do not obey your law, as you used to, and hold to neither faith nor truth instead. We know this, we have learnt it, we have observed it. Tomorrow we shall conquer and defeat you for sure.' Oh what a disgrace for Christians, when heathens rebuke us on matters of faith! We should blush violently for this and penitently correct our sins with weeping.

III.5

Battle was joined on the following day, as I said, and it was very hard fought. For a long time victory was doubtful for either side, until the Almighty forced the Turks to flee and splendidly aroused the Christians against them. Yet the Turkish attackers scattered them in troops to such an extent that even as far as Antioch they did not pause and they were unable to reassemble into their companies any more during the battle. Nevertheless, God scattered the Turks, since some fugitives got home to Persia, others indeed entered the city of Aleppo for the sake of saving themselves. Moreover, the king of Jerusalem and the count of Tripoli with their men were like allies of the glorious Cross, and those who had taken it to war were like slaves serving their lady, always fighting with honour around it and not deserting it; they stood manfully on the battlefield, and almighty God, through the virtue of that same most holy and precious Cross, powerfully snatched them from the hands of that most wicked race and saved them for some purpose of his own sometime in the future.

And when the king had guarded the battlefield for two days and none of the Turks had returned there to fight, he took the Lord's Cross and went to Antioch. And the patriarch of Antioch came out to meet the Holy Cross, and also the king and archbishop who was carrying it, and all gave thanks to God and sang sweet-sounding praises to almighty God, who through the power of

---

[6] In contrast to Walter, Fulcher places this battle near Zardana rather than at Tall Danith. Walter the Chancellor, II.12, pp. 152-3, n. 213. His estimate of the distance between Antioch and Zardana is fanciful.

his glorious Cross had given victory to the Christians and had brought back that same Cross safely to Christendom. They wept piously, they sang joyously, and with adoration they knelt many times in turn before the venerable Cross, rising again and giving thanks with uplifted faces.

> For two days the sun offered light to the Virgin's star
> when the war was waged in which the Persians were defeated,
> and then the bright horns of the tenth moon glowed red.

III.6

After the Franks had refreshed themselves in Antioch with a short period of rest, they decided to return to Jerusalem with the Lord's blessed Cross, as was fitting. And, with as many soldiers as seemed appropriate, the king sent the Cross to Jerusalem, and on the day when they celebrated the feast of its Exaltation, just like Heraclius when he brought it back from Persia when he returned as victor, they entered the holy city with it, rejoicing, and everyone in the city welcomed it with inexpressible joy.

III.7

However, the king remained in Antioch, since the situation there demanded it, in order to arrange to give the lands of the dead nobles to the living after due deliberation, and in pious compassion to marry widows, of whom there were many to be found there, to husbands, and to put right many other matters with necessary restitution. For just as up to now he had been king only of the Jerusalemites, so with the death of Prince Roger of Antioch he was made king of the Antiochenes by the addition of a second realm.[7] Therefore I admonish the king and pray that he may love God with all his heart and all his soul and with all his strength and that he subject himself to God from the bottom of his heart and with thanksgiving, like a faithful slave, and acknowledge that he is His humble slave, who found the Lord so great a friend to him. If God raised up his predecessor so high, how high will this king be raised? He made others possessor of one realm, this man He has granted two, which he gained without trickery, without bloodshed, without troublesome litigation, but peacefully by divine command. Indeed, God handed to him land far and wide, from Egypt all the way to Mesopotamia.

---

[7] For a discussion of Baldwin's status within the principality see: Baldwin of Le Bourcq, pp. 32-4.

God had towards him a generous hand; let the king beware lest he have a sparing one towards God, who gives abundantly and without reproach. If he wishes to be king then let him take pains to rule righteously.

Moreover, when he had dealt with these matters and many more, the king returned from Antioch to Jerusalem, and with his wife he was crowned with the royal diadem in Bethlehem on the day of the Lord's nativity.

III.9

However, when we had reached the sixth month of this year[8] in Jerusalem, envoys came from Antioch and told the king and all of us who were there that the Turks had crossed the Euphrates and had entered Syria to inflict harm on Christendom, just as they had used to do in the past. So we took counsel, as the emergency required, and the king most humbly asked for the Lord's victorious Cross to be handed over to him by the patriarch and clergy, saying that he and his men who had to go to war should be protected by it, because he believed that the aforesaid Turks could not be driven out of our land, which they were already laying waste, without a major battle. And since he did not put his trust in his own strength, nor in the great army that he had, with the Lord's inspiration and favour he would rather have that very Cross than many thousands of men. Otherwise, without it neither he nor others dared to set out for war. As a result, as was to be expected, there was a split between those who were going to war and those who were staying in Jerusalem, as to whether the Cross should be taken to Antioch in such an emergency for Christianity, or whether the Jerusalem Church should not be deprived of its great treasure. And we said: 'Alas, wretched us! What shall we do if God allows us to lose the Cross in battle, as the Israelites once lost the Ark of the Covenant?'

What more shall I report? Necessity commanded, reason instructed; we did what we did not want to do, and we agreed to do that we were unwilling to do. And when, piously weeping many tears for it and singing hymns in praise of it, the king and patriarch, and also all the common people, had escorted the Cross barefoot outside the city, the king left with the Cross, weeping, and the people returned to the holy city. It was the month of June.

---

[8] 1120.

So they went to Antioch, which the Turks had by now blockaded so closely that the inhabitants dared go scarcely a mile outside the circuit of the ramparts. But when the Turks heard of the king's approach they at once withdrew and moved off towards the city of Aleppo, where they would be safer; there they were joined by three thousand Damascene soldiers. The king, inspired to boldness, approached them to join battle with them, and on both sides many fell either wounded or dead from arrowshots, yet the Turks refused to fight, and after three days of this struggle, with the outcome always in doubt, our troops returned to Antioch while the greater part of the Turks went home to Persia. As for the rest, the king reverently sent back the Holy Cross to Jerusalem and he himself stayed in the region of Antioch to protect the land. Therefore on 20 October we welcomed back that same glorious Cross of the Lord into Jerusalem with great joy.

Albert of Aachen

Albert of Aachen's narrative account, 'Historia Hierosolymitana', recorded the course of the First Crusade largely from the point of view of Godfrey of Bouillon and the Lorraine contingent and then went on chronicle events in the Levant up to 1118. He may have composed his narrative of the crusade, covered in books one to six, shortly after the expedition and then added books seven to twelve, which dealt with later events, in the early 1120s. His account ends in spring 1119 and he therefore does not mention the battle of the Field of Blood.

Albert was almost certainly not an eyewitness to any of the events in the Latin East which he recorded. The evidence he provides must, therefore, be used with care and we certainly cannot expect him to have been consistently reliable on points of detail, such as numbers of manpower or the attribution of specific titles to individuals.[9]

The extracts given below were translated from S. Edgington's forthcoming edition of Albert's 'Historia'.[10]

XII.19

In the second year after Maudud's murder, Bursuq of the realm of Khorasan marched out, and Ridwan king of Aleppo,[11] and Cocosander of the state of Lagabria,[12] with forty thousand Turks, and they set out into the land of Antioch with much equipment and irresistible weaponry, pitching their tents on the plains of the towns of Rossa and Roida[13] and Apamea, destroying and subduing their suburbs with stone-hurlers, and as they were not able to harm Apamea at all, they devastated the whole district in that place with looting and fire. They overcame the towns of Tonimosa, Turgulant and Montfargia[14]

---

[9] For a further discussion of Albert as a historian see: S.B. Edgington, 'Albert of Aachen reappraised', *From Clermont to Jerusalem: The Crusades and Crusader societies 1095-1500*, ed. A.V. Murray (Turnhout, 1998), pp. 55-67.

[10] Forthcoming with Oxford Medieval Texts. An earlier, less accurate edition is currently available. Albert of Aachen, 'Historia Hierosolymitana', *Recueil des historiens des croisades. Historiens occidentaux*, vol. 4 (Paris, 1879), XII.19-20, pp. 701-2.

[11] Albert is in error here as Ridwan had died in 1113.

[12] This individual is unidentifiable.

[13] This may be reference to Rugia and Rubea in the Ruj valley to the south of Antioch.

[14] Tonimosa and Turgulant are unidentified, but Montfargia may be Montferrand.

with their great strength and strong army, and took away William de Perche,[15] a Christian prince and ruler of these fortresses, captured and conquered; of the rest whom they found in the towns, some they destroyed with capital sentence, others they took captive. They are reported to have settled in these parts for the days of eleven weeks.

King Baldwin was stopping in Jerusalem at that time. He had been summoned to assist Christ's soldiers, so, taking five hundred knights and a thousand footsoldiers, and Tughtegin, prince of Damascus, now bound by oath to that self same king, he hastened on his way to Antioch with very many cavalry.[16] Pons, son of Bertrand of Tripla, which is Tripoli, was in the same company with two hundred cavalry and two thousand infantry; he set out on the royal road all the way to the state of Talamria,[17] where Roger of Antioch and Baldwin of Edessa met them with ten thousand cavalry and infantry, and they pitched camp and stayed in this land for eight days. When the Turks heard about the king's arrival and the strength of his forces, they decided to flee into the mountains towards the state of Melitene,[18] because they were afraid to fight with him. King Baldwin, realizing that the Turks had retreated, arranged to return with his men, but he brought with him Tancred's widow who was the daughter of the king of France,[19] and she was married to that same Pons on the king's advice, with the wedding celebrated splendidly and with all plenty and abundance in the town of Tripoli, which was left to him by his parents by the law of inheritance.

XII.20
After the king's return, the Turks at once went back in their strength to Baghras,[20] and Harim[21] and Sinar,[22] towns belonging to the Gauls,

[15] This may be William of Percy, a major figure in northern England, as lord of Topcliffe, and founder of the well known Percy family from Normandy. William went on the First Crusade and is known to have died in the Levant. 'Cartularium abbathiae de Whiteby, I', *The Surtees Society*, vol. 69 (1878), ed. J.C. Atkinson, p. 2, no. 1; 'The Percy Fee', *Early Yorkshire Charters*, vol. 9, ed. C.T. Clay (Yorkshire, 1963), p. 1.

[16] Albert suggests that Tughtegin was allied to Baldwin I rather than Roger of Salerno.

[17] This may be a reference to Tall 'Ammar.

[18] Albert is the only source to suggest that Bursuq fled as far as Melitene, a town to the far north of Antioch.

[19] Cecilia of France, the daughter of King Philip I of France and Bertrada of Montfort. Married to Tancred c. 1106.

[20] A castle c. 10 miles to the north of Antioch.

invading the land and laying waste unsparingly everything found there.[23] Roger and Baldwin, hearing this, were very greatly troubled about the king's return journey, because he was already going far away and could not be called back. And for that reason they took counsel and decided not to send messengers to him in vain, and assembled as many as fifteen thousand of their men, of all kinds, Franks and Armenians alike. For the Turks were divided into three companies above the River Farfar,[24] which makes a channel between the two towns of Caesarea Stratonis[25] and Apamea. Then at very first light, on the day of the Exaltation of the Holy Cross, Roger and Baldwin formed battle-lines and attacked those very Turks in their camp where, when battle was joined, fifteen thousand Turks fell, but few of the Christians were found to have died. When the first army was destroyed in this way, while Roger was making for the second amidst great shouting, all the enemy were stricken by terror and took flight to the waters of the aforesaid river, in which some five thousand were swept away by the waters and died by drowning. Then while the third army, dumbstruck by this triumph of the Christians, was scattering along ways it was unsure of, by chance it arrived in the region of Camulla,[26] in a certain valley next to the castle Malbech,[27] where Tughtegin met them with eight thousand, battled with them hard, and three thousand of them were killed and a thousand taken prisoner. For there were among these fugitive Turks many of Maudud's offspring and blood, who were often greatly opposed to Tughtegin, making complaints among greater and lesser people of the land of Khorasan concerning his treachery and the wicked murder of their relative, and demanding vengeance for their relative's murder. On this account Tughtegin was always suspicious and careful, and now he was allied to King Baldwin and the Christian faithful he stuck to them completely, and he did not desist from harming the Turks in every way he could.

---

[21] A town to the east of Antioch, lying on the western fringe of the Jabal Talat.

[22] This site is unidentified.

[23] Albert is alone in asserting that Bursuq ravaged the region around Antioch rather than the Jabal as-Summaq.

[24] The Orontes River. Albert is alone in asserting that this battle took place near the Orontes.

[25] This is a reference to the Mediterranean coastal port of Caesarea.

[26] This may be a reference to the 'valley of Camels', al-Buqai'ah, the plain of Aakkar in northern Lebanon. P. Deschamps, 'Le Crac des Chevaliers', *Les Châteaux des Croisés en Terre Sainte*, vol. 1 (Paris, 1934), p. 110.

[27] This may be a reference to Mehelbeh.

Matthew of Edessa

Matthew wrote an Armenian 'Chronicle' of events in northern Syria up to 1136, which he probably composed at around that date. For the period from 1051 to 1101 he based his account on the testimony of eye-witnesses, while for the later period up to 1136 he relied heavily upon his own observations of events. His work provides us with an important counter-weight to both the Latin and Arabic authors, and in some ways he can be regarded as an impartial source for Antiochene history. In general Matthew's account is supported by a detailed and accurate chronology and is particularly valuable for the insights it gives us into Armenian attitudes to life under Latin rule. A.E. Dostourian has recently published a new English translation of this text, which for the first time, offers the English speaker a full modern edition of the text of Matthew's account.[28] This translation was, however, made from the French edition produced by E. Dulaurier in 1858.[29]

III.67[30]

This same year[31] God's anger burst upon His creatures. God, in His omnipotence and His wrath, turned His gaze towards them. He was angry with the sons of men who had strayed, turning aside from the path of righteousness, in accordance with the prophet's words: 'In this time there is no one, not prince, nor prophet, nor chief, who practises justice; not a single one of them.' It was in this way that everyone eagerly followed the road of perversity, they conceived a hatred of God's commandments and precepts: priests, warriors, men of the people, prelates, priests, monks - none kept strictly to the good way. They all gave in to inclinations of the flesh, to worldly pleasures, things which the Lord considers to be sins in the highest degree. And so this threat of the prophet came to pass: 'He looks on the earth and makes it tremble.' When God had turned his wrathful gaze upon His creatures they could not prevent themselves from being cast down by the terror of His prodigies. This is how it happened. On the 12th of Mareri, a Sunday, day of the Feast of the Invention of the Cross, a terrible phenomenon

---

[28] Matthew of Edessa, *The chronicle of Matthew of Edessa*, trans. A. E. Dostourian (Lanham, New York, London, 1993).

[29] Matthew of Edessa, *Chronique*, ed. & trans. E. Dulaurier (Paris, 1858).

[30] To facilitate cross-referencing Dostourian's chapter breaks have been adopted.

[31] 1114-1115. 563 of the Armenian era.

struck, a sign of anger such as had never been manifested in man's memory for centuries past, or in our own time, such as was never mentioned among those in Scripture.

While we were deeply asleep, suddenly a horrible noise was heard which resounded throughout the whole world. An earthquake was felt; the plains and higher places were raised up with a crash; the mountains and the hardest rocks cracked open and the hills gaped. The mountains and hills, violently shaken, resounded, and like living animals they were restless and breathing. This din struck the ears like the voice of the multitude in the camp. Like a confused sea, creatures rushed from all directions, overcome by the fear which the Lord's anger inspired in them; for the plains and the mountains reverberated with the resonance of bronze and they shook to and fro like trees tormented by the wind. The groans of the peoples escaped as a muffled din, like the moans of a man who has been ill for a long time, because of their fright they raced to their ruin. The earth was like a fugitive at bay in its convulsions, and distressed like a condemned man, uttering tearful lamentations and groans. This noise was to be heard after the earthquake for about an hour that night.

In this disaster each person believed that it was the end of his life. They all shouted: 'It is our last hour! It is the day of the last judgment!' Indeed, that day presented a predetermined and distinct date, for it was a Sunday, marked with the note var,[32] and, what is more, the moon was waning. Thus it brought together all the signs of the last day. Everyone was plunged into despair, as if he were under sentence of death and without hope of reprieve. This night saw the ruin of many towns and provinces, but they were only in the lands belonging to the Franks; in other lands and those belonging to the infidels nothing serious happened. At Samosata, Hisn-Mansur, Kesoun, Raban,[33] and at Marash, the devastation was terrible, and forty thousand people lost their lives, for these were densely populated cities and no one escaped. It was the same in the town of Sis,[34] where an innumerable multitude of the inhabitants perished. Many villages and religious houses were destroyed and a large number of men and women crushed. In the famous

---

[32] A chant in Armenian liturgical practice.

[33] These four towns were to the north of Antioch and to the west of Edessa and the Euphrates.

[34] A town in the Taurus mountains of Cilician Armenia.

Black Mountain,[35] at the monastery of the Basilians, holy monks and Armenian teachers had assembled for the consecration of the church. While they were engaged in celebrating the divine office the building collapsed on them, and thirty monks as well as two teachers were swallowed up under the debris, and their bodies have been buried there to the present day. An identical accident happened near Marash: the great monastery of the Jesuans crushed beneath its ruins all the monks. As soon as the shocks stopped, it began to snow, and the country was buried beneath deep drifts. The famous Armenian teacher Gregory, surnamed Mashgavour, died in the same place.

This was how disaster after disaster and frightful misfortunes afflicted the faithful as punishment for their sins, for they had abandoned the true path of divine precepts and had thrown themselves eagerly into the way of error, straying from the rules laid out in the holy books and behaving like madmen. And like those madmen who, in Noah's time, ate and drank right up to the day of their destruction, so richly deserved by their blameworthy deeds, these men continued to give themselves up to merriment right up to the moment when the Lord reached out to them and destroyed these workers of iniquity because they were committing enormous crimes.

III.70

This same year[36] the commander-in-chief of the Persians, the emir Bursuq, having once again assembled troops, arrived before Edessa. After halting there for a few days he crossed the Euphrates and came to Aleppo. From there he went on to capture Shaizar, a Muslim town, then he made up his mind to sack Tall Bashir[37] and the territory of Antioch. At once all the nation of Franks assembled at Antioch with Count Roger.[38] The king of Jerusalem and Baldwin, count of Edessa, quickly arrived too and met in the district of Shaizar. At the same time the powerful Persian emir Il-ghazi, son of Artuk, arrived at the Frankish camp: he had come with a considerable army to find Roger, for Il-ghazi was the sworn enemy of Bursuq. The emir of Damascus,

---

[35] This mountain, in the region of Antioch, was a significant centre of monastic and eremitical activity in the twelfth century. A. Jotischky, *The Perfection of Solitude: Hermits and Monks in the Crusader States* (Pennsylvania, 1995), p. 81, n. 39.

[36] 1115-1116. 564 in the Armenian era.

[37] Also known as Turbessel. A town in the county of Edessa, formerly held by Joscelin of Courtenay. See: pp. 170-71, n. 287.

[38] Matthew wrongly styles Roger as 'count'.

Tughtegin, was also seen to arrive. They joined the Christians and made an alliance with them and swore friendship with a solemn oath. The emir of Aleppo assembled likewise.[39]

The army of the infidels and that of the Franks were encamped there for four months without the Turks' daring to join battle, after which Bursuq stealthily withdrew, unbeknown to the Franks. When they realized he had suddenly retreated the king of Jerusalem, the count of Tripoli, the emir Il-ghazi, Tughtegin and the emir of Aleppo each went back to his own country. Bursuq, learning of the Christians' departure, marched towards Antioch with the intention of ravishing the territory of this city. When he heard this the count of Edessa returned to Antioch and, taking with him Roger and seven hundred cavalry, he advanced against Bursuq in the district of Aleppo.[40] Taking him by surprise with this tactic, he pounced on him and achieved a total victory, forcing the emir to flee. The Franks took some distinguished officers captive and carried off considerable booty, gained by pillaging the Turkish camp. The infidels who escaped from this defeat took to their heels ignominiously.

III.78

In this same year[41] the great count of the Franks, Roger lord of Antioch, called up his troops and came to attack 'Azaz, a city belonging to the Moslems and situated not far from Aleppo. The Armenian prince, Leo son of Constantine son of Roupen, joined him with his army on this expedition. Roger besieged 'Azaz for thirty days, preventing the Turks from bringing in reinforcements. After this he handed responsibility for the assault over to the Armenians. He called Leo and said to him: 'Tomorrow you are going into battle in order to show in some small way the Armenians' valour.' Leo gave the command to his soldiers who were in the camp to form up around him, and this brave champion of Christ exhorted them one after another to bear themselves well. The following day the Turks shifted themselves to attack the Franks, and Leo, having immediately ordered his men to take up arms to repulse the Muslims, gave the signal for his Armenians to charge the infidels.

---

[39] This is probably a reference to the eunuch Lu'lu, who held the position of atabeg of Aleppo for Alp Arslan ibn Ridwan for a time.

[40] Matthew suggests that Baldwin II count of Edessa was the prime-mover in this campaign.

[41] 1118-1119. 567 in the Armenian era.

Leo, roaring like a lion, leapt on them and pursued them to the gates of the town with his sword at their backs, slaughtering them and taking them captive. After this the infidels did not try to sortie. Leo gained a reputation for bravery that day, and his name became the subject of universal praises among the Franks. From then on Roger took a liking to the Armenian troops. By his repeated attacks he forced 'Azaz to surrender, but he was merciful towards the inhabitants and, far from inflicting any evil on them, he let them withdraw peacefully. A great enmity sprang up between Il-ghazi and Roger, who had previously been close friends, and they became irreconcilable, because Aleppo and 'Azaz belonged to Il-ghazi.[42] This Turkish emir seethed with rage in his heart. .

III.79

At the beginning of the year 568[43] Il-ghazi collected a formidable army, and since he was at this time considered supreme chief by all the Muslims, everyone joined him with their forces. He marched against Roger, count of Antioch, at the head of eighty thousand men. It was with these impressive numbers he arrived below the walls of Edessa. He stayed there four days without undertaking anything against this city, then he made for the Euphrates, which he crossed. His rate of march was that of a steed put out of breath by a long, fast gallop. He sacked many places, for none of the provinces occupied by the Franks was fortified against this sudden invasion. He captured castles, villages, religious houses, slaughtering the inhabitants, even old men and infants. When he came to Buza'ah[44] he halted.

Meanwhile Roger, made arrogant by his powerfulness, had not dreamt of making a single preparation for defence; full of self-confidence, he was remembering the pride of the race from which he was descended, and he deeply despised the Turks. He neglected all the precautions which prudence demanded on this occasion. Without surrounding himself with sufficient troops, without having summoned his Frankish allies, he set out, full of conceit, to meet the infidels.[45] He had under his command six hundred

---

[42] Matthew presumably mentions this previous friendship because of the military cooperation between Roger and Il-ghazi in 1115.

[43] This corresponds to 1119-1120 Christian era.

[44] A town to the north-east of Aleppo.

[45] Matthew provides an interesting summary of Roger's errors leading up to the Field of Blood. See: Roger of Salerno, p. 14.

Frankish cavalry,[46] five hundred Armenian cavalry and four hundred infantry; he was followed by ten thousand men, a rabble recruited from among all sorts of people.

The Turks had recourse to any possible means to ensure victory and had set a number of ambushes. The territory of the town of Atharib was the setting for the terrible battle that ensued. The multitude of Persians engulfed the Christians, who found themselves surrounded on all sides, with no way out. All were put to the sword and the count of the Franks, Roger, died with his men. A few just managed to escape. From the Euphrates to the sea, the Turks devastated everywhere, shedding blood and taking a host of captives. The Christian army was annihilated. This calamity took place on 6th month of K'agh'ots, a Saturday, the eve of 'Fat Sunday' which precedes the Transfiguration.[47]

The king of Jerusalem, Baldwin, came to Antioch and, having gathered together the remnants of the Frankish army, he marched against the Turks. On the 25th Arats, that is to say 16th August,[48] a new battle was joined in the same place as the previous one.[49] The Christians destroyed a number of Turks, then the two armies took flight, both of them, without either being victorious or defeated, for each side had suffered many losses, the infidels as many as five thousand men. It was not only weapons which accounted for so many victims, but also the intense heat. Above all the king of Jerusalem had afflicted heavy blows on the infidels. The Franks all went home and King Baldwin returned to the Holy City.

---

[46] One manuscript gives the figure of '100 Frankish cavalry'.

[47] 28 June 1119.

[48] Walter gives the date of 14 August. Walter the Chancellor, II.12, p. 155, n. 223.

[49] This is presumably a reference to the battle of Tall Danith in 1115.

Orderic Vitalis

Orderic was born in 1075 and entered the abbey of St Évroul, Normandy, at the age of ten, where he remained until his death in c. 1142. From this vantage point he wrote 'The ecclesiastical history' from the birth of Christ to 1141. His account of contemporary events was written from a distinctly Norman perspective and included a description of the First Crusade, drawn almost entirely from Baudry of Bourgueil, and some details of the early history of the Latin East. He may have had access to Fulcher of Chartres' 'Historia' but there is no evidence to suggest that his views were coloured by this work and his other sources for events in the Levant are unclear.[50] *The following passages were probably written between 1135-7. This translation was made from M. Chibnall's edition of 1978.*[51]

XI.25

In the year of Our Lord's incarnation 1111, the fourth indiction, Mark Bohemond died after many hardships and victories in Jesus's name, and Tancred succeeded him for some years,[52] a praiseworthy soldier in the suppression of the heathen. When Tancred died,[53] Roger son of Richard, a kinsman of the aforesaid princes, took over the principate of Antioch, but fortune was against him and he held it for only a brief time. When the death of these invincible princes was heard throughout the whole world, there followed immense grief for the Christians, immense joy for the pagans. And so the emir Il-ghazi, nephew of the sultan, prince of Persia, went to war against the Christians, and with a huge multitude he besieged Zardana, a castle held by the Christians which lay ten leagues from Antioch. Moreover, Roger son of Richard, the prince of Antioch, went to war, even though the patriarch Bernard tried to stop him, and he would not wait for King Baldwin

---

[50] Orderic Vitalis, *The ecclesiastical history*, vol. 1, ed. & trans. M. Chibnall (Oxford, 1980), p. 62. For a much fuller discussion of Orderic's writing see M. Chibnall's introduction in this volume, pp. 1-125.

[51] Orderic Vitalis, *The ecclesiastical history*, vol. 6, ed. & trans. M. Chibnall (Oxford, 1978), XI.25, pp. 104-8.

[52] Tancred had been acting ruler of the principality since Bohemond's return to Europe in c. 1105.

[53] In December 1112.

of Jerusalem whom he had summoned.[54] In fact Roger was a bold and zealous knight, but not the equal of his predecessors because he was unsound and stubborn and rash.

The patriarch, who was concerned for the people, said in a fatherly way to the duke[55] as he set out in such a great hurry, 'As a prudent general you should keep your prowess in check, and wait for King Baldwin and Joscelin and the other loyal nobles who are already coming early to our aid. Your rash haste has harmed too many people and it has snatched away life and victory from great princes. Examine old and new histories, and look closely at the fates of some distinguished kings. Remember Saul and Josiah and Judas Maccabeus; remember the Romans too, who were defeated by Hannibal at Cannae, and take very great care that you do not to precipitate a like destruction for those who are your subjects. Wait for your worthy allies who excel in faith and manifold virtue, and fight against the pagans with them, trusting in the power of almighty God, and with God's help you will enjoy a longed-for victory.' The prudent patriarch said these things and many like them, but the arrogant prince rejected them all and set out, and on the plains of Sarmada he pitched camp with seven thousand men.

Then the emir Il-ghazi and his huge squadrons of heathens quickly abandoned the siege, and suddenly came down from the nearby mountains onto the plains, and they covered the face of the earth with their great number like locusts. Then as the Christians were flocking together to their tents they attacked them fiercely, catching them unprepared, and on the fields of Sarmada they killed Prince Roger with seven thousand men. Robert of Vieux-Pont,[56] however, and other knights or squires who had gone out early to forage, or else had left the tents to go fowling or for other reasons, saw the sudden attack and sped across the seven leagues to the city where with their dreadful reports they brought out the citizens and roused them to the defence of their native land. Some hundred and forty escaped by being outside the camp, and they were saved by God's mercy for the protection of the faithful.

---

[54] For a discussion of Orderic's attitude to Patriarch Bernard see: Historiographical background, p. 10.

[55] From the Latin 'dux'. Probably intended to denote the status of 'general'. See: Walter the Chancellor, I.Prologue, p. 77, n. 2.

[56] Orderic seems to have had a particular interest in Robert as a Norman knight originally from Vieux-Pont-sur-Dives in Calvados.

When he realized this, Patriarch Bernard acted decisively to protect the city with all the clergy and lay-people he could find. Cecilia as well, the daughter of Philip king of the Franks, who was Tancred's wife, knighted Gervase the Breton, son of Viscount Haimo of Dol,[57] and she called up many other squires to knightly service against the pagans.[58] The gentiles, moreover, elated by so great a massacre of Christians, flocked en masse to the city, planning to take Antioch by surprise now all the defenders were killed, but by God's intervention through the hands of a few of His faithful they were entirely repulsed from the Antiochene defences.

After fifteen days the king of Jerusalem and Count Pons of Tripoli met at the castle of Harim[59] with their forces, and having joined battle in the gracious name of Jesus they won and destroyed the wings of the pagan armies. There the new knight Gervase killed the emir Il-ghazi,[60] and Christian strength confounded the heathen forces. And so the Christians were made rich by the spoils of the pagans, and they gladly gave thanks to God.

Then as there were no more members of Tancred's family, King Baldwin obtained Antioch and for some years he held it against the heathens. Later young Bohemond came to Syria from Apulia, and he was welcomed by all with great rejoicing, and married the king's daughter, and recovered all his father's possessions.[61] He followed in his father's footsteps for some four years and did remarkably well, but like a very beautiful flower he suddenly withered away.[62]

---

[57] Gervase is mentioned in Orderic's account on a number of occasions, but is otherwise unidentifiable. M. Chibnall suggests that his actions were reported in semi-legendary, *chanson*, terms. Orderic Vitalis, XI.25, p. 108, n. 2.

[58] Orderic may have confused Cecilia of France, the former wife of Tancred who was now married to Pons of Tripoli and presumably resident in that county, with Cecilia of Le Bourcq, the recently widowed spouse of Roger of Salerno, who is more likely to have been in Antioch at this point.

[59] Orderic is probably in error here as other sources indicate that the armies gathered at Antioch and then marched out towards Hab and Tall Danith.

[60] Orderic is certainly in error here as Il-ghazi did not die until 1122. See: Walter the Chancellor, II.16, p. 171, n. 290.

[61] Bohemond II arrived Antioch in 1126 and was married to Alice, daughter of Baldwin of Le Bourcq.

[62] Bohemond II was killed in 1130 during a campaign in Cilician Armenia.

William of Tyre

William wrote an extensive history of the Latin East from the First Crusade to the 1180s, whose exact title is debated but which can be referred to as the 'Historia Hierosolymitana'. William was an important figure in the kingdom of Jerusalem, becoming chancellor of Jerusalem in 1174 and archbishop of Tyre in 1175. He probably composed the following sections of his narrative between 1170 and 1184, drawing heavily from the accounts of Walter the Chancellor and Fulcher of Chartres, and in places attempting to reconcile their versions of events. This translation was made from the Huygens edition of 1986.[63]

11.23 *An enormous earthquake shakes the districts around Antioch; also Bursuq, a very powerful Turkish general, ravages the same region.*
In the year of the Lord's Incarnation 1114 so great an earthquake shook the whole of Syria that it utterly destroyed many cities and countless towns, most of all around Cilicia, Isauria and Coelesyria. For in Cilicia it threw to the ground Mamistra, with many towns, it also cast down Marash with its suburbs in such a way that scarcely a trace of some of them remained: towers and walls were shaken and quite large buildings were falling down in a dangerous manner, there was an immeasurable slaughter of people, and very spacious towns, built like ramparts of stones, became burial mounds for the crushed, and were tombs for their destroyed occupants. The ordinary people fled in alarm their city-dwelling, terrified of the ruin of their homes, and when they hoped to find peace in the open air, terror-stricken, they suffered in dreams the crushing which they feared while awake, interrupting their sleep. Nor was this danger, so great as it was, in one region only, but this plague spread widely, right to the furthest boundaries of the East.

Also, in the following year, as was his custom, Bursuq, a very powerful Turkish leader, assembled an infinite horde of that same race and invaded the Antiochene region. After marching across all that province, he camped

---

[63] William of Tyre, *Willelmi Tyrensis archiepiscopi chronicon*, ed. R.B.C. Huygens, 2 vols (Turnhout, 1986), XI.23, pp. 529-31; XI.25, pp. 532-3; XII.9-12, pp. 556-62; XII.14, p. 564. The best discussion of William of Tyre as a source is provided by P.W. Edbury & J.G. Rowe, *William of Tyre, historian of the Latin East* (Cambridge, 1988). A full translation of William's account is also available. William of Tyre, *A History of deeds done beyond the sea*, trans. & ann. E.A. Babcock & A.C. Krey (New York, 1976).

between Aleppo and Damascus, waiting for an opportunity to arise for them to attempt incursions into some or other of our lands. At once Tughtegin, king of the Damascans was extremely suspicious of these Turks' manoeuvres, and feared that they had assembled here rather with the intention of striving for the ruin of him and his kingdom than advancing to fight against the Christians whose strength they had often experienced, so he became concerned: for Bursuq blamed him for the death of the aforesaid nobleman[64] who had been killed at Damascus, believing the murder of this man had proceeded from his conspiracy.

So when he heard of the approach of the Turks and fully understood their intention he sent envoys with an enormous quantity of splendid gifts both to the lord king and to the lord prince of Antioch, seeking a truce for a fixed period and beseeching them, offering oaths and hostages, promising that for the entire period of the truce he would faithfully observe an alliance with the Christians both of the kingdom and of the principality. Meanwhile, the prince of Antioch, seeing that they were in the territory neighbouring his and having learnt from some reports that they were intending to invade his land, summoned the lord king to his aid, and also urged Tughtegin, who was no less bound to him by an oath of alliance, to call up his troops and come with his men. Moreover, the king, who was extremely concerned for the safety of the region, assembled his feudal army and, surrounded by his honourable retinue, made his way there with all speed, taking with him Count Pons of Tripoli; he arrived in a very few days at the place where the lord prince had assembled his forces. Tughtegin, since he was even closer, arrived before the lord king's army, and joined our men's camp as an ally. So with all the forces collected together before the city of Shaizar, where they had earlier heard the enemy to be, they stood as one; when the enemy realized this, and saw that they could not withstand our men except by a fierce battle, for the rest they feigned a retreat as if they were not going to return, and so our side separated one from another and returned home.

11.25 *Bursuq once again causes trouble on the Antiochene frontiers, but he is confounded by Prince Roger who marched against him with his allies, and put to flight, with his legions scattered.*
Therefore, while these things were going on in the kingdom, Bursuq, of

---

[64] Maudud of Mosul.

whom we spoke earlier, who had feigned flight and departure from Antiochene territory at the approach of the lord king and other nobles who had marched against him, now saw that the king and the prince of Antioch, and also Tughtegin, had separated and returned home to deal with domestic concerns, thought that they would not easily be able to assemble anew and he again attacked Antiochene territory and overran the whole region, burning estates, reducing suburbs to ashes and afflicting with rape and pillage anything they could find outside the garrisoned fortresses; they also divided their forces into companies and sent them off to various districts to inflict slaughter here and there, and when they met unwary inhabitants either in the fields or on a journey they were to drag them off as prisoners or put them to the sword. And they did not only attack estates without walls with their assaults, they also invaded violently even walled towns, such as Ma'arrat and Kafartab, and, having seized all the citizens in them, they put them to the sword or bound them in fetters and cast them down to the ground, and, occupying the whole region, they were daily carrying off booty from everywhere and Christians as slaves.

When this was announced to the prince he summoned to him the count of Edessa and on 12 September he marched out of Antioch and made with all speed for the town of Rubea with his expeditionary forces, and from his position before the town he sent out scouts who would inform him accurately about the size of the enemy and their position, while he drew up his battle-lines and composed his marching-columns, girding himself valiantly for battle. While he was keenly engaged in these preparations in accordance with military discipline, loyally supported by the lord count, a messenger arrived, hurrying with all speed, and announced that the enemy were encamped in the valley of Sarmada. When they heard this the whole army rejoiced exceedingly as if they were already within sight of victory.

Bursuq himself, when he heard of the arrival of our men, ordered his own men to arm and exhorted his fellow-soldiers to draw up marching columns and to do their utmost; wishing nevertheless to look after his own safety, with his brother and certain of his household he took possession of a neighbouring hill, called Danith, before our men approached, from where he could see his men fighting and better inform them about battle tactics. So it happened that while he was busy with these things our men's lines, with their banners raised, began to advance, and when they saw the enemy, a scattered horde of them,

Lord Baldwin, count of Edessa, who was in the vanguard with his regiment, charged them fiercely with a violent attack which shattered all their army. The remaining lines followed his example and merged their formations into the midst of the enemy, pressing hard with swords and blades the better to repay the injuries which they had so freely inflicted on villeins and poor people. The enemy, therefore, hoping to resist the first waves of the attack, boldly tried very hard to drive our men back, but eventually, marvelling at our men's forces, their charge and their wonderful steadfastness, the enemy's lines were thoroughly dispersed and they were put to flight. Bursuq, seeing the defeat of his men from the hill-top, and that our men were prevailing, escaped with his brother and household, whom he had assembled on the hill, abandoning his banner, his camp and all his baggage in his flight, and saved his life. Our men pursued closely their troops, dispersed and put to flight, and killed the fugitives with their swords, inflicting infinite slaughter for some two miles. Moreover, the prince with his division stayed for two days on the battlefield as victor and waited for his men who had pursued the enemy in different directions. When they returned and delivered up to him all the spoils, he offered suitable shares to his companions in victory: for when the enemy had abandoned the camp all of them, even the most important, forgot to take with them when they fled the super-abundance of all sorts of commodities and enormous wealth; so our men received both booty and spoils, which they had brought together from different places, and at the same time our prisoners, whom they had thrown in chains, and they rejoiced in sending them back home with their animals, wives and children. More than three thousand of the enemy are said to have fallen in that battle. After these transactions the prince sent ahead horses, mules and the great number of prisoners, and with a variety of all sorts of riches going before him he entered Antioch as victor, to the great acclaim and happiness of his people.

12.9 *Il-ghazi, a very powerful satrap of the Turks, overruns Antiochene territory with enormous forces, devastating everything.*
In the same year[65] a certain prince of the infidels who was greatly feared among his own people, prince of a miserable race and a treacherous people, that is to say the Turcomans, Lord Il-ghazi by name, who had as allies Tughtegin king of Damascus and Dubais the powerful satrap of the Arabs, invaded Antiochene territory with enormous forces and all the weight of

---

[65] 1119.

numbers of his men, and camped this side of Aleppo. Since he was forewarned of his approach, Lord Roger prince of Antioch, the brother-in-law of the lord king, sent word to the princes positioned around, that is to say Lord Joscelin count of Edessa,[66] also Lord Pons count of Tripoli, even the lord king himself, and told them about the emergency, warning and beseeching them with all his might to come at once with all speed to bring help against the pressing danger. Therefore the king collected to him all the military forces he could assemble from his kingdom at such short notice, and he reached Tripoli by a forced march, and there he urged the lord count, who was equally ready for the expedition, to ally himself with him on the journey he had undertaken.

But the lord prince, meanwhile, who was impatient by nature, and unaware of the common law governing the futures of mortal men, marched out of Antioch and was encamped around the town of Artah. Moreover, this place was well enough supplied with food for the armies, for there was free and easy access for those who wanted to go to the army from our territories, and hence there was a very great abundance of provisions on the expedition and as great a supply as might be found in the towns. When he had waited there for some days for the arrival of the lord king and the count, although the lord patriarch, who had followed him even here, forbade it, and also some of his nobles disagreed, he ordered the army to set out, arguing forcefully that he would await no one's arrival. For there were certain of the nobles of the region who were urging him to this, not so that they might improve the situation of the army, but so that they might by the presence of the army improve the security of their own lands, which were close to the enemy camp. Therefore, following the advice of these men, the prince withdrew from that place where he was previously and rashly brought disaster on himself and his men by ordering the camp to be relocated to the place which was called the Field of Blood. And when his army was counted, seven hundred cavalry were found and three thousand infantry in battle array, not counting the traders who were accustomed to follow the camp for the sake of buying and selling.

When the enemy realized the prince's camp was located very near, in order to be able more convincingly to achieve the effect of concealing the plan they had conceived, they struck camp and pretended to be moving their lines

---

[66] Joscelin may not have held the county as early as June 1119. See: pp. 170-71, n. 287.

towards the city of al-Atharib, and when they arrived there, since they could not do anything useful that night, they camped around the districts. The next morning the prince sent out scouts, wanting to know whether the enemy were moving to besiege the town or were making for the camp to join battle with our men; and while he and his men were preparing for battle as though they were expecting to fight straight away, the messengers raced back and announced with one voice that the enemy, in three divisions, each having twenty thousand, were advancing on our army at a rapid pace. When he found this out the prince made four battle-lines and rode around them, circling them earnestly and inspiring the drawn-up lines with suitable words, and while he gave his attention to this, behold, the enemy's lines with their banners on high were almost on top of our army. And so battle was joined, both sides pressing fiercely, but because of the weight of our sins the opposing side came out on top. For the battle-lines led by Geoffrey the Monk and Guy Fresnel, noble men and valiant in arms, which were appointed the first to charge the enemy, being best, advanced in accordance with military discipline, and violently dispersed the greater formations and denser cohorts of the enemy and almost forced them to flee; but the line led by Robert of St Lô, when it should have charged the enemy fiercely following the example of the others who had preceded it, wrongly stood still and allowed the enemy to re-muster their forces, and then took flight and scattered the prince's line, which was standing by to bring reinforcements to the others, by escaping through their midst and taking a part of them with them in flight, in such a way that none could possibly be called back.

Something else happened in that battle which is worthy of report. For while they were striving keenly to and fro in this very conflict, behold, a huge whirlwind came forth from the north and everyone saw it in the middle of the battlefield clinging to the ground and creeping along, taking with it so much accumulated dust that it got in the eyes of both sides with its huge quantities of dust so that they could not fight, and, drawing itself up in a spiral like a pot burning with sulphurous fires, it carried itself off into the air. And so it came about by misfortune that the enemy were superior and our side was destroyed, and nearly all our men were put to the sword.

12.10 *Prince Roger falls in his battle line and our army is overthrown.*
Moreover the prince was fighting manfully in the midst of the enemy with his few men, like a man valiant in arms, while he tried in vain to recall his men.

But as he was launching an attack against the enemy's greater forces, he was pierced through by swords and died. Those, however, who had attended the baggage and equipment took themselves onto the neighbouring hill; those indeed who were seen to flee the enemy's weapons, removing themselves from the tumult of battle, when they saw our men on the hill-top, thinking they had the forces to resist and they could be saved with them, approached them eagerly. When everyone had arrived there the enemy, having put absolutely everyone who was on the plains to the sword, turned their attention to them and sent cohorts there who dragged all of them to their deaths in a moment of time.

Rainald Mazoir, one of the greater princes of that region, took himself off with some other nobles into the tower of a certain neighbouring town, called Sarmada, for the sake of safety. When this was afterwards made known to the aforesaid prince of the Turks, he flew there at all speed and violently forced the aforesaid noble men who had reassembled inside, to surrender, and thus it came about on that day that of the many thousands who had followed the lord prince, because of our faults which deserved it, scarcely one escaped to tell the tale, while of the enemy few or none were killed.

Moreover, it is said that this same Prince Roger was a most corrupt man, unchaste, parsimonious and a known adulterer. Over and above this, he had made his lord Bohemond the younger, son of the elder Bohemond, who was still in Apulia with his mother, an alien from Antioch, which was his paternal heritage, for as long as he had held the principality: for Lord Tancred of good memory had committed the principality to him on his deathbed, on condition that he would not refuse Lord Bohemond or his heirs if they demanded it back.[67] But it is said that on that expedition, on which he was stabbed and died, he had made confession of his sins to God with contrite and humble heart in the presence of Lord Peter, the reverend archbishop of Apamea, who was present in that same emergency, and who promised the deserved fruits of penitence on the Lord's authority, and so he rode into the trial of battle as a true penitent.[68]

---

[67] William is the only extant source for this death-bed arrangement.
[68] For a discussion of William's attitude to Roger's character see: Roger of Salerno, p. 23.

12.11 *The king and the count of Tripoli hurry to Antioch to resist the aforesaid Il-ghazi.*

Meanwhile, the king and the count of Tripoli were approaching and they had come to the place which is called Mount Nigra.[69] When the aforesaid Il-ghazi realized this, he sent ten thousand picked cavalry to meet them, and if possible to hinder their approach. As these troops left they separated into three divisions, one making for the coast towards the Port of St Simeon, the other two aiming to cut off the king by different routes. It happened, moreover, that he met one of the two divisions and by the Lord's outstanding mercy he dispersed it violently, killing many and taking some captive, and put it to flight. From there he reached Antioch through Laitor and Casabella, and was welcomed by the lord patriarch, the clergy and people with utmost enthusiasm, and at Antioch he entered into discussion with both his own men and those Antiochenes who had survived the aforesaid battle, as to what he should best do at that point of dire necessity.

Meanwhile, Il-ghazi by-passed the towns of 'Imm and Artah, and besieged al-Atharib, the more boldly because he had heard that Alan, the lord of that same place, had been summoned along with his retinue by the lord king, which was true. So, approaching the fortress and finding the place unprepared, he sent in miners on different sides to undermine the hill on which the said town was sited, and put in beams propping it up to be burnt up afterwards by introducing fire, so that they would overthrow the towers and the walls on top of it when the rampart gave way. The townsmen, fearing that when the rampart was undermined the whole fortress would collapse headlong, surrendered the place on conditions concerning their lives, safety and free return to their own people.

Il-ghazi took an army from there to the castle at Zardana and blockaded the place, which he also took in the same way within a very few days when the inhabitants of the place handed it over. Then, being impatient by nature, and so being very sure that no one could withstand him, he treated the whole region as being under his authority, so that for the inhabitants within its boundaries there was no hope of escaping the yoke of such a prince.

---

[69] The Black Mountain.

12.12 *The king and that same count engage with the aforesaid Il-ghazi and, having put him to flight, they destroy his battle-lines, killing very many, and the care of the principality is committed to the king.*

The king, with the count and the army, as many as he could muster, came out of Antioch and, thinking they would find the enemy at al-Atharib, they marched towards Rubea; from there they passed through Hab and camped on the mountain which is called Danith. When Il-ghazi heard this he called together his princes and ordered them under threat of death not to sleep at all that night but to devote it all to attending to their weapons and horses with utmost care, and at daybreak, before first light, having carefully prepared, they were to charge the king's camp and, finding them still asleep, to run them through with their swords, so that not even one of them would be allowed to escape death. But indeed, divine clemency had ordained a very different outcome. The king and his men were no more remiss in looking after their responsibilities, and he stayed up all that same night to look after matters necessary for the coming battle, and the reverend man Lord Evremar, archbishop of Caesarea, who had followed the lord king to those regions with the wood of the Lord's Cross, was advising and exhorting the people. Therefore, armed and girded ready for battle, early in the morning they were manfully awaiting the enemy's expected attack. Therefore nine battle-lines were assigned on the king's command in accordance with the discipline of military affairs - for he is said to have had seven hundred knights in that battle - and when they had been placed in proper order, they awaited the Lord's mercy.

Three lines were therefore sent forward to precede all the marching columns; the lord count of Tripoli held the right wing with his men; the Antiochene princes were placed on the left; he put the infantry companies in the middle, and the lord king himself, ready to reinforce the rest, followed with four battle-lines. And while they were drawn up in this way, waiting for the enemy, behold, they arrived with an enormous din, with a blaring of trumpets and a dreadful noise of drums, charging against our men. But they had a great reliance on their countless numbers, while for our men hope in the presence of the most victorious Cross and in the confession of the true faith was greater and unfailing.

Therefore, when the battle-lines were joined and the legions were intermingled in hostility, battle was fought at close quarters with swords and, spurning the laws of humanity, as if against monstrous wild beasts; it was fought on both sides with burning enthusiasm and insatiable hatred. And when they realized the violent and dangerous situation presented by our infantry companies, the enemy exerted themselves with all their might to destroy the divisions of infantry, and it came about that God permitted them to perish for the most part on the enemy's swords that day. The king, however, seeing the infantry companies were being pressed beyond their strength, and that the vanguard lines lacked reinforcements, leant forward and charged into the midst of the columns with those of his men whom he had kept with him, and, pressing keenly with his sword he scattered the densest formations of the enemy, and he and his companions from those same battle-lines who were faithfully sticking close to him and bringing to others who were now forsaken strength and encouragement by their words and example, charged against the enemy as one, and, when they called down assistance from the heavens divine mercy attended them and there was an incalculable massacre of the enemy, while the remainder who could resist no longer they put to flight.

About seven hundred of our infantry are said to have fallen there, and a hundred of our cavalry, but of the enemy the number was as high as four thousand, not counting the mortally wounded and prisoners in shackles. Il-ghazi, escaping with Tughtegin, king of Damascus, and Dubais, prince of the Arabs, left their men to die, while our men pursued them and rode out to various places. The king occupied the battle-field with a few men and stayed on there until the first parts of the night, when eventually, forced by lack of food, of necessity he took himself off to the neighbouring town called Hab for the sake of taking refreshment. In the morning he returned from there to the aforesaid battlefield, and he sent messengers to his sister and to the lord patriarch with his own ring as a token of victory, signifying the gift of victory conferred upon him from heaven by God's grace. Yet on that day he did not leave the battlefield until it was fully evening, until he had received news for sure that the enemy who had been scattered were not going to return. Eventually, having brought together as many of his men as he could have at that time, he entered Antioch in triumph, with the victory palm, and all the clergy and people of the entire city met him, with the lord patriarch. Moreover, this victory was granted to our men by God in the year of the Lord's incarnation 1118,[70] and also in the second year of the reign of Lord

---

[70] This date should of course be 1119.

King Baldwin II, in the month of August, on the eve of the Assumption of Mary, holy mother of God.[71]

The king sent the wood of the holy life-giving Cross back to Jerusalem with the lord archbishop of Caesarea and an honourable retinue, so that it would be received honourably on the day of its Exaltation by the clergy and people, with hymns and religious songs. But he was obliged to stay in the province of Antioch on account of the serious situation in the region, and there both the lord patriarch and all the nobles, together with the clergy and the people, by common desire and freely given assent handed over to the king the care and every kind of authority over the Antiochene principality, so that in this way he would have a free hand in the principality, just as he had in the kingdom, to establish, remove and deal with all things in the role of judge. The possessions of those who had fallen in battle were granted to their children or other blood-relations in any degree, just as reason or custom demanded; also widows were placed in marriages with men who were their equals and matched them in status, and also fortresses were carefully garrisoned with the men, provisions and weapons which seemed necessary, and then at a time when he had their leave, the king returned to his kingdom. There he was crowned with his wife in the Bethlehem church on the feast day of the Lord's nativity.

12.14 *Once more Il-ghazi renews his campaigns and invades Antiochene territory; when the king meets him, Il-ghazi is affected by apoplexy and dies.* In the following year[72] the aforesaid very tenacious and indefatigable persecutor of the Christian name and faith, Il-ghazi, like a restless worm always seeking out someone to harm, seized the opportunity offered by the king's absence, called up his military forces and also appointed some of them to besiege our people's fortresses. When they realized what was about to happen, they called on the lord king most urgently, and he hastened energetically to those parts, taking with him the wood of the salvation-bearing Cross and an honourable retinue of clergy; Lord Joscelin of Edessa was also summoned, and with the Antiochene nobles he moved his camp against the aforesaid powerful man. And when they had arrived there, hoping to join battle on the following day, it happened that the Lord's hand touched him with

---

[71] 14 August.
[72] 1120.

a disease, which is called apoplexy. As a consequence, the noblemen who were in his army, being deprived of the support of their prince, took good advice and wisely declined to go to war, and, carrying their lord away half-dead on a stretcher, they hurried to Aleppo, but before they reached the city he is said to have given up his wretched ghost, handing it over to eternal fires.

The king also, having made a delay at Antioch which seemed necessary at the time, returned safely to his kingdom by the Lord's doing, and with both peoples, in his kingdom as well as in the principality, because his merits demanded it, he was very much loved and welcomed; and he certainly managed both administrations faithfully and devotedly - that is to say, the kingdom's and the principality's - although they were very far apart. Nor was it easy to tell which of them concerned him more: although the kingdom was his by right and he could even bequeath it lawfully to his successors, the principality was entrusted to him and he seemed to demonstrate an even greater diligence on behalf of the Antiochenes' condition. He continued in this good faith until the arrival of Lord Bohemond the younger, as is told in the following pages.[73]

---

[73] Bohemond II arrived at Antioch in 1126.

Charter (a) 1114

Roger, prince of Antioch, confirms whatever his barons, he himself and the wife of his uncle, Tancred, have granted to the church of St Mary in the valley of Josaphat.[74]

In the name of the holy and indivisible Trinity, Father and Son and Holy Spirit. I Roger, by God's grace prince of Antioch, in response to demands of certain of my barons that I for my part might consent and agree to the alms and grants which they have made for the redemption of their souls to the church of the holy and glorious virgin Mary in the valley of Josaphat,[75] wishing to share in the prayers of the holy men who serve there night and day, I graciously accede to their goodwill and just petition, and whatever they have individually in small measure granted to that same aforesaid church I have confirmed and established as fixed and firm by my seal.[76] Moreover, these are the people who have bestowed these things: Robert fitz-Fulk, who bestowed a casal[77] called Merdic;[78] Robert of Vieux-Pont, another casal called Burio;[79] Robert of St Lô, at his fishery Agrest,[80] 500 pounds of fish every year; Guy Le Chevreuil 200 pounds of fish every year and 100 mecuchia[81] of salt and one casal which is called St Paul's,[82] and in the casal called Oschi,[83] two carucates of land;[84] Robert of Laitor,[85] one casal called

---

[74] The charter comes from the cartulary of the abbey Our Lady of Josaphat. *Chartes de Terre Sainte provenant de l'abbaye de N. D. de Josaphat*, ed. H.F. Delaborde (Paris, 1880). This translation was made from Hagenmeyer's edition of this single charter, which appears as an addendum to his edition of Walter the Chancellor. *Galterii Cancellarii, Bella Antiochena*, ed. H. Hagenmeyer (Innsbruck, 1896), p. 314.

[75] This Benedictine monastery was in the kingdom of Jerusalem. See: A. Jotischky, *The Perfection of Solitude*, pp. 51-3.

[76] For a discussion of the imagery used in Roger's coin issues and seal see: M. Rheinheimer, 'Tankred und das Siegel Boemunds', pp. 75-93.

[77] The term 'casal' indicates a small settlement or village.

[78] Merdic can been identified as Mardikh about twenty six kilometres south of Zardana. P. Deschamps, 'La défense du comté de Tripoli et de la principauté d'Antioche', p. 221.

[79] Burio has been identified as the village of Bouraya in the mountains near Jabala. P. Deschamps, 'La défense du comté de Tripoli et de la principauté d'Antioche', p. 55, n. 3.

[80] This site is unidentified.

[81] An unknown weight or quantity.

[82] This site is unidentified.

[83] This may be a reference to the village of Oshin in Cilicia.

Anadi[86] ......Bonable,[87] one casal called......[88] I, moreover, wishing to share and associate in the grants to the church as aforesaid, as much for my own salvation as for that of my father[89] and mother and my uncle Tancred, and also all my relations, have granted every year as a perpetual right, for the provisioning of the holy men 500 eels, and the casal which my uncle Tancred's wife[90] granted to that same church at Jabala for his soul, as much as concerns me, I also grant, and the land which lies next to the town, just as it was marked out by us, and one house within the town where the brothers are lodged when they come there, which they may possess as a perpetual right. This grant was made in the year 1114 from the Lord's incarnation, in the seventh indiction, and witnessed by those who have signed below.[91]

---

[84] Guy Le Chevreuil, the main Latin landholder in Cilicia, had previously issued his own charter detailing these donations. The only specific variation was that only one carucate of land near Oshi was listed in this earlier document. 'Chartes de l'abbaye de Notre-Dame de Josaphat', pp. 115-16, n. 4.

[85] Robert can probably be identified with Robert of Sourdeval as descendants of the Sourdeval family are known to have held Laitor. *Cartulaire général de l'ordre des Hospitaliers de S. Jean de Jérusalem (1100-1310)*, vol. II, pp. 175-176, n. 1441-2.

[86] This site is unidentified.

[87] Bonable appears to have been one of the major Latin landholders in the Jabal as-Summaq. Albert of Aachen described him as 'holding the town of Sarmin' in 1111. C. Cahen argued that Bonable also held Kafartab from an early date. C. Cahen, *La Syrie du Nord*, p. 243, n. 7.

[88] There are two *lacunae* in the edition at this point.

[89] Richard of the Principate.

[90] Cecilia of France.

[91] The witness list to this charter is not extant.

Charter (b) 1118

Roger, prince of Antioch, approves and confirms all the gifts which have been made to the Jerusalem hospital in all the realm of Antioch, 4 June 1118.[92]

In the name of the holy and indivisible Trinity. Let all men know, both present and in the future, that I, Roger, by God's grace prince of Antioch, approve and confirm in writing all the gifts and alms which have been made to the Jerusalem hospital in all the realm of Antioch[93] up to the present day, whether casals or tenants, whether houses or lands or anything which may profit men, for this reason: that no man or woman from today and henceforth should dare to disturb, diminish or steal them from the aforesaid hospital and Christ's poor. Firstly, I approve and confirm the gift which Lord Bohemond made to the Jerusalem hospital, that is to say, of three casals which are in the mountains of Antioch. Also I confirm my gift, that is to say of certain houses within the walls of Antioch with one piece of land, and of a certain dwelling which I gave to Lord Gerard[94] when I was in Jerusalem, in the square of the aforementioned town. Besides I approve and confirm to the aforesaid hospital a certain casal which Roger of Florence[95] gave it in the territory of Harim, and another which Bonable gave in the land of Kafartab, also that which Robert[96] gave in the territory of Delthio,[97] also, moreover, the tenants which knights gave to the hospital in all the land under my authority. Lastly as well, so that God may have mercy on me and the soul of my father[98] and

---

[92] This charter comes from the cartulary of the Hospital of Jerusalem. *Cartulaire général de l'ordre des Hospitaliers de S. Jean de Jérusalem (1100-1310)*, 4 vols, ed. J. Delaville Le Roulx (Paris, 1894-1906), vol. 1, p. 38, no. 45. This translation was made from Hagenmeyer's edition of this charter, which appears as an addendum to his edition of Walter the Chancellor. *Galterii Cancellarii, Bella Antiochena*, ed. H. Hagenmeyer (Innsbruck, 1896), p. 315.

[93] From the Latin 'in omni regno Antiocheno'.

[94] The Grandmaster of the Hospital of Jerusalem between (c.1099-c.1118).

[95] Roger may have held this land as a rear-vassal of Guy Fresnel, the Latin lord of Harim. Albert of Aachen, XI.40. Roger was also mentioned among a group of men who had agreed to grants made to the Genoese in a charter issued by Tancred of Hauteville, dated 9 December 1101. *Liber Privilegiorum ecclesiae Januensis*, p. 42, no. 25.

[96] It is not clear whether this is a reference to Robert of St Lô who appears in the witness list to this charter.

[97] This site is unidentified.

[98] Richard of the Principate.

all my relations, or indeed all the faithful who are dead, in every way I am able to I approve and confirm to the Jerusalem hospital all those things which it has acquired up to today, and holds at that time and possesses in all the realm of Antioch.[99] I wish it always to hold them and without any contradiction as long as the world shall endure: if anyone should try to steal them or to diminish them in any way, may he be excommunicated and excluded from the body and blood of Christ until he comes to his senses and makes amends.

Moreover, this charter of gift or confirmation is made on 4 June in the year 1118 from the Lord's incarnation.
Signed. Roger, prince of Antioch.
Signed. Guy Fresnel.
Signed. Robert of St Lô.
Signed. Peter the subdeacon, who wrote this charter of confirmation on the day and year above.

---

[99] From the Latin 'in omni regno Antiocheno'.

Bibliography

PRIMARY SOURCES

Walter the Chancellor – Editions

Edition employed for this translation

Galterii Cancellarii, Bella Antiochena, ed. H. Hagenmeyer (Innsbruck, 1896).

Earlier editions (in chronological order of publication)

Gesta Dei per Francos, vol. 1, ed. J. Bongars (Hannover, 1611), pp. 441–67.
Patrologia Latina, vol. 155, ed. J.P. Migne (Paris, 1853), pp. 995–1038.
Quellenbeiträge zur Geschichte d. Kreuzzüge, vol. 1, ed. H. Prutz (Danzit, 1876), pp. 1–55.
Recueil des Historiens des Croisades. Historiens Occidentaux, vol. 5, ed. P. Riant (Paris, 1895), pp. 75–132.

Latin Sources

Chronicles

Albert of Aachen, 'Historia Hierosolymitana', *Recueil des historiens des croisades. Historiens occidentaux*, vol. 4 (Paris, 1879), pp. 265–713.
'Anonymi Florinensis Brevis Narratio Belli Sacri', *Recueil des historiens des croisades. Historiens occidentaux*, vol. 5 (Paris, 1886), pp. 356–62.
'Ex Historiae Francicae Fragmento', *Recueil des Historiens de Gaule et de la France*, vol. 12, ed. L. Delisle (Paris, 1877), pp. 1–8.
Fulcher of Chartres, *Historia Hierosolymitana*, ed. H. Hagenmeyer (Heidelberg, 1913).
—— *A History of the expedition to Jerusalem 1095–1127*, trans. F.R. Ryan, ed. H.S. Fink (Knoxville, 1969).
Gesta Francorum et aliorum Hierosolimitanorum, ed. & trans. R. Hill (London 1962).
Orderic Vitalis, *The ecclesiastical history*, ed. & trans. M. Chibnall, 6 vols (Oxford, 1969–80).
Ralph of Caen, 'Gesta Tancredi in Expeditione Hierosolimitana', *Recueil des historiens des croisades. Historiens occidentaux*, vol. 3 (Paris, 1866), pp. 587–716.
Raymond of Aguilers, *Le 'Liber de Raymond d'Aguilers'*, ed. J.H. & L.L. Hill (Paris, 1969).
William of Tyre, *Willelmi Tyrensis archiepiscopi chronicon*, ed. R.B.C. Huygens, 2 vols (Turnhout, 1986).
—— *A History of deeds done beyond the sea*, trans. & ann. E.A. Babcock & A.C. Krey, 2 vols (New York, 1976).

Collected documents and other sources

Carte dell'Archivio Capitolare di Pisa, ed. E. Falaschi & M.T. Carli, 4 vols (Rome, 1969–77).
'Cartularium abbathiae de Whiteby, I', *The Surtees Society*, vol. 69 (1878), ed. J.C. Atkinson.
Le Cartulaire de chapitre du Saint-Sépulchre de Jérusalem, ed. G. Bresc-Bautier (Paris, 1984).
Cartulaire général de l'ordre des Hospitaliers de S. Jean de Jérusalem (1100–1310), ed. J. Delaville Le Roulx, 4 vols (Paris, 1894–1906).
'Chartes de l'abbaye de Notre-Dame de Josaphat', ed. C. Kohler, *Revue de l'Orient Latin*, vol. 7 (1899).
Chartes de Terre Sainte provenant de l'abbaye de N. D. de Josaphat, ed. H. F. Delaborde (Paris, 1880).
Italia Sacra, ed. F. Ughelli.
'Liber Jurium republicae Genuensis', 2 vols, *Monumenta Historiae Patriae*, vols 7, 9 (Augustae Taurinorum, 1853–57).
Liber Privilegiorum ecclesiae Januensis, ed. D. Puncuh (Genoa, 1962).
Oxford Book of Medieval Latin Verse, ed. F.J.E. Raby (Oxford, 1959).
Papsturkunden für Kirchen im Heiligen Lande, ed. R. Hiestand (Göttingen, 1985).
'The Percy Fee', *Early Yorkshire Charters*, vol. 9, ed. C.T. Clay (Yorkshire, 1963).
Regesta Regni Hierosolymitani (MCVII–MCCXCI), ed. R. Röhricht, 2 vols (Oeniponti, 1893–1904).

Eastern Christian Sources

Matthew of Edessa, *Chronique*, ed. & trans. E. Dulaurier (Paris, 1858).
—— *The chronicle of Matthew of Edessa*, trans. A.E. Dostourian (Lanham, New York, London, 1993).

Arabic Sources

Gabrieli, F., *Arab Historians of the Crusades* (London, 1969).
Ibn al-Athir, 'Kamel Altevarykh', *Recueil des historiens des croisades. Historiens orientaux*, vol. 1 (Paris, 1872), pp. 189–744.
Ibn al-Qalanisi, *The Damascus chronicle of the crusades*, trans. H.A.R. Gibb (London, 1932).
Kemal ed-Din, 'La chronique d'Alep', *Recueil des historiens des croisades. Historiens orientaux*, vol. 3 (Paris, 1884), 578–690.
Sibt ibn al-Jauzi, 'Mir'at ez-Zeman', *Recueil des historiens des croisades. Historiens orientaux*, vol. 3 (Paris, 1884), pp. 517–70.
Usamah Ibn-Munqidh, *An Arab-Syrian gentleman and warrior in the period of the crusades*, trans. P.K. Hitti (New York, 1929).

SECONDARY WORKS

Asbridge, T.S., 'The significance and causes of the battle of the Field of Blood', *Journal of Medieval History*, vol. 23.4 (1997), pp. 301–16.

Bahat, D., *The Illustrated Atlas of Jerusalem* (New York, 1990).

Brooke, R. & C., *Popular religion in the Middle Ages: Western Europe 1000–1300* (London, 1984).

Brown, P., *The Cult of the Saints* (Chicago, 1981).

Bull, M., *Knightly Piety and the lay response to the First Crusade* (Oxford, 1993).

Burns, R., *Monuments of Syria: a historical guide* (London, 1992), p. 201.

Cahen, C., *La Syrie du nord a l'époque des croisades et la principauté franque d'Antioche* (Paris, 1940).

Constable, G., 'The Second Crusade as seen by Contemporaries', *Traditio*, vol. 9 (1953), pp. 213–79.

Deschamps, P., 'Le Crac des Chevaliers', *Les Châteaux des Croisés en Terre Sainte*, vol. 1 (Paris, 1934).

—— 'La défense du comté de Tripoli et de la principauté d'Antioche', *Les Châteaux des Croisés en Terre Sainte*, vol. 3 (Paris, 1973).

Du Cange, C., *Les Familles d'Outremer*, ed. E.G. Rey (Paris, 1869).

Edbury, P.W. & Rowe, J.G., *William of Tyre, historian of the Latin East* (Cambridge, 1988).

Edgington, S.B., 'Albert of Aachen reappraised', *From Clermont to Jerusalem: The Crusades and Crusader societies 1095–1500*, ed. A.V. Murray (Turnhout, 1998), pp. 55–67.

Epp, V., *Fulcher von Chartres: Studien zur Geschichtsschreibung des ersten Kreuzzuges* (Dusseldorf, 1990).

Frolow, A., *La relique de la vraie croix; recherches sur le développement d'un culte*, 2 vols (Paris, 1961).

Geary, P.J., 'Humiliation of Saints', *Saints and their cults: studies in religious sociology, folklore and history*, ed. S. Wilson (Cambridge, 1983), pp. 123–40.

—— *Furta sacra: Theft of Relics in the Central Middle Ages* (Princeton, NJ, 1990).

B. Hamilton, *The Latin Church in the Crusader States. The Secular Church* (London, 1980).

—— *Religion in the Medieval West* (London, 1986).

Holt, P.M., *The Age of the Crusades: The Near East from the eleventh century to 1517* (London, 1986).

Jamison, E.M., 'Some notes on the *Anonymi Gesta Francorum*, with special reference to the Norman contingent from south Italy and Sicily in the First Crusade', *Studies in French Language and Mediaeval Literature Presented to Professor Mildred K. Pope* (Manchester, 1939), pp. 183–208.

Jotischky, A., *The Perfection of Solitude: Hermits and Monks in the Crusader States* (Pennsylvania, 1995).

Kedar, B.Z., 'The subjected Muslims of the Frankish Levant', *Muslims under Latin rule, 1100–1300*, ed. J.M. Powell (Princeton, N.J., 1990), pp. 135–74.

Kennedy, H., *Crusader Castles* (Cambridge, 1994).

La Monte, J.L., *Feudal Monarchy in the Latin kingdom of Jerusalem, 1100 to 1291* (Cambridge, Mass., 1932).

Lilie, R.J., *Byzantium and the Crusader States 1096–1204*, trans. J.C. Morris & J.E. Ridings (Oxford, 1993).

Lot, F. & Fawtier, R., *Histoire des Institutions Françaises au Moyen Age*, 3 vols (Paris, 1957–62).

Mayer, H.E., 'Jérusalem et Antioche au temps de Baudouin II', *Comptes-rendu de l'Académie des inscriptions et belles-lettres*, Novembre-Décembre 1980 (Paris, 1981), pp. 717–33.

—— 'The Concordat of Nablus', *Journal of Ecclesiastical History*, vol. 33 (1982), pp. 531–43.

—— 'Mélanges sur l'histoire du royaume latin de Jérusalem', *Mémoires de l'Académie des inscriptions et belles-lettres*, nouvelle série 5 (1984), pp. 126–30.

—— *The crusades*, 2nd edn, trans. J.B. Gillingham (Oxford, 1988).

—— 'Die antiochenische Regentschaft Balduins II. von Jerusalem im Spiegel der Urkunden', *Deutsches Archiv*, vol. 47 (1991), pp. 559–66.

—— *Varia Antiochena: Studien zum Kreuzfahrerfürstentum Antiochia im 12. und frühen 13. Jahrhundert* (Hannover, 1993).

—— *Kanzlei der lateinischen Könige von Jerusalem*, 2 vols (Hannover, 1996).

Metcalf, D.M., *Coinage of the Crusades and the Latin East in the Ashmolean Museum, Oxford*, 2nd ed. (London, 1995).

Munro, D.C., 'A Crusader', *Speculum*, vol. 7 (1932), pp. 321–35.

Murray, A., 'Baldwin II and his nobles: Baronial faction and dissent in the kingdom of Jerusalem, 1118–1134', *Nottingham Medieval Studies*, vol. 38 (1994), pp. 60–85.

—— '"Mighty against the enemies of Christ": The relic of the True Cross in the armies of the kingdom of Jerusalem', *The Crusades and their sources: essays presented to Bernard Hamilton*, ed. J. France & W.G. Zajac (Aldershot, 1998), pp. 217–38.

Phillips, J., *Defenders of the Holy Land* (Oxford, 1996).

Prestwich, J.O., 'The military household of the Norman kings', *English Historical Review*, vol. 96 (1981), pp. 1–35.

Rheinheimer, M., 'Tankred und das Siegel Boemunds', *Schweizerische Numismatische Rundschau*, vol. 70 (1991), pp. 86ff.

Riley-Smith, J.S.C., *The First Crusade and the idea of crusading* (London, 1986).

—— *The crusades. A short history* (London, 1987).

Rowe, J.G., 'The Papacy and the ecclesiastical province of Tyre', *Bulletin of John Rylands Library*, vol. 43 (1960–61), pp. 160–89.

Runciman, S., *A history of the crusades*, 3 vols (Cambridge, 1951–54).

Siberry, E., *Criticism of Crusading 1095–1274* (Oxford, 1985).

Smail, R.C., *Crusading warfare 1097–1193* (Cambridge 1956).

Stargardt, J.A., *Europäische Stammtafeln*, vol. 2 (Marburg, 1984).

Ward, B., *Miracles and the Medieval Mind: Theory, Record and Event 1000–1215*, rev. ed. (Aldershot, 1987).

Index